ISBN-13: 978-0692338063
ISBN-10: 0692338063

PUBLISHED BY: AMB/KENERLY PRODUCTIONS
COVER ART: AMB BRANDING DESIGN
EDITED: NICOLE BROOKS

FIRST PRINTED IN THE UNITED STATES
AMB-KENERLY PRESENTS

To order additional copies of this book, contact:
Kenerly Presents at shauntakenerly@yahoo.com
Follow me on Twitter @shaunkenerly
Follow Rio Jonz on Facebook

THE ULTIMATE BREAK

ACKNOWLEDGEMENTS

First and foremost I thank my Heavenly Father for the hedge of protection that He has around me. For without that, there is no me. I want to thank my mother, Ms. Joyce Ann Gaines. She has been there with me when the whole world gave me the cold shoulder. In the streets, and in prison, she's still rockin' with her Son. I want to thank my ex-wife for putting the flame under my creativity. I have to thank my cousin Carl Coleman for giving me the seed money for my business venture. You don't have to come looking for me, cuz! I'll find you…with my checkbook open. My family: Brother Ronnie, sister Tamra, my baby sister Marti; my cousin Rochelle—with her wild butt—has always been there for me. ALWAYS! My cousins Sharon, Kieshalon, Cynthia, Victor, Jamila, Maria, Wren, Feleta, my Real One Rory, his wife Candy, and his bro Robert. My Aunt's Helen, Arlene, Carolyn, and Barbara Jean; may she rest in peace. To my team at AMB Branding; Shaunta Kenerly and Aija Monique. Teamwork Makes The Dreamwork! To the City of Compton for never dealing with me with an iron fist. I love my City…and I get the love in return. To all my homies behind the wall: This is a HUB & DUB thang! For Life! I finally got it right, ya'll. If I left anyone out, It's for a real reason. They know the deal.
AND LAST BUT "NEVER" THE LEAST!!
I want to acknowledge my woman, my future wife; my life…
Zanavia Ann Clark.
"I love you, admire you, and thank you for putting up with my excited self. For if it wasn't for you settling me down, no one would even know…that I wrote a book. You slowed me down long enough to see this project come to life. So, in essence, you brought me back to life.
THANK YOU, BABY! 8-3-1

Chapter One

The phone rang.

"Yes," answered René.

"Is this room 221?"

"The house of fun! And who is this?"

"I'm here to pick up René for her date this evening. My boss got tied up and asked me to come."

"If he didn't send you with my bread, don't even bother comin' up."

"Oh, I have it for you."

"Well, what are you waitin' for? Come on up!"

"René, why do you talk to them like that? That's a three thousand dollar date for two hours! That's fifteen hundred an hour!"

"Oh yeah…Karin? Let me tell you something, girl. I'm tired of flat-backin' and jaw-jackin' for my bread. The only reason I'm datin' this fool tonight is because Bone is comin' home tomorrow, and three G's is a whole lot better than the two hundred that state will give him. He's been gone forty months, and thirty of that forty, I wasn't there. This is the least I can do to show some type of love.

"Yeah, but he knew you were still getting' high back then."

"I ain't on that page no more though, and this will be my proof of it."

The truth was that René had been clean for nine months, but the last two weeks had been a little rough on her sobriety. With her mother still threatening to take her kids from her, René slipped; A dime rock – one red eye flight – led her to a fifty piece. Her next move was a quarter piece, and when she had gotten down to the last gram, Bone called…

"Hey, baby girl," cried Bone!

"My baby will be home in two weeks! I'm so glad 'cause these kids out here are game goofy," René said.

"I thought you left those kids alone nine months ago? Don't play with me René!" Bone was upset. "If you still in them

streets when I get out, that's where I'm leavin' you. I ain't got time for no two-dolla-ass street games. I just spent the last forty months of my life in prison for playin' that game. That's too many months for some crumbs. I want more outta life. Come on, baby! We've been over this already right?"

"You're right baby," agreed René, "I'm cool. I'll be at the front gate waitin' on you."

"What about the boys," asked Bone? René has two sons; Zackery is ten, and Xavier is eight.

"They still got their little doubts about you, but they trust my judgment. It's open arms waitin' fo' ya', baby. Just come home."

***

René snapped out of her daydream with Karin pulling on her arm, "Your ride is at the door, girl," she said, "You want me to get it or what?"

"Nah," René said, "I got it." She swung the door wide open, and was about to be very rude, when the man at the door thrust a small manila envelope into her hand. She opened it up and took out thirty crisp one hundred-dollar bills. Stuffing the money back into the envelope she finally looked at the man that was at her door. He looked like a hockey player stuffed in a business suit; square chin, broad shoulders, and a military crew cut.

"Man, you look like da' po-lease. Let me see your dick."

"Are you serious?" he asked. His face turned beet red.

Karin pushed passed René and said, "Here, let me help you." She grabbed the man by his belt buckle and pulled him into the room.

"Okay ladies. The jokes on me," he said after regaining his composure.

"Oh, she ain't jokin' big boy. If you don't show us your dick, and let me hold it...," Karin smiled, "then you can take your money and your square-chin-ass outta here. Now drop'um or get the fuck out." Karin stood with her hands on her hips.

He slowly unbuckled his belt and unzipped his slacks. Karin was right up on him waiting to see. She really hoped that he wasn't a cop because this was her kind of man; big, blond, and dumb. Any man who spends over a hundred dollars for some ass on Artesia Blvd. had to be dumb, Karin thought. He wasn't buying. He was transporting. If Karin played it right, he would drop René off with his boss and come back for some fun with her. He was kind of cute, thought Karin. She would come up with a cool price for the night.

"Here, let me help you," said Karin. She slid her hand through the slit in his trousers. She pulled out his cock, caressed it in her hands, and looked him straight in his eyes. She said over her shoulder, "He ain't no cop, girl. He's just horny."

"Let him go then, and I'll send him back to you. What's your name dude?" asked René.

"John," he stated.

René looked at Karin who was trying to avoid eye contact. That was all of their tricks names: John; birth name or not, when they hit the "A Line" looking for love - last name Trick, and first name John.

"I'll be here waiting," said Karin, with more humor in her voice than she wanted.

"Okay uh, John, let's go," René said. Before they walked out of the room, René turned to Karin and said, "I will send John back to you, girlfriend."

They both roared with laughter.

As they got ready to get in John's truck, Rene saw Alisha come out of Room 119. *Who was in that room*, she thought. Then it hit her. *Brooklyn!* As John got ready to open her door, she said, "Hold on one second, John. I'm gonna bring my girlfriend along with us. I'm sure your boss wouldn't mind two for the price of one, now would he?" Before John could respond, she walked towards Alisha.

"What's up, girl?" asked Alisha.

"Is Brooklyn still in that room, or is a trick in there?"

"Brooklyn's still scrapin' up the rent money. What's up?"

"Step back in the room, and I'll tell you my pretty," René did her impression of the wicked witch of the West.

As they walked into the room, Brooklyn dropped her pipe in her beer. She didn't want René to know that she was still getting high; at least she wasn't going to get high in front of her. *How come Alisha didn't knock?* thought Brooklyn. Alisha had her key. *I'll have to get that back before she leaves again*, she thought.

"We didn't mess your red-eye flight up did we, Brook?" René laughed. She knew that's exactly what they did, "We'll be out of your way in two minutes. As soon as Alisha changes them Nike's for her brand new sandals, we're gone."

"Where we goin' that I need to show off my feet?" Let the whole truth be told Alisha had more than just pretty feet. She was what the old school playaz called a brick house - French vanilla colored skin, long wavy hair like an Indian, firm pointed breast, small waist, flat stomach, and wide, pear-shaped hips. Alisha was built like an old Coke bottle with an upside down heart shaped booty, and those pretty ass feet. "Better be more than a hundred René."

"How about five hundred, and you get half of it right now?"

"Put the money in my hand right now," Alisha said, "Wait! How many dudes?"

René had picked up the phone to call upstairs, "Oh, just one. Can you handle that? I thought so," She spoke into the phone, "Get me three of them out of that envelope I left up there and dropum' down…I'll be standing under you in ten seconds." She hung up the phone and headed for the door. As she got ready to open it, she looked back at Brooklyn who was drinking her beer. She was taking big gulps, so she could get her pipe out of the can. René shook her head and said, "If you stop chasin' that pipe, you'll probably make some money, girl."

"Ya'll just leave my key on that table before ya'll step, so I can get high in peace," Brooklyn tried to be sassy, but the truth was she was hiding her hurt feelings.

In all of her time on the streets, Brooklyn had never made five hundred dollars on one date. Hell, she had never made five hundred dollars in one night. Well, she might have, but the dope man was getting her money so fast she never even tried to keep count.

René stepped out of the room and looked up. Karin stood there with the money folded in her hand. When she dropped it down, she said, "You found your stunt dummy, huh?"

"You know it, and Mr. Bossman is gonna replace what I pay her. Bone called me the Ghetto Madame, so I might as well live up to it."

"Might as well. You've been twistin' girls like that before you met Bone. You just be careful. Who you takin' anyway?" Karin asked.

After a brief moment, René said, "Alisha." She hesitated on telling Karin because she didn't feel like hearing her mouth.

René had stopped taking Alisha on V.I.P. dates because she always half-ass did her job, and that caused the trick to spend his money elsewhere.

"Don't worry, Karin. I'll make sure the job gets done."

"Just be careful, René," Karin stated, "You know how that bitch is. She ain't to be trusted."

Karin was right, but it wasn't like she was going to be there by herself. As long as René was there, nothing could go wrong. Could it?

René walked back into Brooklyn's room and gave Alisha the money. Alisha's eyes lit up.

"Damn! Who is this dude, René?" Alisha's mind raced.

"Don't trip girl. Our feelings ain't in this situation. This is bizness. Remember that Alisha, or you can stay your high yellow ass here."

"Fuck Karin," Alisha yelled! "You wasn't thinkin' like that about me until you and her started sharin' that room. I know how to handle bizness and you know that!"

"That's why I'm down here girlfriend," René said softly just like the seductress she was.

On the way out the door, Alisha put the key and a hundred dollar bill in Brooklyn's hand. She squeezed her hand and said,

"At least pay your rent again before you go on one," and left the room.

Back at the truck René said, "I'm sorry we took so long, John. My girlfriend couldn't find her sandals, but we're ready now."

"He's cute," said Alisha.

René glared at her like she would choke her out right there.

John's truck was a little high off of the ground. It was a Chevy Suburban, all black with twenty-four inch rims on it. Alisha needed some help getting in, so she turned to John for some assistance.

"Could you give me a boost, please?" Before John could step up and assist her, René slid between them, grabbed Alisha around her waist, and boosted her so hard that she hit her head on the door jam.

"Ouch," Alisha cried. Embarrassment kept her from turning around.

John winced when he heard the thud. René winked her eye at him, and he just shrugged his shoulders. He boosted René in behind Alisha; he didn't want them to be seen.

As he drove out of the parking lot, he could hear René whispering harsh words to her girlfriend. He hoped that she would get the message. If she didn't, there was a bigger price to pay than just a bump on the head.

***

They made a right off of Ocean Blvd. into the Marina. You could hear small laughter and music in the parking lot but all was quiet at the end. The more elite crowd kept their forms of entertainment a little more contained. They didn't want the whole world to know just how far their passions extended.

John double parked next to the last walkway and let the girls out. He punched the access code in the gate, heard the small click, and let them down to the craft called 'Eve.'

She was a fifty-foot Pershing yacht; a fast boat for fast women. Eve was midnight blue with smoked gray flames flowing off of the tip. You could only see the flames at an angle because of the deep pearl in the paint. The name Eve was in bright red flames along the back of the boat; an Albino Python was painted under her name.

René looked at Alisha and said, "I don't think this is a good idea."

"It's too late for all of that, girl," Alisha reminded her, "This is bizness, remember? Tuck your feelings in yo' bra until we get home."

"I ain't wearin' no bra!"

While they were going back and forth, John walked back to his truck and drove off. He was going back to see if Karin could satisfy his lust for the evening. He was glad for the invite, so he wouldn't be forced to join his boss in his wild sexual fantasies. John didn't enjoy hurting women.

"So, what kind of treat did John bring me?" Came a voice out of the speaker somewhere around the girl's feet. They both stepped back and looked down at the walkway.

From inside the boat emerged a stubby little man wearing some blue khaki shorts and a Hawaiian shirt. A potbelly white man, with thinning gray hair that was thicker around his ears than it was on top. The top was covered by a hand full of hair combed over from the far left of his head; an easy mark for the ladies of the night.

René had seen this man before. She hadn't dated him, but his little fat face stood out; he looked like a miniature John Candy. Plus, his eyes showed recognition at the sight of her. It would come to her. It always did. Let's just hope it didn't come too late in the game. She had a bad vibe about him. It would come to her. It always did.

"And you must be René," he said looking her up and down.

René had on some pink Capri pants with a pink and white string bikini top. Her feet were tied onto a high heel with the laces meeting the bottom of her pants: Hebrew sandals with a twist.

"And what might your name be, little man?"

"Ha-ha-ha," he laughed heartily, "My name is Adam on these special occasions."

"And Eve is this special lady here," said Alisha pointing at the boat.

"You're very observant young lady. And what is your name?"

"On special occasions like this, I go by Medusa," Alisha did a short belly dance as she said Medusa, and René almost spit in her face from trying to hold in her laugh.

René needed that because it eased the tension that she was feeling within herself.

"My friend here is the best crowd pleaser there is," René said, "I never leave home without her."

"Well, let's just hope I don't turn into stone before the show is over," Adam extended his hand first to René and helped her onto the craft, then to Alisha. When she climbed aboard, he whispered in her ear, "You're gonna love this." As Adam walked down the steps into the belly of Eve, he said, "Follow me ladies."

"This is gonna be easy," whispered Alisha.

"Yeah," René agreed, "Let's just make it quick. I got a bad vibe."

The inside of this boat looked nothing like what you might see in a Show Boats International Magazine. Instead, it looked like a room in one of your more expensive bathhouses. They would call this room, The Pain Freak.

To the left of the entrance, there was a four-foot high bar mounted along the wall, an assortment of liquors, and three leather encased ice buckets.

As Adam opened the ice buckets, he said, "Coke, weed or speed."

The girls looked at each other and smiled thinking about a catch phrase that Bone always used to say. They both finished Adam's statement with, "You pass me by you don't get high," and broke out laughing.

"That's catchy right there ladies. So, you know all about this world then?"

"We know about this stuff on the bar," said René, "But we don't know nothin' about this other stuff. And, if you think for one minute that we're cool with it, think again."

The other two walls had an array of whips, chains, handcuffs, and boxing gloves with spikes embedded in them. In the center of the room, was a miniature pool table with straps at all four corners. Against the back was a modern let-out couch with two pullies mounted above it on the ceiling. On the floor next to the couch was what looked like a gigantic medicine ball with four straps attached to it. It looked like you would hug it and someone would strap your wrists and knees to it. It was severe beatings going on here, and the drugs were supplied to keep your mind twisted until it was over.

Alisha looked at René and said, "I ain't down with this girl!"

"Huh! Me neitha', girl. We ain't finta stay here," René spun around on Adam and said, "Look here, love, you got the wrong girls for this. We ain't into getting tied up and shit."

"Oh, I don't want to tie ya'll up. I want to be tied up, but first, I want to get high."

The girls looked at each other, shrugged their shoulders, and sat down at the bar.

"Listen Adam, before we start..."

"I know, I know. I owe you for bringing Medusa," Adam reached in his back pocket, "This was gonna be your bonus if you stayed an extra hour, but Medusa is real sexy, so here you are."

He handed René the same type of manila envelope that John did. She didn't look in it because she knew it was filled with hundred dollar bills.

She would slide into the bathroom later and tuck it in her special inside pocket. For now, she just stuck it in her front pocket.

Alisha watched her like a hawk. By René not looking into the envelope, was a sure sign that it was a stack of bread, so she leaned over and said, "You'll break *that* envelope in half home girl."

"Don't start, girl," whispered René.

"No," growled Alisha! "Don't make me start."

"I'm going up top for a sec," Adam said.

Once he was up the stairs, René resumed the conversation, "You just stay away from that white powder in that bucket and you'll get your half."

"I ain't got no problem with the ye'-yo baby. You do!"

Alisha could tell that René was getting high again. They had known each other too long; they had gotten high together. Plus, the pants René wore Alisha bought them for her. They were supposed to go back and exchange them for a bigger size. Tonight, she wore them with a belt.

"Okay," René said. She knew Alisha had noticed some weight-loss, so she let the comment ride, "This is chronic," she grabbed a bud out of the ice bucket in the middle, "One joint of this, and we'll be cool."

"Yeah, and some of this Level Vodka, and we'll beat da' shit outta fatboy with the fat pockets." Alisha winked her eye at her long time girlfriend, "We'll lace yo' man's pockets real nice tomorrow.

"How do you know Bone is comin' home tomorrow," René asked?

"Girl, please. You ain't the only bitch he's been keepin' up with. Who you think was there for him those thirty months you was in a fog? Let's not go there right now; let's get this money."

René was really slipping in her game. She left her man for dead, and her best friend slid right under him. All of that would change after tonight because tonight René was going to change the game; tonight's game was Russian roulette with all six bullets.

"Adam," René said when she saw him coming down the stairs, "Show me the little ladies room, so I can freshen' up."

"Now, if you were a little lady I'd be more than happy to. What are you six-two?"

"Six-one and a half, baby."

"Okay. The *'big'* girls use the one next to the couch." He turned to Alisha, "And you Medusa, can use the one by the stairs when you need it."

They both got up and headed to the bathrooms; René to stash the money, and Alisha to get naked. It was time to get down to business.

When they both came out a couple of minutes later, Adam said, "Wow!" Alisha had stripped all the way down while René still had on her bikini top and a pink lace thong.

René still had on her heels, so her stroll was a lot more seductive than Alisha's. It was as if René couldn't compete with her, though; Alisha's body was firm, like a track star.

Her short frame was stacked, and it wasn't soggy. Unlike René, whose body was slowly becoming a product of cocaine use, it was as if her hips were pouting like a sad clown at the circus. To the untrained eye, she looked fabulous. To Alisha, she looked like she needed to sober up. No matter what though, Alisha and René were hot, and they were home girls for life.

Alisha was the closest to the bar, but this was René's show. She would respect that tonight. She sat down next to Adam and waited for her cue.

"So, Adam," began René, "What would you like to drink?"

"Hell, I'll have both of you with a twist of lime," he laughed, "But since I don't have a glass that big, I'll have a double shot of Grand Marnier with an orange juice back."

René nodded at Alisha and she poured the double shot. René glided over to the refrigerator and got the orange juice. She handed that to Alisha and stood next to the three ice buckets. With her right hand, she touched each top.

"Coke, weed, or speed?"

"We're gonna set the go fast aside. I wanna see if I can get numb for this adventure."

"You sure have enough coke here to get numb with," added Alisha.

"Yeah, we'll see," Adam, muttered.

Alisha looked at René confused. René just shrugged her shoulders.

René pulled a silver spoon out of the ice bucket of coke and dumped it on the bar. She crushed the chunks down with a shot glass, and with a razor strapped to the bucket top, she made six lines. As she played with the lines to make them long, a chill went down her spine and her stomach bubbled. The urge hit her so hard that she just stopped. She pulled a straw off the top and handed it to Adam.

"Here you go baby," she said as she backed away from the bar.

Alisha slid the drink next to his left arm from behind him. She looked over at René and said, "Grab one of them buds and let me roll a couple, girlfriend."

René grabbed a bud, the papers off of the bucket top, and handed them to Alisha. Alisha held on to René's hand. Looking her in her eyes and said, "I got you, girl."

"Thanks," mumbled René. She grabbed two snifters and filled them halfway with Remy Martin. She handed one to Alisha, "We'll have to do that Level shit when Bone gets home. I need this cognac right now."

Regaining her composure after a stiff drink, and a hit of that good weed, René went to work. She dumped some coke into a shot glass and headed to the pool table.

"Adam can you come and snort some of this off of my body?" He was in the middle of snorting his second line off of the bar.

"Can I? I thought you would never ask," He got up and walked over to the pool table.

René had lain back on the table. Alisha came over, took the glass, and trailed the dope from René's breast to her naval.

"Now the fun begins," Adam said as he bent over René.

She popped her right breast out of her bikini top, and Adam licked her nipple.

Alisha slid behind him and unbuckled his shorts. They immediately feel to the floor because he didn't have enough ass to hold them up.

Adam started sniffing, and Alisha grabbed a leather barber strap off of the wall. She didn't know how to use a whip, but the barber strap was like a thick belt. Before Adam got to her naval, Alisha whacked him across his ass.

"Aaah!" he cried, "What the fuck was that?" He looked back to see Alisha with one hand on her hip and the other one swinging the strap.

"Oh, you girls are full of surprises. I forgot I had that there. Actually, I've never used that for entertainment. I use that to sharpen my straight razor. Do that again," he bent over René again and sniffed some more. Right before he was done, Whack! "Oooh, yeah," He was ready for that one.

Adam stood up straight to unbutton his shirt. As he did this, Alisha hit him again, Whack! "Aaah! Hot damn," he cried, "I'm startin' to think you like this more than me." She hit him really hard that time because his voice went up a couple of octaves.

"Hold on little lady. Let me get into my outfit," he took off his shirt and revealed bruises all over his back. Around his nipples was a circle of puncture wounds. They both winced at the sight of the man's body. He looked like a badly beaten prisoner of war.

As he walked around the pool table, he grabbed his drink off of the bar and said, "I lost all of the feeling in my body from nerve damage. I fell off of a two-story building and messed up some damn nerves that control my feeling. The only feeling I have as you've already found out is in my ass."

"You mean you can't feel this?" Alisha grabbed his cock and pinched it.

Nope. Here, come over to the closet, "He opened the closet and pulled out his outfit. It was a leather G-string with two straps that came off of the back and over his shoulders; it clamped onto his nipples. He pulled on the G-string, Alisha pulled the straps up, and laid them on his shoulders.

René got up off of the pool table and faced him. She checked out the ends on the straps. They both had six half-inch long spikes.

"Push them into my chest," Adam directed, "Right over my nipples.

René grabbed the straps and pushed. When they wouldn't go in easy, Adam grabbed her hands and helped her. With one swift jerk, they went into his skin. He didn't flinch.

Adam closed the closet and went back to the pool table. He bent down and went into the front pocket of his shorts. He pulled out a glass pipe and some rock cocaine. At the sight of the pipe, René passed gas and her stomach fluttered.

"I had my neighbor rock some of that junk up for me. His old lady's a real fiend, so he had no problem with the task. Free crack keeps his old lady off the track." Adam smiled at that. "Hey, new catch phrase for you girls." They didn't laugh. "Anyway, strap me down."

He handed the rock and pipe to René. Her desire was that evident. He knew that she wanted a hit. The scent from her passing gas went straight to his nose. Her vice was ready to show its ugly face.

René set the stuff down on the bar and strapped his arms down to the pool table. Alisha strapped down his legs.

"Grab that small torch and melt some of that stuff down," Adam ordered.

René did that without hitting it.

"Now, stick it in my mouth and let me hit it. Make sure that pipe gets real hot."

She stuck the pipe in his mouth and he pulled on it. He pulled on it for at least a minute with the flame straight on it. She pulled the pipe out of his mouth.

Through a cloud of smoke, he said, "Now unzip the front of my G-string and touch my dick with that pipe."

She hesitated.

"I paid you good money for this, bitch. Now burn me!" That pissed René off. She unzipped the front of his G-string and thrust the hot pipe into his cock.

He didn't even flinch.

Adam's eyes were open. Smoke was trailing out of his mouth, evaporating before his eyes.

He didn't see it.

"Okay, I believe you. Your nerves are dead. Now what?"

René leaned over him, "Adam. Adam!" His eyes were glazed over. She looked up at Alisha.

Alisha rushed to unstrap his wrist. She checked for a pulse. Nothing

"Damn," cried Alisha, "We gotta get da' fuck outta here."

"Slow down girl. Not so fast."

"What do you mean slow down, René? How much dope did you put on that pipe anyway?"

"Bout a gram."

"You busted his heart! Why?" asked Alisha?"

"I told you I knew this fool from somewhere, remember? Well, it hit me when I seen them holes around his nipples. You remember that night when Shelley came through with that big spender and Bone was tryin' to convince him into rentin' a room at the Budget Inn?"

"When Jo-Jo had a room next to fat boy Dee? We seen Shelley the next day laid out on the bus stop with pipe..."

"Burns," finished René, "Shelley told me about a trick with holes around his nipples. That was this fool right here. I had to stay with that girl for two weeks nursin' them damn burns. She wouldn't let me take her to the hospital."

"She's the reason you stopped getting high?"

"You damn right," cried Alisha, "Ain't no high in the world worth the pain I saw that girl go through. What do we do now?"

"Get dressed and wipe everything down you think we touched."

Alisha opened up the closet and pulled a duffel bag out of the top, "And we ain't leavin' empty handed," she said. She ran to the bathroom, got her clothes, and got dressed right next to the pool table.

Once she was dressed, she went to a drawer next to the refrigerator and opened it. It was an odds and ends drawer. She pulled it all the way out and set it on the floor.

All the way in the back of the drawer was a roll of duct tape. She grabbed it, ran to the bar, and taped all three ice buckets. She set them in the bottom of the duffel bag. Next, she grabbed the Remy Martin and the Grand Marnier. She opened the side pockets on the bag. Before she stuffed the bottles in there, she stuck her hand in. She pulled out a pair of thin leather gloves; the kind a car thief wears. She slid them on her hands and stuffed the bottles in the bag.

René came out of the bathroom dressed, with two towels in her hand, "I wiped everything down in there."

"Go wipe that front bathroom down for me," Alisha said. She picked up Adam's shorts and stuffed them in the bag.

René grabbed a roll of paper towels off of the top of the refrigerator and threw them at Alisha, "Wrap up the glasses girlfriend."

"No shit," Alisha winked, "Thanks." She grabbed both snifters and downed the rest of the Remy in them.

She wrapped up both of the snifters, the shot glasses, and Adam's glass. She dropped them in the bag. She grabbed the duct tape off of the bar and dropped that in the bag too. You could tell by the way she was moving that this wasn't her first clean up job.

She went back to the junk drawer, found a pair of shears, and went to work. She unstrapped Adam's limbs and cut the straps off of the pool table. She cut Adam's outfit off of him as well.

When she dropped that stuff in the bag, she saw his shorts and went in the pockets. No wallet but the front pocket had a big roll of money in it. She looked up to see if René was coming, and when she didn't see her, she stuffed the money down the front of her pants. You could see it if she put the wad in her pocket. You had to conceal your private stash.

Alisha was no fool.

René finally came out of the bathroom. Alisha was done stuffing the bag. She wiped down the bar.

"You movin' too slow girl! Give me that towel," Alisha demanded.

René slowly tossed her a towel.

Alisha looked at her funny. She continued to wipe down the bar; she wiped off the junk drawer, stuffed it back in the slot - wiped down the refrigerator, inside and out, and hit the bar one more time.

"What else? Oh!" She walked over to the closet and wiped the door down real good. She stopped to examine her girlfriend because she was moving to slow.

"You didn't hit that shit did you?"

"Please. I'm too nervous for that." Rene' lied. The truth was that she had hit it twice in, both bathrooms. That's why she was moving so slow; she was trying to listen. She was paranoid.

"Okay. Let's get off this boat," Alisha said.

René went up the steps first. Alisha came up the rear wiping as she walked. She had the duffel bag on like a backpack with her arms laced in the handles.

When they stepped onto the walkway, Alisha said, "Shit! I forgot the joint." She jumped back on the boat, ran down the steps, and grabbed the joint.

Before going back up the steps, she opened the bathroom door. She wanted to make sure she hadn't dropped anything in there. When she hit the light, she stared at a pipe and a torch. It was crumbs of dope sitting on the counter, too.

René hit the dope.

When Alisha came up the stairs, René was climbing back onto the boat, "I forgot somethin'."

"Oh, you mean this?" Alisha showed her the paraphernalia.

"Yeah," she mumbled as she grabbed it.

Alisha knew it wasn't the time to jam her up about it so she said, "You got your phone on you?"

"Huh," René asked. She was waiting to get cussed out.

"Your phone," growled Alisha, "You got it?"

"Oh, yeah, I got it. Here," René handed it to her.

As they started walking up the walkway, she called the motel. "Room 119, please," she waited. "Brook, listen. No questions. Are you by yourself? Good. Go outside and tell me if you see a big black Chevy Suburban on rims. Hurry!"

"Give me that joint girl," René needed to calm down; bring her coke high down.

Alisha dug in her pocket and gave her the joint. "You say it's leaving", she said into the phone. To René she said, "That dude John just left Karin."

"Let me…call…her," René choked on the weed.

"Okay, wait," into the phone, Alisha said, "Brook, I'll give you another hundred if you hang up right now and pack your shit. Hello?" Alisha laughed, "Didn't have to tell her twice, huh? Here," she handed René the phone.

"What's the number?"

"Just press send again," instructed Alisha, "And pass the joint."

They walked out of the Marina toward the gas station. Alisha heard René saying, "Hello? Room 221." She waited. "Who is this? What chu' doin' in my room?"

"Who is that," asked Alisha?

"Marie's nosey ass," she grunted, "Put Karin on the phone. Don't ask me no questions! Give Karin the phone!"

"What happened?" Karin asked. She knew if René was calling her in the middle of a date, it was a problem. She told her not to take Alisha.

"Tell Marie to leave, grab any and all money, go downstairs, get Brooklyn, and get the hell out of there!"

To Marie, Karin said, "I'll talk to you later love. I got another date comin'," as she searched for her shoes, she asked, "What did you do, René? I told you no…"

"I don't have time for all that," she interrupted Karin. "We're walking out of the Marina to the gas station. Two cabs are sitting in the parking lot. We're gonna jump in one of them and meet ya'll at the Motel 6 off the 605 and Slauson. Don't forget

Brooklyn. Please don't leave that baby girl behind like that," René started crying.

"That serious, huh?" It wasn't a question. *Okay,* Karin thought. "Get yourself another phone card in that gas station 'cause you ain't got no minutes on your phone."

"Oh yeah," René sniffed. "Thanks for reminding me."

"You got both my cell numbers?"

"They're in my phone," answered René.

"Hey," Karin cried, "Are you in the Shell by that 7-Eleven?"

"How did you know?" René sounded confused.

"I'm a Long Beach whore that's how," Karin said sarcastically. "Go in 7-Eleven to get the phone card, and while you're in there..."

"Get you a Cisco," René finished.

"Thanks love. See ya' soon."

***

When John pulled up to the gate in the Marina parking lot, he knew something was wrong. The boat was still in the slip. His boss always went out for the second half of the show, so no one would hear those poor girls scream. Eve should've been a mile out in the water twenty minutes ago.

He got out of the truck, punched the access code to the gate, and slowly descended down the walkway. He slipped a seventeen shot Ruger out of his holster and stepped to the boat like a cat burglar. He didn't hear anything, only the water slapping the body of the craft. He carefully stepped onto the boat, walked halfway down the steps, and stopped short. From where he stood, John saw his boss' feet pointed toward the sky on top of the pool table. He backed up and stood on deck.

He put his gun away then pulled out his phone.

"Tino." He hesitated. "You there or what?"

After a pause, "Yeah, dad, I'm here."

"I need you down at the Marina."

"He burnt another broad?" Tino asked.

"No. This time he got burned," answered John.

"Oh shit! Holy shit!" Tino bounced out of his bed.

"Yeah. I hope he made his peace with God." John hung up the phone then went down into the boat. He looked at the bar and saw that all three ice buckets were missing. "Figures."

He walked around the old man without even looking at him. He didn't want to remember him in this way; smothered by his own vile passions. He opened the closet door and looked up on the shelf; the duffel bag was missing. He snatched everything out of the closet. No duffel bag.

He pressed send on his phone again, "I'm getting on the freeway right now," Tino said.

"Go back and get Little Johnny."

"Holy shit! What's goin' on down there?"

"The bag is gone."

"We'll be there in fifteen minutes."

"Twelve." John hung up.

He stepped off of the boat and walked back to his truck. Inside the back, were two five-gallon jugs of gasoline. He unlatched them and carried them down to the yacht; the once beautiful Eve that he now despised. Everything she represented now was evil; all things evil must be burned.
And burn she would.

Chapter Two

When they pulled up in front of the motel, they saw the little red BMW. Alisha jumped out with the bag while René paid the cabbie.

"How much," she asked him?

"Just give me an even fifty." The meter read: $62.75.

The cabbie said, "An even fifth." Any time black ladies *walked* out of the Marina all they had were solid hundreds. He would tell them he didn't have change, and they would say, "Just keep it," and go on about her business. In spite of women walking the streets to get money, they always had a slight embarrassed look to them. The extra fifty would be the keep-this-between-me-and-you money: hush money.

Sure enough René handed him a hundred.

"I'm sorry," said the cabbie, "I don't have any change." As he got ready to fold the bill, and stick it into his pocket, she grabbed it.

"Well, would ga' lookie there," René said in country drawl, "Why this here looks a like a motel. I reckon they got bills ta' change dis' up." She slid out of the back seat and walked into the office.

"Bitch," mumbled the cabbie.

As Alisha walked over to the BMW, Karin got out. Brooklyn wasn't in the car. That made Alisha angry. This would be her reason to get off in Karin's ass.

"Don't look at me like that, girl. The youngster's up in the room already."

"Where is it?" Alisha demanded.

"Right above the office. I figured since you did..."

"I did?" Alisha stopped her. "You did good to get the room where you did. You do bad in your analogy of this situation."

"Big words for a little girl," Karin teased.

"Don't start, Karin," Alisha barked, "What number?"

"Two fifty-two. Knock twice." Karin walked toward the office, and Alisha headed for the stairs.

"Here ya' are, Mister Cabbie," said René as she handed him a fifty and a twenty, "See, I gots me some manners," she continued in her southern drawl.

"Yeah thanks," he mumbled then sped off slapping her arm with the car as he left.

"Wow!" You really made friends with that kid," said Karin.

"Fuck him! Come on girl. Let's get in the room."

"No. You get in the car first," Karin instructed, "I got somethin' for ya'." She grabbed the paper bag from René. "I believe you have somethin' for me in here." She slipped the bag down until the top of the bottle was exposed. She opened it up and turned the bottle up like a dunk sailor. "Now I can deal with this a little better."

Inside of the car Karin opened up her purse and slid René a .38 snub-nose pistol. Whatever happened out at the Marina, Karin knew that if it was bad enough to make René cry, then it was bad enough for her girlfriend to carry some heat.

"Don't tell me what happened right now, 'cause you ain't even got it sorted out in your own head yet. Plus, I think by the look on your face right now, I'm gonna need more than one Cisco."

"We got some Remy in the bag. Let's get up there before that ho starts stuffin' on me."

"Now that's my girl right there. Tuck them feelin's in yo' pocket, girlfriend!" Karin smiled a warm sincere smile at René and squeezed her leg. "Come on."

They got out of the car and walked around the whole motel before going up to the room. They looked for anything out of place; anybody sitting in a parked car. They had to be on their toes, because if they slipped, the fall was six feet down.

They knocked twice on the door. The peephole went dark as Brooklyn immediately opened the door. The room had two beds, but René didn't think it was going to be any sleeping tonight. She had to figure out how much she was going to tell Brooklyn and Karin. They both had big mouths. Brooklyn would give up information for a dime of crack, sometimes less. It just depended on when you caught her. Karin, on the other hand, was a little more refined. Although she looked a lot like a younger version of Barbara Walters, she could hold her tongue once she deemed it a necessity.

"Okay, first things first," René had everyone's attention. "I want to slide this dresser against this chair, against the door." She was a pro at keeping the door secure. She just hoped that they wouldn't use the window to get in if they found them.

She put the back of the chair underneath the doorknob, and Alisha and Brooklyn pushed the dresser against the chair. Next, they pushed the bed closest to the window all the way up against it. Then they stacked the other bed on top of that one.

Karin stood by the bathroom watching and drinking. When they finished the task at hand, she said, "René, you're more scandalous than us all. Nobody thinks to stack the beds at the window, unless they've had bad trips with tricks comin' back for revenge. Damn, girl! You ain't datin', you're robbin' tricks."

"Why do you think I never stay in rooms after a date? I ain't stupid." She looked at Alisha and Brooklyn.

René gave them rooms before and the trick always came back looking for her. Now they both stood there with their jaws almost hitting the floor in awe.

"Come on, Alisha," René said, "Let's see what we got in that bag and split up this money."

"Okay, but I get to keep the bag," Alisha said.

"I don't care, girl. Let's split da' bread!"

Alisha went in the bathroom to get the bag. When she came out, the girls were sitting in a circle on the floor. She cut the TV on loud so no one could hear them talk. She also cut the air-conditioner on; it was beginning to get stuffy.

They all sat around in a circle looking at each other. Four street whores about to share in the spoil from a date that turned ugly - ugly for the trick, good for them.
So far.

Karin gave René the envelope with the twenty-seven hundred dollars. René laid it in the center of the circle they had formed on the floor. She went into her pocket; her secret pocket sewn on the inside of her pants, and pulled out the cash Adam gave her on the boat. She tossed that onto the floor.

Alisha pulled out the Khaki shorts, and tossed them to René, who started searching the pockets. Then Alisha pulled out all three ice buckets.

"Ya'll gonna love what's in these," she said. She pulled out the two snifters, the two shot glasses, and Adam's glass. "Brook, go wash these out. This one," she held up Adam's glass. "Wash it, and then break it in the toilet. Please make sure you flush all the pieces, too."

Brooklyn got up and took the glasses into the bathroom.

As Alisha pulled out the Remy Martin and Grand Marnier, Karin said, "You did good bringing them. Yeah, we're gonna need them."

"You got dat' right, girlfriend." Alisha smiled at Karin nodding her head in agreement. They didn't hate each other but they were jealous of one another at times.

"We need some ice, Karin," Alisha said.

"Send Brooklyn," she said flatly. "She ain't been seen."

It was true, thought Alisha. John only knew about René, Alisha, and Karin. Brooklyn would do all of the running.

"It ain't nothin' in these shorts but some chump change." René tossed some crumpled bills in the pot on the floor. She folded up the shorts and put them back in the bag.

Brooklyn returned with the glasses then Karin said, "Youngster, go get us some ice, kay?" She wasn't asking her.

"What do I look like, Karin? I ain't no..."

"Come on, Brook," broke in Alisha. "We ain't got no room in here for no bitchin'. Just run down there, fill up a small trash can, and come on back."

"Should she take this?" René was holding up the pistol.

"Nah," said Alisha, They ain't gonna catch up to us that damn fast. The only one that knows we're here is the cab driver, and he ain't been gone fifteen minutes. Plus, ain't nobody seen her with us tonight."

Brooklyn looked from Alisha to René, and back to Alisha. They made her nervous, "Let me hurry up and go get this ice before I get too scared to go." Karin pulled back the dresser. Brooklyn moved the chair and was out of the door.

The bag was empty. The only items left were the straps from the pool table and Adam's shorts. Alisha folded the bag up and stuffed it in a drawer.

"Strip," René demanded. She looked at Alisha with fire in her eyes.

"What?" Alisha looked astonished.

"You heard me. Get naked. I think you stuffed on me."

"Okay. You get naked too, bitch!" Alisha was mad.

"No problem," They both stood up.

René pulled off her clothes and Alisha did the same. When they were totally naked, they exchanged clothes so that they could go through each other's pockets. They found nothing.

"You want me to squat and cough, too?" Alisha was real mad.

"Nah," René said calmly, "My bad, girl. I'm just on edge." René still thought she had something, though. She would just watch her.

They got dressed. As Alisha pulled her top over her head, she heard two knocks at the door. She froze.

"Girl, that's just Brooklyn," Karin said, "You *really* need a drink."

"No shit."

Karin opened the door. Brooklyn came in with the ice and they all sat back down on the floor, all except for René.

She moved the chair in position under the doorknob, and by herself, slid the dresser against it. When she turned around to sit down with her girlfriends, they were all looking at her; shaking their heads.

"What?" René said with a smile on her face.

"You are scandalous," they said in unison.

That broke the tension in the room.

They all fell out laughing.

"Okay," René started. "It's twenty-seven hundred in this envelope and fifteen hundred in this knot. That's forty-two hundred. I'm gonna give Bone three G's tomorrow so that leaves twelve hundred to split. That's three hundred a piece. It's like one-eighty in that bundle. We'll use that to eat or whatever."

René gave everybody three hundred a piece and threw the one-eighty on the nightstand. Then she nodded towards Alisha.

"Now, ladies. This is what's gonna put you over the top. We've been out in these streets talkin' 'bout getting' over da' hump. Once I get x amount of dollaz, I ain't gonna walk these streets no more. I've said it; René has said it," she pointed at Brooklyn and Karin, "And you've both said it. Here is your chance to get that money."

She pushed all three ice buckets to the center of their circle and opened them up. Karin and Brooklyn both let out a gasp and their eyes got as big as fifty-cent pieces.

"What is it?" asked Brooklyn. She could tell the one in the middle was skunk weed; she could smell it. The other two was either coke or speed.

"Coke, weed, and speed," said René.

"Shhh," Karin said, and when they all looked at her with a questioning look she said, "You pass us by. You don't get high!" They all screamed with laughter.

Alisha poured Remy in all four glasses and said, "A toast." They all raised their glasses. "May we all stand tall above it all!" They clinked their glasses together and drank.

As Alisha was talking, René thought that she really had been keeping in contact with Bone. Almost every word that came out of her mouth sounded just like something he would say. Alisha was really in her way. No she wasn't.

"I made this score happen, not her," she whispered softly.

"Huh?" asked Karin.

"Don't get overly excited," René said, "The only thing we're touchin' tonight is that weed and this drank. Everything else will be put away until Bone gets here."

"All of a sudden, you wanna start doin' for Bone," Brooklyn said.

"More than you ever did for him, baby," countered René.

"I ain't never tried to do nothin' for him."

"So be thankful that I included you tonight, and watch yo' little sassy ass mouth!" barked René.

"Yeah, Brook. Kick back," warned Alisha. She knew why Brooklyn said what she said. She was gearing up to give Alisha praise for looking out for Bone and talk down to René. She looked at René as a big sister she didn't like, and Alisha was the sister she loved.

"Okay, kids," broke in Karin, "Put the tops back on that white, tape them back down Alisha, and put them back in your bag. René, get the mirror off the wall, put it on the floor, and dump the weed on it. Brooklyn, you freshen' up our drinks. Me, I'm gonna feed you kids with Domino's Pi---."

"No!" They all screamed, "Pizza Hut!"

"Okay, kids. Pizza Hut it is."

Alisha pulled the duffel bag out and put the two ice buckets in. As she did that, she checked the side pocket to make sure that the little black velvet bag was in there. It was.

When she first got in the room, she stuffed the money out of her pants into that pocket. The little velvet pouch felt like it was holding some kind of stones. If they were the stone she was thinking of, Bone wouldn't even trip with the dope.

She grabbed the pouch, balled it up real tight in her hand, and stuffed it down the back of her pants.

René spotted her looking in the side pocket on the bag. *I got you, bitch,* she thought. She would check the bag later.

"Crafty bitch."

***

Tino and Little Johnny pulled up at the Marina. Big John sat in his truck. He got out and walked over to the gate. When they walked up behind him, he asked, "How many cabs were in the gas station parking lot?"

"One," Little Johnny answered.

"Okay. Let's go down and get this boat ready. By the time we wire it up, the other cab should be back. You two will take it out and do as we planned.

"Where's the gas?" asked Tino.

"It's inside the boat."

They walked down and got on the boat.

John had put a sheet over his boss so they couldn't see him. They started wiring C-4 to a timed detonator. They were going out about a mile and a half dragging a motorized raft to leave Eve out there to explode. Leave Eve to burn.

When they were ready to leave, John said, "Don't forget to pour all of the gas out and bring the cans back with you. When you get back call me, and I'll tell you where to meet me. Don't fuck this up! It has to look like an accident."

"We wired it right," Little Johnny declared, "The Fire Marshall will think the wiring was bad and the gas tank blew from a spark. That's if they get to it in time. Don't worry, Pops, we got this."

John got off the boat, walked up the walkway, and headed toward the gas station. He was going to catch a cab to his next destination.

As he got ready to cross the street, the cab pulled up in the turning lane. John walked up to the cab and got in the backseat.

"José, I need you to take me to where you dropped those two black chicks off."

"I ain't took no black chicks nowhere," José didn't like the man in the backseat. He forgot his name but he knew that box head a mile away.

"Come on, José," John said, "Don't tell me you had a false call or a fare just stiffed you," he pulled out a hundred dollar bill and dropped it in the front seat, "Take me to those women."

José picked up the bill, and while he stuffed it in his top pocket, he said, "I knew they did something wrong!" When the light turned green, he made a u-turn and headed for the freeway.

Money makes the world go 'round, thought John. He guessed the girls were being cheap on their end. *Those girls*, he mused. He wasn't really concerned about them as long as they gave him the bag back. They could keep the drugs. That was crumbs compared to forty million in diamonds. They wouldn't know what to do with them anyway. *Hell, I might give them a couple of them for getting my boss out of the way*, he thought, *Just as long as they give them back.* No harm, no foul.

"They stole from you, huh?" José asked.

"What makes you ask that?"

"The pretty one. She had a big black bag with a lot of stuff in it."

"Oh yeah?"

"Yeah, and they met up with another lady, a white lady."

"Where did you take them, José?"

"I'm taking you right now. They are at the Motel 6 off of the 605 Freeway and Slauson. Don't worry. I'm taking you right now."

They didn't go back to the same motel. They were trying to hide, John thought. The 605 Freeway and Slauson. *That's a little ways from their turf*, he thought. These girls were making trouble for themselves. Big trouble.

***

They got off of the freeway on Slauson. They went left, passed the motel, and then made a U-turn. That was the way you got in. When José made the U-turn, John said, "Don't go in the first entrance. Go down to the end and pull in."

José pulled into the last entrance and drove to the back. The motel was right next to the freeway, so in the back it's real dark, because of the ivy on the wall of the freeway. The lights off of the motel gave very little light to the parking lot.

"Back in next to that dumpster," John ordered. He would wait right there for his sons. "Go to the office for me and see if you can get their room number."

"No problem," José jumped out of the cab and headed for the office.

John looked over the seat at the meter. It had been running the whole time. $62.75 it read. "I'll be damn!" John mumbled.

This bastard couldn't just be satisfied with the hundred. He wanted the fare as well. I'll give him a farewell alright. His phone vibrated against his hip. "Where are you?"

"We're getting in the car right now," answered Tino, "It went perfect! You can see flames a hundred feet in the air right now."

"Do you hear sirens yet?"

"Nope!" Tino smiled at that.

John smiled at that. "Good. Come to the Motel 6 off of the 605 and Slauson." He hung up.

John could see José on his way back. *Greedy bastard.*

"They tell me nothing," he said as he got in, "They told me no two black ladies checked in. No two black and one white lady checked in either.

"Maybe they never checked in then."

"Yeah. You want me to take you back or what? I get off at twelve thirty and it's twelve right now."

"Nah, I'm gonna stay right here."

"Okay, man," José stuck his right hand over his shoulder, "The meter says $62.75, but you can just give me an even fifty."

"Let me see if I got change," John said.

With his right hand he reached for his Ruger, stuck it to the back of José's head, and pulled the trigger. José pitched forward and landed on the horn. John quickly reached over the seat and pulled him back. He propped his head on the window like he was sleeping, dug in his top pocket, and took back the hundred he gave him.

"You won't be needing this anymore, now will you?" It wasn't a question.

***

Upstairs the girls were totally blind to what was going on outside. They were full of Remy and weed and didn't know that their adversary was moving in on them.

The cabbie that René had pissed off had sold them out. His greediness had also got him killed.

Troops were on their way, speeding fast down the freeway, while their commander/daddy was waiting patiently for them in the parking lot.

"Pass the joint…You remember the pantyhose freak…his name was Alex…put some more ice in my cup, Brook."

They were having fun, thought René. She just hoped that it wouldn't be short lived. She was glad that Bone would be home the next day. Then there would be a man around to take control. Her mind was too foggy to think. He would know what to do. He always had a plan. Now was the time for her to start listening to his plans. Listen or die.

***

Tino and Little Johnny pulled into the motel parking lot. As they drove passed the cab, John called them up.

"Where are you?" Tino asked.

"Back up by that cab behind you."

"Oh. We didn't even see you."

"I know dipshit. That's why I'm calling," he hung up and got out of the cab.

Tino backed in right next to the cab. Little Johnny got out and walked over to his dad. He could already see a job that he had to finish.

"Johnny, take this cab and dump it, and we'll meet you here at two. That's a little less than two hours. Bring the Blazer. We might be making a trip to the desert."

"I'll put the shovels in the back." Little Johnny slid on his gloves.

He opened the driver's door of the cab, slid José over to the passenger's side, and got in. He pulled a handkerchief out of his pocket to wipe the windshield off; blood and bone is hard to see through. He rolled down the driver's window and drove out of the lot. He would leave the cab at the park by his house.

It was always something strange going on in the park.

Chapter Three

The phone was ringing but the girls couldn't hear it. The TV was too loud. Brooklyn saw the red light flashing and said, "Hey! Turn that TV down. The phone is ringing."

Karin cut the TV off, and everybody just stared at that awful device, making that awful noise. It could only mean one thing. John had found them.

"Answer it Brooklyn," Karin said.

"Shiiit. Not me!"

"You answer it, Karin. Your voice is deeper than ours. You could easily sound like a man." Alisha slid jokes in when she could.

Karin flipped Alisha off and grabbed the receiver.

It stopped ringing.

It stopped ringing but the red light kept flashing: a message at the office. Karin had told the clerk that she was hiding from her boyfriend and that two of her girlfriends would be with her. If anybody inquired about them, to call, so, she called.

"Damn."

René saw the concern in Karin's face, "What is it, Karin?"

"I told the young girl behind the desk to call me if anybody came in asking about us."

"That cab fool gave us up. Bitch-made cabbie!" René said angrily.

"Now what?" asked Alisha, "We're trapped. Now we gotta come out shootin'!"

"Hold on," Karin said, "Let me call down to the office." She picked up the receiver and pressed zero.

"Front desk," said the young clerk.

"Yes, this is two-fifty..."

"Two fifty-two?" She finished.

"Yes."

"The man that was driving the cab just came in here about fifteen minutes ago. I've been trying to call but you wouldn't answer."

"Yes, well the TV was a little loud. You said fifteen minutes ago?"

"Yeah, but he didn't park up front, so I went outside, and he was parked out back by the dumpster. Someone was in the backseat, too."

Karin put her hand over the mouthpiece and said, "Put everything back in that bag and let's get ready to go." Back in the phone she said, "Do me a big favor, love. Go and see if they're still back there. If they are, go back to the office and call me. But if not, come up and knock twice on my door."

"Okay," She hung up.

"I got her to check out the parking lot. If she knocks, be ready to go. If she calls, we go to Plan 'B'."

"What's Plan 'B'?" asked Brooklyn. She was clearly shaken.

Karin looked over at René. She shrugged her shoulders. She looked over at Alisha. She started looking at her feet. Brooklyn caught on quick.

"There is no Plan 'B'", she muttered. "I guess Plan 'B' is me, huh?"

"Yeah, girl," Alisha spoke quickly because she knew that Brooklyn would listen to no one else. "They don't know you, right? So, uh," she was thinking, "uh, yeah! You put on Karin's coat, right, and you go out, so whoever's watching will just see a person with a big coat on, and a hood. Yeah!" She was making it up as she went along. "Then, you come back, and René will wear the coat---."

"How am I gonna get the coat back upstairs?" René asked flatly.

"We'll send Brook down to get it, and then---."

There were two knocks at the door.

Alisha screamed.

"Okay, kids," Karin said, "That's enough of that hair-brained idea. Nobody's out there waiting for us."

"Whew," Alisha signed audibly.

Karin was laughing at Alisha; payback for that manly voice thing. She pulled back the dresser, moved the chair, and opened the door.

The young clerk was standing there. "The cab is gone, so you're cool."

"Thanks, love." Karin said. "Hold on a sec." As she went to the nightstand to get twenty dollars, the clerk looked around at the room.

"He must be real crazy, huh?" She was tripping on how they had stacked up the beds at the window. They covered about a third of the window.

"He sure is, baby. That's why we're leavin'." Karin handed the clerk the twenty. "Are you on all night?"

"Nah. I get off at one thirty," she said.

"Have your boyfriend come get you, love. I don't want him taking his anger out on you."

"I don't have a boyfriend. Shoot, I don't want one if he's gonna be like yours."

"Good."

The clerk sniffed the air and shyly said, "Uh, do you have anymore of that weed? It smells good."

"We sure do," Karin smiled, reached in her purse, and pulled out a bag. They all made bags out of the trash bags: they all had a corner of a trash bag. Karin opened her bag and handed her a bud the size of your middle finger.

"Wow! Chronic," the girl, said barely concealing her excitement.

"Don't you smoke that with your daddy," Karin teased.

"I won't. Bye."

"Bye-bye. And thanks again," Karin left the door open and said, "Let's go while we can."

"Yes, mommy dearest," teased Alisha. "You sounded like you were talking to your daughter."

"I'm old enough to have a daughter that age."

"You're old enough to have a daughter my age!" cried Alisha.

They all broke out laughing.

"If I had a daughter like you, I'd beat her," Karin said sarcastically.

"Yeah, yeah, come on. Let's get the hell out of here." Alisha grabbed the bag and stepped out. She looked left then right. She went to the right toward the stairs. They all filed out behind her. Brooklyn was close on her heels.

René and Karin were the last ones out. When Karin closed the door, she looked at René, "I hate that bitch!"

"No you don't. She just got you in there," René started laughing again.

"Bitch," Karin mumbled. "Hey, you're gonna tell me what the hell went on out there when we get to the next motel. And by the way, where might that be?"

"Not on this side of town that's faSho'."

"Where then?"

"The Ho-Jo!" said René.

"By Magic Mountain?"

"That's the one."

"Perfect," Karin pointed at René. "Then, you're gonna give me the run down."

They walked down to the car and drove off.

***

A Black Lexus GS300 sat under the freeway by the motel exit. Tino and John sat there watching the girls get in the car. It would be better to follow them away from here than to jump out right now. John didn't want to hurt them, he just wanted the bag back. The way they were looking around they knew he was close. They didn't know what he wanted, but they knew he was on their heels. If he got out now and approached them there would be too big of a scene.

"What do you want to do?" asked Tino.

"We follow, son. We follow."

When the girls pulled out of the parking lot, they turned left onto the street. Ten seconds later, the Lexus followed. They got on the 605 South, so John thought they might be headed to Artesia Blvd. Like a dog going back to his own vomit, or a child that only plays in his own yard; lost outside of the fence.

As they went onto the 91 West, John saw the billboard above the store off to the right: DuVall Diamonds. He missed that old boy. As weird as he was, if it wasn't for James DuVall, John didn't know where he would be today.

"Pull over right here. You see that blue and green awning that says DuVall Diamonds."

"Yeah, Johnny, I see it," said Steve.

"One man inside; no other employee, and he don't even got the door locked. Just walk right in. Hell, I might not even have to pull the heat. The man ain't nothin' but about five feet tall."

"Just hurry up man. I gotta get my mom's car back in thirty minutes."

Steve was a wimpy mama's boy but a damn good driver. If he gets me away from this lick, thought Johnny, I just might give him his full share. "Don't worry, Stevie, you'll get your ice cream after you wash your hands." Johnny talked like Mary Poppins.

"Fuck you, man!"

Johnny jumped out of the car and walked toward the diamond store. When he got to the window he could see the man behind the counter arguing with a customer. He walked in and started looking in display cases.

"I don't give a rat's ass, James. I ain't leavin' this store 'till ya' give me ma' money back. And, I'm 'bout ready ta' come 'round dat' der' counter and git ma' own money. You hear what I say James?"

James DuVall looked passed his rowdy customer, Lee Royce. He was looking at the big boy that had just walked into his store. He looked every bit of six feet five inches and about two hundred and eighty pounds. His body looked mean, but he had the face of an innocent child. Just the kind of man he needed in his store, in his store right now, for a clown like Lee Royce.

"Yeah, I hear you loud and clear Lee," DuVall waved the big boy over. "Hey son! I'm sure glad you came back for that job you were asking about. Come over here a second."

"Who me?" Johnny was shocked, "I ain't...."

"I know you ain't looking for hand outs, but I'll give you a thousand dollars a week plus a twenty percent discount on all merchandise in the store. What do you say to that, son?"

Wow! I came in here to rob this guy and he's offering me a job. A thousand a week? Wow! Looks like I won't be going back to prison no more. "What do I gotta do?" Johnny asked.

"You'll be the head of my security," DuVall looked over at Lee. "And your first job will be to ever-so-kindly escort Mr. Royce out of my establishment."

Johnny looked over at Mr. Royce who was fumbling with his hat in his hand. Lee got the hint and started for the door. When he grabbed the handle, he turned around, "This ain't over, James DuVall. Oh, no! By far is it over."

Present Time
***

As they changed over from the 91 West to the 710 North, John focused back on the task at hand. The girls had gone passed their normal stomping grounds, which meant to him that they were going somewhere to rest, regroup, and try to put everything in perspective. It made sense. When you kill a man, and steal from him, you need some peaceful space to get your thoughts together; rest was a weapon. He would need some rest also. And, he needed to go see Janet. Mrs. DuVall would want to see him; needed to see him.

"When these ladies stop at their next hideout, I'm going to see Mrs. DuVall."

"Why do you keep calling these bitches la...?"

"Hey!" John interrupted, "What did I tell you about that!" John didn't call women bitches. No matter what position in life they chose. He grew up with an abusive father who constantly beat his mother and called her a bitch. He vowed never to raise his sons up in that fashion.

"Give me your brother's new number."

"777-9311," Tino mumbled. "Pops, these 'ladies' just killed Mr. DuVall, and you still respect them enough to call them ladies?"

"To be honest with you, I think he had a heart attack. I didn't see anything that suggested that they killed him. And, you know how I feel about that word. Call them what they are: two-bit whores.

"Whore," Tino smiled. "You're losin' your hipness, Pops. It's 'ho', not 'whore'."

"Yeah, whatever." John dialed Little Johnny's number.

"Hey, Pops."

"Where are you right now?"

"I'm getting up in the Blazer. What's up?"

"Change-up. Jump on the 710 North to the 105 West. They're relocating."

"Why don't you just run them off the road, jump out, grab the bag, and get on?"

"Because if we do that, we'll never get the diamonds, you idiot! Four frantic women on the freeway; shots fired back and forth. Listen, it's one in the morning. They don't know what to do with diamonds, especially at this time of morning. So we let them think that they ditched me while you're watching them the whole time. When the sun comes up, and they come out of whatever motel they're in, then we get them. Is that clear enough for you?"

Little Johnny couldn't stand his father sometimes, and right now was one of those times. He put this finger on the end button and said, "Whatever," before he pushed it.

"Tino, you call that brother of yours back and you tell him, that if he fucks this up, he won't have to meet me in the grass because I'll kill him!" John was furious, "How dare that boy hang up on me?"

"Just calm down, Pops. You're always talking down to him. That's why he did it."

"Well, I wouldn't do that if he exercised his head up top more than he did his head down below. I swear I didn't act like that when I was his age. Little Johnny. Little piss-ant is more like it."

They road in silence the rest of the way. The only conversation in the car was one-sided because John couldn't hear his other son's responses over the phone. All he heard was, "Take the 405 North...yeah, toward the valley...no, we're still on the freeway...yeah, I know...I'll call back when we get off."

Twenty minutes later, they got off on Roscoe Blvd., made a right, and caught the light at Sepulveda. The girls were three cars ahead of them. They turned right. Tino, being impatient, hit the horn.

"Hey, boy!" John cried, "Relax. If by the time we turn, you don't see them, that means that they pulled in there," He pointed to the right at the Best Western Motor Lodge.

And he was right. When they pulled passed the parking lot, they could see two of them going into the office.

"You see them two?"

"The white girl and the sister with the gold hair,"

"The white girl is Karin, and the sister is René. There's one more, but I don't know her name. She might've instigated this whole scheme. When I picked the two of them up René didn't seem like she really trusted her."

"What makes you say that?" asked Tino.

"Oh, just a little something I watched play out while they were getting in my truck."

"What about the fourth 'lady'?" Tino asked sarcastically.

"Straggler," replied John, unruffled. Make a U-turn and go back to that Del Taco we passed. Call your brother and let him know our locale.

***

"This don't look like the Ho-Jo, Karin," René had fallen asleep fifteen minutes into the ride.

"Yeah," Karin conceded, "I got twisted up on the freeways. I don't get out much anymore."

"Where are we?" René asked.

"San Fernando Valley! Home of some Hollywood stars and homosexuals," Karin sounded like a Universal Studios tour guide.

"Yeah, René," Alisha added, "And guess where?"

"Sepulveda," declared René, "Where else? Once a ho, always a ho."

"That's right, girlfriend!" Exclaimed Karin, and gave René a high five.

Alisha just shook her head. She couldn't wait to see Bone so she could get off of this roller coaster ride of a life as a prostitute.

Karin and René got out and went inside of the office. Alisha shook Brooklyn.

"Huh, she said in a low voice," She was half sleep.

"Get up. Hurry!" whispered Alisha.

She snapped up, fear creasing her face. Brooklyn didn't like being led in the blind. And, she wanted to get high: now!

"Alisha I need a...."

"Red eye, huh?" She finished for her.

"Hell yeah! All this runnin' and duckin' and hidin' got me straight on edge."

"So you want to smoke a drug that gets half, no, 80%, of the users paranoid. How do that sound?"

"Don't start with me 'cause all a ya'll know what I'm talkin' 'bout, goin' through, or whatever. A bitch needs a hit!"

Alisha could relate. Too much at times. At twenty-nine years old, she had experienced things in the streets that no average woman could endure. Even other street walking women would never experience, let alone endure the depth of evil that had been bestowed upon her. It was time to hang up her garter belts and start exercising her profession. She was a Registered Nurse and a Certified Chemist. She could make it in right society. All she needed was a real man for support. She needed Bone.

"Look, Brooklyn. I'm gonna make sure you get your red eye flight when we get upstairs. I need you to hold something for 'US', me, you, and Bone. Don't tell nobody! Do you hear me?"

"Yeah, I hear you."

"I'm serious, Brook. This is our ticket out of here," she pulled the bag out and handed it to Brooklyn.

"What's in here," she asked.

"Diamonds!" she beamed.

Brooklyn unloosened the drawstring and stuck her hand in and pulled out a hand full of stones. She gasped and said, "You killed for this, huh?"

"Not me," Alisha locked eyes with Brooklyn and Brooklyn could tell she wasn't lying.

"You sure Bone is gonna take me with ya'll," she asked?"

"You know how he is with me; and you too, girl."

Brooklyn was in love with Bone, but she knew she wasn't his type: she still got high, "I could get my kids---."

"And get your own place, go back to school, bring your punk man, too," Alisha was laughing at the latter part of her statement.

"He ain't no punk!" Brooklyn declared. She always stuck up for that chump.

"Anyway, put them in your pocket, and tomorrow we both give them to Bone. Then we work on you and that dope."

"I'm ready, girlfriend, but not tonight," she pleaded.

"I know. Just wait until we get upstairs. You got a pipe?"

"No, but I'll make one," she said.

"Don't worry about that. René has one." Alisha looked at Brooklyn who had her eyebrows raised. She nodded.

"I knew it!" Exclaimed Brooklyn, "She thinks I'm stupid, but she forgets one thing."

"What?" asked Alisha.

"That I get high too," she declared. Brooklyn was young but she wasn't no fool. She had noticed the weight loss. She just didn't say anything. Wasn't her business to say nothing to René. It was her business to tell Bone. And tell she would.

Brooklyn stuffed the diamonds back in the bag and pulled the drawstring real tight. She put the bag in her left pocket. Her money was in her right pocket, and she didn't want to slip and pull the bag out with her money.

She leaned her head back on the seat and closed her eyes. She was about to start taking some big steps in her life. Was she really ready for them? Time would tell. Right now, she was ready for a flight.

***

The Blazer backed in next to the Lexus. He was still mad at Big John, so he backed in on the driver's side of the car. If Big John wanted to talk to him then let him get out and talk. As the window rolled down on the Lexus, he became angrier because his dad was behind the wheel.

"I'm only going to say this once, so listen carefully. If you fuck up, you know where to meet me: the grass. Once this little situation is over, you still meet me in the grass. I will not tolerate disrespect. The red four-door BMW 325I, in the Best Western parking lot behind you. Four women: three black, one white. The white chick is Karin, heavy chest and blonde hair. Two light skin sisters, one dark skin: one has reddish-blonde hair, the other looks like Alisha Keyes. The dark skin girl looks like a little boy with an Afro. They move before I get back, you call *ME*. Don't call your brother to call me, *you* call me. You got that?"

"Yeah," Little Johnny mumbled.

"I can't hear you," said Big John through clenched teeth.

"Yeah, I got it. When are you comin' back?" his son asked.

"I should be back around seven in the morning. I'm going to see Mrs. DuVall and then I'm going through the old neighborhood." He handed his son a large cup of coffee and a box of donuts: surveillance food.

"Let me park right before you leave." Little Johnny pulled all the way around the Del Taco and backed into the parking slot. This time he pulled up on the passenger side. His brother rolled the window down and stuck his tongue out at him then smiled. "Fuck you," he whispered back as they pulled out and left.

***

Upstairs in their room, the girls began kicking off shoes and going through clothes bags. René had been standing at the window since they came in transfixed on the scene in the Del Taco parking lot.

When they first walked in the room, the curtain was open. When she went to draw it closed, she saw John getting out of a Lexus. He was switching places with the driver. She closed the drapes enough so she couldn't be seen but she could see, and she watched.

Now the Lexus was gone but this big Blazer took its place.

"Karin!" René yelled.

"What girl?" Karin started toward the window.

René turned away from the window and looked her girlfriend in the eye. She was trying to be strong but she needed a boost: she wanted a hit.

"We need to talk."

"How many are out there?" asked Karin.

"Just one. Four against one," she headed to the bathroom.

After about ten minutes, Karin knocked on the bathroom door.

"Who is it?" asked René. She sat up on the counter taking a hit. She had been holding the pipe and the rock between her butt cheeks. Now she had the rock broken up on the counter with a little weed and was loading the pipe up. There was no use in hiding it because Karin already knew she was back getting high. Even if it wasn't Karin at the door, she didn't care at this point. She was more worried about her life than her image.

"It's Karin, girl. Open the door."

When she opened it, Karin looked straight passed her and down at the counter, "No more shame, huh?" It wasn't a question.

"No time for shame right now," René said.

"Well, you might as well let Brooklyn join in. You know she needs one too."

"In a minute. Let me tell you what happened out there on that boat. The trick was that one fool who was going around burning girls, remember?"

"You mean datin' them then takin' his money back?" asked Karin.

"No. I mean burning them! Pipe burns, cigar holes. That kind of burn."

"Shelley's trick!" exclaimed Karin. She remembered those horrible days. About ten girls had been a victim of his sting. She almost dated him. The only reason she got out of his truck was because he wanted to get high first. Karin didn't date tricks that got high anymore, too many problems.

"So, you burned his ass and took all that dope from him. Good girl!" She beamed.

"It's a little more to it than that. I put about a quarter ounce of powder up his nose then about a gram on the pipe for him to hit and..."

"And *boom!* Out go his lights!" Karin finished, "So, John is looking for you two because you killed his boss?" It was a declaration more than it was a question.

"That's about the size of it," René sighed. She felt a whole lot better now that Karin knew the story. "Now get out and send Brooklyn in here so we can take ultimate flight."

"Don't tell her the whole story. She's the Barbara Walters of Artesia."

"She needs to know what we got her into, Karin," René persisted.

"Leave out the part about poppin' his balloon. Just tell her you stole all that dope."

"Yeah. Send her in here," René would feel her out with the conversation. Then she might give it all to her. Brooklyn was young but she wasn't stupid. Not that stupid.

Karin came out of the bathroom and said, "Brook. You're up."

Brooklyn got off of the bed and shuffled toward the door.

"'Bout time," she said. When she got in there, she saw the dope out on the counter and said, "Let me pee first. And don't put no weed on there. I want a straight flight."

"Ain't you trippin' on seeing me getting high again?" asked René.

"Girl, that's between you and yourself. I got my own hang ups to deal with."

With that answer right there, René would tell her the whole story. She loaded the pipe, handed it to Brooklyn while she was on the toilet, and said, "Let me tell you what happened…"

***

Alisha chewed on cold pizza when Karin came out and Brooklyn went into the bathroom. She knew what was going on in there but she couldn't worry. Everybody dealt with their own hang-ups their own way. She just hoped that it wouldn't be a distraction that would get them all killed. She wouldn't let that happen. As long as she wasn't high, they would live. She'd beat them all up if she had to. She would too.

"Karin? You still getting high?" she asked.

"Hell no, girl! I stopped doing that about a year and a half ago. Nineteen months as a matter of fact," she said with pride.

"Good. At least two of us got a clear mind in here."

"I'm actually very proud of you Alisha. After that experience you had with Shelley, you have not been back and you've still been hangin' around it. You beat that demon, baby!"

The truth was that Alisha was really Karin's strength out there. Karin had been watching Alisha every since she stopped getting high on cocaine. Through all the weird trips in the streets, nothing got to her that made her turn back to crack. Karin admired Alisha far more than she let on.

"René told me the whole story. That freak deserved what he got."

"I just hope we don't have to pay the price for it," said Alisha. "We gotta get a Press-Telegram in the morning to see if it was front page news. The way John was on our heels, is on his heels, at least one person wants us to answer for it."

"So, you froze the man's heart?" said Brooklyn, "I ain't mad at cha', girl. You ain't gonna freeze mine up in this bathroom, though. I'm out of here. For some reason, it don't even feel the same."

"You didn't get high?" asked René who was beyond sparked.

"It's not that I didn't get high," said Brooklyn, "It's just that I want to feel that high Alisha, Karin," she hesitated, "And you feel, or at least you felt. I want to feel that sober high. I want my babies back!"

Brooklyn started crying. She and René both had been fighting with their mother's for their children. René knew exactly what she was going through. René walked over to the toilet with the pipe. She dropped it in there. She swept the rest of the dope in her hand and dropped it in. She looked over at Brooklyn.

Brooklyn walked over to the toilet and put her hand on the handle. She looked at René; she nodded her approval. Brooklyn winked at her, cracked a smile, and flushed the toilet.

"Just wave those troubles down the drain," she said. She let go of the handle and gave René a great big hug. They both cried, but Brooklyn felt that the tears they were sharing were tears of joy, tears of freedom, and tears for a new beginning. She leaned back and looked René in her eyes and said, "I won't tell him."

"Thanks Brook."

***

Outside the Del Taco parking lot was Little Johnny. He sipped coffee and ate donuts. He hated just sitting and watching. Why did he get all of the dumb work and Tino got to run around with Big John? Because he is the favorite, that's why. Tino was the favorite and junior was a mama's boy, *"and since you wanna be up under your mama all the time,"* was the beginning line every time he got left behind. While they entertained, he made sure nobody got out of line. He was never a part of the reindeer games. He was always left the shit detail.

So here he was sitting in this big ol' truck all alone. *Well, since I'm so close I might as well pick up some action on*

Sepulveda, he said to himself. He fired up the truck and pulled out on Roscoe. When he got to Sepulveda, he made a right. He was going to pick up a hooker. Little did he know that the one he picked up would cost him so much.

Chapter Four

They were all seated at the table. It was time to make a plan to get the observer in the Blazer off their tail, remove him, and contact John. Find out just what his intentions were *IF* they met up again.

"Okay ladies, before I go into my plan, let me just tell you that Brooklyn, on her own, flushed the pipe, and the crack. She made a decision to stop getting high, and she is looking at us for support."

Brooklyn was looking shy, timid, and vulnerable. She was not expecting the reaction she received.

"That's great, girl!" said Karin. She got up and gave her a big hug. "Now we can hang homegirl. Get some real money."

"Yeah, and get them babies back," said Alisha. "I am so proud of you! I gotcha back. Don't even trip."

"Okay. Now to the bizness," René blurted out. "Don't be nervous, but I saw John outside in the Del Taco parking lot when we got up here."

"What...we gotta go..." Alisha and Brooklyn were rising out of their chairs.

"Relax," said Karin, "Here. Fire this joint up."

"Yeah, kick back. He's gone, but he left a big white Blazer in his place. Now I can see out the window from where I'm sittin' but the truck is gone," said René. "Trust me, he ain't gone far. What I want to do is get that fool and find out what they want."

"They want to kill us René!" said Alisha "We killed his boss so he kills us. That simple."

"I don't think so. If it was that easy, he would've did a freeway shootin' and just kept on about his business."

"You got a point there, girlfriend," Karin said. "So, that means you gals got something he wants back."

"The dope," said Brooklyn.

"Whatever it is," said René, "We gotta catch the watchdog, tie his ass up, and contact his master. I'm too old to be runnin' scared. I'm damn near forty years old; way too late in the game to start runnin'."

"So, how do we catch this watchdog?" asked Alisha who already knew.

"We catch a dog with a stray cat," said René.

"You seen a stunt dummy already?" asked Karin.

"No, but if we hit the street like the gangsta hoes we are, I'm sure it won't take but a minute."

Brooklyn fired up the joint, hit it real hard, and passed it. As the joint rotated, they discussed a strategy. They tied down each other's hair and then changed clothes.

"Damn, Karin you didn't bring but one extra outfit?" asked René. "I can't fit nothin' Brook's got in her bags."

"Girl, you said grab money and go. The only reason that outfit is up here because it was in the trunk of the car."

"What cha' gonna do about the stuff in your room?" asked Alisha.

"The maid'll pack that shit up and put it in the storage room. You know that, girl."

"Check out time!" screamed Brooklyn. "You pay now or you leave now." She said, imitating mamason. They all broke out laughing.

Once they were all dressed, and looking a little different, René said, "Get a little bit of that powder cocaine and put it in the plastic on your cigarette pack. Get some of that speed and put some in this one. That's for the stunt dummy. She's on one or the other."

Alisha did it and rolled them up. She gave them to René.

"Okay. Let's go catch us a dog," said René.

Before they stepped out in the hallway Karin said, "Meow!"

"You see the sign on the side of that donut shop?"

"Yeah."

"Okay. Look about three cars..."

"I see it," interrupted René, "Let's get a little closer."

They started walking. About ten yards from the corner they stopped and sat down on some apartment stairs.

"I see a chick in the donut shop," Brooklyn said.

"Okay, Brooklyn," Karin said, "You're up. Ask her two simple questions: do you get high, and do you have a pipe? If she answers 'yes' bring here over here."

"That's dumb. Let me go..."

"No, Alisha," Karin persisted, "We need a dumb one like that. That way she'll do as we say instead of coming up with a better idea for 'our' plan. We don't need no half-ass smart bitch ruining what we're trying to do."

"You're right," conceded Alisha, "Brook, you ready?"

"As I'll ever be," she walked off pulling the hood over her head. She wore Karin's big jacket with the hood on it, hiding. She ran back across the street so she wouldn't have to cross the intersection twice. She didn't need to be seen that long in the light.

As she got to the corner, the light turned green, so she ran across. She walked into the donut shop and headed right to the booth the woman was sitting in. She was about five feet tall, dark like Brooklyn, with a purple mini skirt on, and some white high heels. The high heels had seen better days, so did the white sweater she was wearing.

Brooklyn sat down and blurted, "Do you get high, girlfriend?"

"Ha!" She cried. "I must really look like I need a hit for you to just walk up and that be the first thing to come out of your mouth. Do I look that bad, girl?" She asked as she pulled out her compact.

"Nah, I just need a hit that bad," Brooklyn sighed. "So, do you got a pipe or what?"

"Yeah, but we can't hit it right here."

"Come on. I got a spot."

"Hold on, girlfriend," she hesitated, "What's your name at least, so I'll know what to call you in case we get stopped?"

"Lorraine," Brooklyn said after some thought, "Tipi Lorraine."

"Your daddy must've played a lot of dominoes."

"Huh?"

"Never mind. They call me D.L."

"Down Low?" Brooklyn asked.

"Dark and Lovely," she declared as she stood up.

They walked out of the donut shop, down to the corner, and waited for the light to change. When the light turned green, Brooklyn wanted to run across but she couldn't because D.L. had on heels./' Plus, she didn't want to spook the girl.

Behind them the Blazer pulled out, and was about to make a U-turn.

When they got ready to cross over to where the crew was waiting, Brooklyn heard Alisha yell, "Wait up!" Brooklyn pulled D.L. back.

The Blazer drove by and honked the horn.

That spooked D.L. "Is something wrong, Tipi?"

"Nah," Brooklyn said coolly. "We cool. Come on, my girlfriends are over there." Brooklyn started across but D.L. held her place. Brooklyn went back to the curb and said, "Look. Ain't nobody gonna do nothin' to you. Trust me, kay?" She grabbed D.L. by her hand, gave her a reassuring look, and they crossed the street.

"We didn't think she was gonna come," René said, when they made it across the street.

"I had faith in you, Brook," Alisha said.

"What's this all about? 'cause it damn sure ain't about getting high." D.L. was being sassy.

"It's about some money," René barked. "You down for makin' that, right?"

"Depends."

"Depends on what, love?" Karin asked calmly.

"How many of ya'll I gotta do," D.L. replied.

They all looked at her, looked at each other, and again back at her; they busted out laughing.

"She's gonna do you first…Shiiit! I'm first…where do I fit in…" They were teasing each other back and forth when René pulled her to the side.

"What's your name?"

"They call me Dark…"

"No, baby. I asked your name. My name is René," she said in her seductive, disarming voice.

"Tish. My name is La Tisha."

"Look Tish. Did you see that big truck that honked at you before you crossed the street?"

"Yeah."

"We want to catch that fool. He ain't no kind of freak or nothin'. We just need to set a trap for him." She was keeping it simple.

"And I'm the bait? Nah, I'm cool." D.L. started to walk off.

René pulled out the dope, "You fuck with crack?"

"Sometimes. That don't mean I'm some dumb ass strawberry out here, though."

"I didn't say that," René eased up. "All we want you to do is pull him up on that street behind the Best Western…"

"Langden?" She replied.

"Yeah. Pull him up over there and get his pants down. Once you get his pants down, accidentally hit the horn, and we'll take it from there. I'm gonna give you this," she waved the dope, "Plus twenty dollars for your pocket. Is that cool?"

"I ain't gonna get hurt am I?" She asked.

René pulled the pistol out of her back and showed it to her.

"Okay," she agreed.

"Look!" Karin pointed, "He's on his way back."

They all sat back down on the steps. He drove passed, looking around.

"Let's go ya'll," René ordered. To D.L. she said, "Let him pass you up one more time, Tish, then get in. By that time, we'll be in position."

"Okay," she replied. "Hey! When do I get paid?"

They were all running across the street. René yelled over her shoulder, "When the job is done."

***

Little Johnny saw the chick hit the street, but she was walking with some dude in a hooded jacket. He pulled out anyway and made a U-turn. As he passed them up, he honked his horn. He was using that as a signal. I'm next.

The next time he doubled back he didn't see her, so he figured that she was taking care of her business. The next time she surfaced he would be right on top of her. He made another U-turn for another pass. He was going a little too fast this time, but he could've sworn her saw her. "Damn," he said out loud.

One more pass.

Back the other way, he saw her on the opposite side of the street, and she was watching him pass. "I'll be right back," he said out of the window but not too loud. He made another U-turn, slowed down next to her, and pulled to the curb. He cut his lights off and jumped in the passenger seat. The truck was way too high to talk from the driver's seat.

"What's going on this morning, baby doll?" He asked.

"You tell me, big daddy in the big truck."

"I'm just lookin' for some quick fun before I go to work."

"You don't work for L.A.P.D. do you?" Tish asked.

"Hell no!" He cried, "Never have and never will." He opened the door and said, "Here. Let me help you get in." He jumped down.

She walked up to him.

"I hope you're strong enough, big boy," she said.

"Just put one foot on that step and grab the door."

When she did that he gripped her hips and boosted her into the truck. He closed the door and went around to the driver's side. When he got in he said, "Do you have a room?"

"What do you want this morning?" she asked.

"Just a little head," he replied.

"That's all? We don't have to go to my room for that. Go up to the light and make a left. I know a quiet spot right around the corner by Del Taco."

When she said Del Taco, he thought, *I can have my candle blew out and still watch the motel for those chicks. Cool!* He cut the lights on and pulled away from the curb.

Little Johnny was letting his other Little Johnny get him in trouble. Big trouble.

***

"Did you hear that chick, René?" Alisha asked, "How many of ya'll I gotta do? She's freak nasty. It must not be no dudes out here hustlin' with these girls."

"Yeah. She's a lonely kid," acknowledged René.

"What's her name, Brook?" Alisha asked.

"Dark and Lovely." Brooklyn replied.

"Figures."

They were walking into the front entrance of the Best Western. They walked straight down the hallway to the rear entrance. It was a small laundry room on the left of the hall. You could almost see Roscoe Blvd. from inside. Brooklyn would wait in there with the drawstring from the drapes. Karin had removed the string from the drapes with no problem. Tying guys up was nothing new to her.

"Just wait right here, Brook," René said. "If anybody starts to come out when we attack this dude you let us know. Karin, you and Alisha go sit on those apartment steps across the street. I'll be in between the buildings on this side."

They stepped out into the early morning air. It felt good to their warm, excited skin. Their adrenalin was already pumping. They were going to take down the hunter's dog. Catch him up in a clever trap laid out by some sharp pussycats. They may have played in some alleys with stray cats, but their fur wasn't that matted together. They didn't have many patches missing.

The Blazer turned down Langden and drove passed them. As it got ready to turn around at the end of the street, René said, "Get ready ya'll."

"You ready Karin?" Alisha asked.

Karin flashed her .380 and said, "The Wild Wild West, baby!" She had traded coats with Brooklyn for the second half of the show. She flipped the hood up on her head.

Chapter Five

"Just pull up under this tree right here," Tish said, "This is my regular spot."

Little Johnny didn't like it because he couldn't see the motel parking lot, "I'm gonna pull up a little further in the light. It's too dark right here." He was trying to make it seem like he was nervous.

"The kinda bizness we're doin' don't need light, baby. Don't worry I won't bite cha'." Tish winked at him. He smiled back.

Gotcha!

He cut the truck off and scooted his seat back as far as it would go. He began to unbuckle his belt and Tish stopped him.

"Let me do my job, big boy." She sat up on the armrest and unbuttoned his pants. Then she straddled the armrest and said, "Lift up a little."

He lifted his butt and she slipped his pants down to his ankles. As she did this, her right elbow hit the horn.

"Watch what you're doing bitch!" He growled. He couldn't afford to get caught up like this. He put his left arm behind his head, grabbed the back of her head with his right hand, and pulled.

"You ain't gotta be so rough, big boy," she snatched away from him, "I'm gonna take care of you." Tish glanced to her right and saw two figures coming her way. "Close your eyes, big boy, and enjoy the ride." She shifted her weight on the armrest just as one of the figures grabbed the door, so he would think that she was making the truck rock.

A hooded figure appeared in the window with a pistol.

"Freeze, big boy!" Karin hissed, "You move and I blow your little pecker off."

Little Johnny snapped his eyes open and saw somebody on the side of his truck with a pistol. He gripped Tish's head and was going to swing her in front of the pistol. She grabbed his balls.

"Okay, okay, okay," he said real fast.

She dug her nails into him; they felt like hot daggers piercing his body.

René opened the passenger door and climbed in. She had her .38 pointed at his head. "D.L., reach under the seat and feel around."

With her left hand she held his nuts, and with her right she felt around. Tish came back up with a .357 Magnum: Dirty Harry.

"Wow!" Karin cried, "You're trying to stop cars with that thing."

"Look. Just take it," he said flatly, "My gift to you. I got a few bucks in my wallet too. Take it all. My gift to you."

"Oh, we're definitely gonna take all that," René said matter of factly, "But that's not why we're here. First things first," she pulled off her scarf, "Take this, D.L., climb in the backseat, and tie his hands together."

Tish handed Karin the gun, who handed it to Alisha. As Tish climbed in the back, Karin said, "Go get Brook, Alisha, so we can tie our dog up in the yard. This concrete yard that is." Karin let out a sinister laugh as Alisha ran to the back of the motel.

It didn't take long for Little Johnny to figure out whom these chicks were. While he was watching their car, they were watching him. How did they know, though? I guess that didn't matter now. His pops was going to kill him.

"What do you want with me?" he asked René.

"I should be asking you that question. You're the one watching us," Alisha and Brooklyn walked up.

René opened the door and let them in, "You got his hands tied good, D.L.?"

"Tighter than a gnat's ass," she declared. Tish looked at Alisha for approval.

"You did this before, huh girl?" Alisha asked.

"I've been in these streets fifteen years. He ain't the first trick to get tied the fuck up."

They all laughed at that.

"Okay, Karin stated, "Drag him in the back and finish the tie. Hands to ankles and go around them knees, too."

Tish and Alisha pulled Little Johnny into the backseat. Brooklyn tied up his ankles and his knees. She climbed into the far back and pulled on him as Alisha pushed him over.

"Man, what the fuck do you bitches want?" Little Johnny was pissed off more at himself than anything. If he had not acted on his sexual urges, he wouldn't be in this situation right now; hogtied with his pants down around his ankles.

"We want your phone and some soap for your mouth, little boy."

Karin looked over at René and asked, "How come all the guys with little dicks drive big trucks and talk shit?"

"Good questions," René said. She hollered over her shoulder, "Hey, teeny weenie, answer that question for us."

"Fuck you!" He yelled.

They all started laughing again.

"Can you drive this big 'ol thang?" René asked.

"Girl, please," Karin slid the seated forward and fired it up.

Alisha had gone into his pockets to get the phone and the money.

"Here," she handed René the phone.

René watched Alisha stuff the money in her pocket. She wouldn't trip on that, "D.L., where you going?"

"Back to the donut shop," she said. She stuck her hand out as René went into her pocket.

"Good job, girlfriend," René said as she handed her both bags of dope, and a hundred dollar bill.

Tish looked at the money and both bags of dope: coke and speed. A lot of it, too. She had enough to go and get her a room for a couple of days and set up some deals to sell the speed. She wouldn't have to subject herself to the nasty John's that loved to ride up and down the street, trying to satisfy an evil lust. She could rest her feet for at least a week, then it was back to the grind; sex for sell.

"Anytime you need me," Tish stated, "I ain't hard to find."

Karin pulled into the donut shop parking lot. Tish pulled her heels off and jumped out of the truck. René waved at her as they drove off. Brooklyn looked out the back window at her.

Tish waved, "Bye, Tipi."

"Who you workin' for, boy?" René asked. She already knew that John had left him there. She just wanted to see how fast he would give him up.

"Fuck you!" He yelled.

"That's what we'll do if you don't tell us," Alisha said. "Do you got that toy, Karin?"

"Sure do," she replied, "I never leave home without it." She reached into her jacket pocket and pulled out a foot long dildo. She tossed it back to Alisha.

Alisha said, "Jump on the freeway so nobody will hear him scream." She slapped him on the ass with the dildo and showed it to him. "You'll probably like this, you freak."

"You stick that in my ass and I'll..."

"You'll what? It's too many guns in here for you to do anything."

"I'll ask you one more time," René said, "Who do you work for?"

"You know damn well who I work for!" He barked.

"That's not an answer." René handed Alisha a jar of hair gel. "Baby girl? Stick him!"

"I think he wants it anyway," Alisha stated. She stuck her fingers in the gel. "Spread his cheeks, Brook."

Brooklyn turned him to where his butt was facing the back seat and spread his cheeks wide open.

Alisha ran her fingers down the crack of his ass and wiped her hand on his pants.

"Hey!" He cried, "You ain't gotta do all that?"

"Name and number," René was going through the phone. She found the feature "Recent Calls" and pulled up the last incoming call. It said, "Big Bro" and the one before that said, "Doe-Doe Dad." Was John this boy's daddy?

"Some guy named Bill. I ain't got his number. He called me."

"Wrong name," René said, "There ain't no Bill in your phone. Stick him, Alisha."

Alisha maneuvered six inches of the dildo into his ass.

He screamed, "Aawww! You bitch"

"Stick your scarf in his mouth, Brook," Alisha said. "Give him something to chew on while I serve him the rest of this thang."

"No wait!" He gasped, "My dad left me out here. My pops is John.

Brooklyn and Alisha looked at René. She nodded. Karin looked a little pale, but she held her strength in her voice, "Call that man and see what he wants."

"Go back to the motel," René said. She went to "Doe-Doe Dad" in the phone and pressed send. Over her shoulder, she said, "Pull that thing out of that boy before he starts to like the way it feels."

***

"They tell me the boat exploded, John," Janet sounded tired. "He died in an explosion. Is that it, John? Nobody else got hurt did they? No girls got hurt with that bastard did they?"

"No, Jan."

Janet DuVall knew all about her husband's late night excursions. She knew about the drugs, the women, and the toys. She knew about it all. She knew because he included her in the beginning.

"Good," she grabbed John's leg. "I need you this morning."

Janet was a forty-five year old stallion; five feet seven, a hundred and forty pounds; jogged two miles a day, and Tai-Bo three times a week. With honey blond hair down to her waist, who could resist?

"I'm taking care of other business right now, Jan."

"More important than me?" She stood up and put her hands on her hips.

His phone rang: saved by the bell.

She walked to the bar to refill her drink.

His caller ID read: Lil John. "What are they doing? They moving?" John asked.

"We sure are movin'!" René replied, "Movin' in a big ol' Blazer with a cute young man tied up in the back. Why are you following me?" René firmly asked.

Now how in the hell did that happen? John's blood started to boil. His pissant son couldn't keep his dick in his pants. That's how that happened. "This is a surprise, René."

"Don't try that sweet talk, John. Why are you on my tail like this?

"I ain't gonna hurt him. I'm gonna make him enjoy this dildo if you don't start talkin'."

Wow! That boy is really in a jam, John thought. *I should make her use it on him*, he considered, then changed his mind. "You killed my boss and you expect me not to look for you to find out what happened?"

"I didn't kill him," René said matter-of-factly, "He had a heart attack. It's not nice to fool with motha' nay-cha'!"

"You could be right about that," John agreed, "But it's still not nice to steal.

"I believe when I picked you up you didn't have three ice buckets with you." He didn't want the dope back. He wanted the bag they used to carry it out in.

"Oh, thaaat," René said, "Well, I'm keepin' them for all of the stress your boss caused me."

"Speaking of stress. Can I talk to my son?"

"Alisha, put this to the kids ear," she handed her the phone.

Alisha gave the phone to Brooklyn. When she put the phone to his mouth, he started yelling, "They got me hog tied, Pops, and they stuck a dil…"

Brooklyn handed the phone back to Alisha who passed it on to René. "Does that relieve your stress?"

"Well, at least I know he's still breathing." John thought that they were giving him what he deserved. Maybe not the dildo."Listen," John continued, "The authorities think that my boss died in a boating explosion, so you and your girlfriend are in the clear."

"That remains to be seen," she said flatly, "Until I can read a newspaper, I'm gonna have to stay away from that area." A boating explosion? If he blew up the boat, and didn't say anything about the dope, what does he want?

"We need to meet René. You took something of mine off of that boat, and I need it back."

"And what might that be John?" she turned in her seat so that she could look at Alisha in her eyes: she did stuff on her.

"You say we took something of yours?" René pulled the phone away from her face, "What is he talkin' 'bout Alisha?" She spoke through clenched teeth.

"I don't know, girl," Alisha replied smoothly. "You need to stop looking at me like that."

"Yeah, you took something of mine. We'll talk about it face-to-face." He hung up.

**

Janet was at the bar smoking a cigarette. She was deep in thought. She couldn't stand James DuVall, but they had been married twenty-four years. That was too much history to just immediately move on from. "Damn you, Jimmy," she whispered.

"I gotta go," John ran his hand through her mane. "One of my boys are in a jam."

"Little Johnny?" It wasn't a question.

"I'll call you when I straighten this mess out," he kissed her on her forehead and walked out.

Tino had dropped him off at his truck, so he was solo again. He had to go save his other son, Junior, who always thought with the head in his pants.

**

They pulled the truck up in the Del Taco parking lot. René knew that John was on his way so his son wouldn't be tied up long. Another hour, hour and a half. The traffic was still pretty light at three thirty in the morning.

They all jumped out of the truck and walked toward the back door of the motel. They were going upstairs to gather their things and relocate. René slowed her pace and grabbed Alisha by her arm.

"Why you holdin' out on a bitch?"

"I ain't holdin' out on you, girl. Don't listen to that fool. He wants to kill us."

René changed the subject, "He said the po-lease think Adam died in a boat explosion. Why would he blow the boat up with him on it like that?"

"Maybe we did him a favor by killin' that fool," Alisha embraced the subject change. "I know we did a whole lot of hoes a favor; one less weird ass trick to worry about."

"He wants the dope, then. I figure between the coke and the speed we got at least four or five pounds," René said matter-of-factly.

"You think so?"

"Hell yeah! Street value is about a hundred thousand." René knew so much about big figures like that because she came from a family of drug dealers. She had a sister that was in a federal prison for transporting two kilos of cocaine to Texas.

"There it is there," Alisha declared. "That's enough to chase us down, don't you think?"

Alisha was right. René was right. René wasn't stupid, though. She knew her girlfriend had something stashed in that duffel bag.

In the room Karin asked, "Where to my lovely fugitive?"

"The Ho-Jo, Karin. You think you can get us there this time?" René was clowning.

"Don't take the car! You'll kill yourself!" Alisha never missed a chance to clown Karin.

"Keep it up, bitch!"

Chapter Six

John pulled up in Del Taco just a little before five a.m. He saw the Blazer parked right where it was when he left. His son wasn't sitting in it. He looked over in the motel parking lot. The BMW was gone.

John got out of his truck and climbed up on the Blazer. He could faintly hear mumbling from inside, but the door was locked. He took out his pistol and smashed the window.

"Um bap ear, bap ear." Little Johnny was talking with a scarf in his mouth.

"I hear you. Just relax." John climbed in the back seat. When he looked over the seat, he couldn't hold back his laughter. The girl's hog tied the boy, and tied his knees together. Clever chicks.

What was funny was the foot long dildo they left wedged in the crack of his ass. He reached over and undid the gag.

"I wish I had a camera," John said. "How long you been sitting here like this?"

"'Bout two hours. Can you untie me now?"

John pulled the dildo from between his cheeks and slapped him in his head with it.

"Hey, man!"

"Shut up you idiot," he slapped him on his ass with it. "Your dick is gonna get you killed." He looked at the way he was tied: slipknot. He pulled one string and his wrist and ankle came loose. He untied his hands and climbed out of the truck.

Five minutes later his son climbed out. "Thanks, Pops."

"That's the only reason I came, son. You're an idiot but you're mine."

***

In the Howard Johnson, down a couple of miles from Magic Mountain, everybody was asleep, except René.

She was on the phone talking to her best friend in the whole world, Jo-Jo. Jo-Jo had stopped hanging out because she was getting too old for foolish games. She had been too old, but her addiction kept her out there. Now that she was clean she stayed away. She had different friends: clean and sober friends.

"The only reason I'm doing this René, is because you truly sound sincere, and because it's Bone who I'm going to get. Other than that, I can't be involved."

"I know that, girl. That's the only reason I called you. If he sees you, then he'll know that it's something serious. If I ain't there to pick him up, he told me he didn't wanna ever see me again." René pleaded with her girlfriend.

"Look," Jo-Jo hated a whiner, "I said I'll go get the boy. Stop pleadin' your case with me."

"Thanks, Jo. I love you."

"How much did you say you took?"

"'Bout five pounds."

"Yeah," she sighed, "I'm really stayin' the hell away from ya'll." She hung up.

Everything would work out now. Bone would get out tomorrow, no, today. Damn.

The sun would be up in about thirty minutes. Things would smooth out today.

René went downstairs to get newspapers. She bought The Press-Telegram, The Los Angeles Times, and The Daily Breeze. If a story about a boat explosion wasn't in one of those three papers, there wasn't an explosion.

Chapter Seven

"Braxton!" yelled the officer in Receiving & Release. Officer Gomez was the head of R&R. He had one damn good clerk and three goofball porters. His clerk was going home this morning. He sure would miss him.

Willie Braxton, also known as Bone, had really showed him that all convicts weren't idiotic sub-human creatures. Bone had taught Gomez how to separate the real from the fake. He showed him how to be a people person not a C.D.C. robot, and for that, he was grateful, because as an officer you don't want to make enemies. It makes your job harder, and you just might be on the wrong end of a knife one day.

"Braxton!" Gomez yelled again.

"I been standin' here," Bone stated, "You was day dreaming. Probably thinkin' about your lunch at eight in the mornin', fat ass!" Bone smiled.

"Fuck you," Gomez said flatly. "Get your box with your clothes, and sign right here for your gate money. They're finally letting your red ass out, huh?" It wasn't a question.

"Yeah, I'll miss you, Gomez, for about five minutes," he started laughing but Gomez knew he meant it. Bone had been working in R&R for two years straight. It would be hard not to miss him.

"Listen," Gomez whispered, "Don't pull that phone out of your pocket until you get off these grounds. Got it?"

"Don't trip, potato chip," Bone declared, "I wouldn't front you off like that."

Gomez had let Bone get away with a lot of stuff; cigarettes, porno books - you name it. If you couldn't have it on the yard, Bone had it. If they took something from you out of your package, talk to Bone.

"Hey Braxton, the front gate called and said some lady named Jo Ann was here to pick you up. You gave me René."

Why was Jo-Jo at the gate? "Can you get her cleared?" They didn't like last minute changes. Neither did Bone. This last minute change had trouble written all over it.

"Only for you, you red haired homosexual," Gomez said. He smiled at Bone because he knew he would come back with something funny.

"You've been chasin' my dick for two years you drag queen," Bone countered. They both laughed.

"I'll take care of it," Gomez waved him away, "Go get dressed." Gomez picked up the phone to clear Bone's transportation.

In the tank, Bone's thoughts were on René. She had too many flaws and gaps that weren't filled in. Now she wasn't even at the gate because she had made some kind or shady move; playing everybody she ran across too close.

Alisha had stepped up to the plate, though. From the very first day Bone hit L.A. County Jail, all the way until now, she was there every step of the way. If he had to choose which one to run with right now, Alisha would be the one. With the FUBU short suit he was putting on, along with the Kenneth Cole sandals (she knew Bone liked to have his toes out in the summer), it was crystal clear who was campaigning for his affection.

"The van is here, fellas," Gomez announced. "Let's go."

Bone lagged back so he could be last. When Gomez handed him his envelope with his gate money in it, he looked at Willie Braxton, a.k.a. Bone, square in his eyes, "It's been a pleasure working with you friend." They shook hands.

"Don't get all misty eyed on me Gomez. It's been real, man. You're alright for a fat ass cop," they laughed. Bone patted him on his back and said, "Don't call me, I'll call you." He hopped in the van and they drove off.

"Take care Bone." The van had turned the corner.

"What did you do beat René up and tell her you were madly in love with me? I know. You slipped her a Mickey and me and you are headed to Vegas to get married."

"Boy, you are crazy!" Jo-Jo walked up to Bone and gave him a hug, "Welcome home Willie," she whispered in his ear.

"Thanks for coming, Jo-Jo. Your face is truly the one I would rather see, anyway."

Bone had known Jo-Jo way before all of the other women on the block, and he didn't meet her on the block. Their mutual friend Freddy had taken Bone to her place and formally introduced them. "I'm just puttin' two real hustlers together," Freddy said. And that he did. They made a good team. Bone and Jo-Jo were the Bonnie and Clyde of Artesia Blvd. They never slept together, though. In fact, she would pick the girls that he messed with. Most of the time.

Jo-Jo was retired from the life now, but she taught Bone so much that he would be forever in her debt. Bone would kill for Jo-Jo.

"Now," she said, "Let's get the hell away from this place." As they walked to the car she said, "Boy, it seems like only yesterday that we was hangin', huh? Boy, you ain't been gone no five years."

"No, but you have. You retired before I got caught."

"And you still came over my house everyday. Went to sober dances with me and all that."

"I had to make sure your ass stayed away," Bone said. He wouldn't go by her house everyday; every other day. He was going to be her support system in whatever she wanted to do. His admiration and respect for her out weighed anything else. Jo-Jo was twenty years older than Bone, and in the world of sex, drugs, and rock & roll, you respect your G's.

"Now look," she turned serious, "I don't know who these hoes robbed, but they got a key of powder and a key and a half of that speed shit." Jo-Jo was giving him the business; lacing his boots to the top hole.

"That speed shit is glass," he corrected her.

"Whatever. It's a bunch of weed, too. It's René, Alisha, Karin, and Brooklyn." She waited for him to respond to the crew of renegades she just named. He didn't.

"Somebody is on their heels about it, 'cause René and Alisha killed the mark. The guy chasin' them around town worked for the mark and they took something besides that dope. He wants that back. René claims they ain't got nothin' else."

"Somebody stuffed," he said.

"Exactly," she agreed. "They trapped a kid watchin' them this mornin', tied him up, dildoed him, and relocated.

"Ouch."

"Yeah. Now they're scared to death!" She cried. "That's the third hotel they done been to. Whoever is chasin' them was hot on their asses."

That was enough information for now, Jo-Jo thought. She would let René and Alisha fill in the gaps. Karin and Brooklyn had been dragged into the situation. They were innocent as far as Jo-Jo could tell.

"So," Bone sighed, "Fresh out the gate I gotta be Captain Save-a-Ho."

"Ain't nothin' changed."

"Stop at the store, baby girl. I need a drink."

"Boy, please!" She reached under her seat and pulled out a pint of Remy Martin. Then she went in her bra and pulled out a bag of Kush. She handed them both to him, "Bone's specialty!"

He laughed and said, "Riiight!"

***

René had a cup of complimentary coffee on the table as she flipped through the front page of The Press-Telegram.

Nothing.

She laid out the "local news" section. At the bottom of the left column there it was:

> Press-Telegram
> "Local News"
> Friday – July 15, 2005

Belmont Shores -

A boating accident last night around ten o'clock took the life of James

DuVall. Our source in the Coast Guard Said, "Mr. DuVall's yacht exploded after some loose wires sparked and ignited the gas tanks." Mr. DuVall was a mile and a half away from the shore so no one else was injured.

James DuVall was the owner of three diamond stores in Southern California. He is survived by his wife of twenty-four years; Janet DuVall who declined all comments.

After René read the article she woke up Alisha.

"Alisha," she whispered, "Alisha." She shook her, "Get up, girl. I got something to show you."

"I'll get it, baby. Let mommy rest five more minutes," she mumbled.

"Five more minutes, mom?" René teased her.

"Yeah, baby."

"Okay mommy, I'm gonna smoke your last joint, kay?" René laughed.

Alisha's eyes snapped open. René stood over her with her head tilted to the left. Alisha pushed her face with her hand.

"Girl, I thought you was Alasia. I was ready to get in her ass. Smoke my last joint at three years old. I heard that." She sat up on one elbow, "What's up?"

"This," she handed her the newspaper.

"Give me that coffee." Alisha sat up in the bed. She sipped on the coffee and just stared at the paper. She didn't know what to read. Alisha was still half asleep. "Read what, girl?"

"Read this," René pointed out the article.

As Alisha read the article, her eyes got wide. He was murdered, but John made it look like he was killed in an accident. When she finished reading it, she smiled. You could see in that smile a wave of relief. It was an accident. Case closed.

"Now we gotta get John off of our back," she said.

With that business out of the way, René walked over to the closet and pulled out the duffel bag. She unzipped the side pocket and pulled out a wad of cash, "You stuffed on me, girlfriend."

"René," Alisha said nervously, "I can explain that."

"I got you, my pretty!" Karin was up.

And in rare form.

***

"Baby…girl," he coughed and coughed, "What kinda weed is this?" His lungs were on fire.

"My son gave me that for you. Some new stuff he's pushin'. Roll that window down, boy. You know I can't stand that smell," Jo-Jo only let Bone smoke weed in her car. He could get away with just about anything with her.

Anything within reason.

Bone pulled out his phone to punch in his mother's number. She would have a fit if he didn't call her first. When he cut the phone on, the screen displayed Alisha wearing nothing but a thong. Over her head it read "welcome" and under her ass it read "home." He showed Jo-Jo.

"Who is that?" she asked.

"That's Alisha. The one with the two little girls."

"I remember. That's the one that's been campaigning to be Mrs. Bone, huh?"

"For forty months straight," Bone knew Jo-Jo was going to give her opinion.

"René is a good girl. Strong willed. Sometimes she uses it wrong," she added, "But she means well. But, Alisha stood up for you when you really needed someone in your corner. A decision between the two don't take too much thought, Willie. If you plan on elevating one of these girls to somethin' different in your life then make a choice."

"Later," he said flatly. He dialed his mother's number.

"Hello…Hello?"

"Hey, Ms. J!" Bone cried. Ms. J. was short for Ms. Joyce. The nickname made her feel young.

"Well, well, well," Joyce said warmly, "If it isn't my long lost son." That was her way of saying, "Welcome home." "Come by the shop when you get in town."

"I don't need no haircut!" He teased her.

"I heard that, boy," she said firmly. "You better check in wit' cho' mama."

"I'll be there in about thirty minutes."

"Is Alisha with you?" Joyce asked. She liked Alisha. She was respectful, loyal to her son, cute, and clever.

"Nope. Jo-Jo came and picked me up."

Joyce knew that she was his old running buddy. She felt that her son was up to something already, "I'll be here waitin'." She hung up.

Jo-Jo wanted Bone to do the right thing. She would show him off to some of her new girlfriends, "Come by the house next Friday and we'll hit a sober dance - clean chicks, working good jobs, own pad; the works, baby boy."

"I'll come dance, and I'll let you show me off, but I think I'm gonna give Alisha a shot."

"Good choice," she had love for René but she hadn't stood the test of time. She wasn't ready.

They made small talk on their drive into L.A. They talked about her kids and his daughter. They talked about overcrowded schools and racial tension. Things were changing in the streets of Los Angeles. It was getting more violent.

"I thought you stayed away from the life, Jo?"

"I still keep my ear to the street. I got a boy in the life."

"Does he have any kids yet?"

"If he do, I ain't seen them. If granny ain't seen none, there ain't none. I told him a long time ago, if a girl is tryin' to trap you with a baby just bring the baby to me. I'll let you know if it's yours or not."

Twenty minutes later they pulled up in front of the shop. Jo-Jo looked towards the chicken joint. Bone said, "Not just yet, Jo-Jo. Don't be tryin' to duck moms." Although Bone's mother was only about eight years older than Jo-Jo, she was always reluctant to go in the shop. I guess she looked at her as a big sister. Joyce treated everybody around Bone like they were his kids

"Hey, ya'll," Joyce, said, "Just have a seat. I'll be through in a minute." She was finishing a man up in her chair. She dusted him off and he got up. "That'll be fifteen," she told him. He gave her a twenty and waved off the change. "Thank you, baby. See you next time." To Bone and Jo-Jo she said, "Come on out here." Joyce was real serious about keeping people out of her business, so they stepped outside.

She gave her son a warm hug and looked him over, "The only thing that's changed is that gray hair in your beard." She gave Jo-Jo a hug and asked, "What is this boy tryin' to get you into, girl?"

"Oh, he knows better than that," Jo-Jo stated.

"I ain't tryin' to get into nothin' my damn self. I don't know what you talkin' about." Bone tried to throw his mother a curve ball.

"Boy please," Joyce wasn't going for it, "I ain't gonna ask a bunch of questions right now, but you and Alisha better come by the house at seven tonight. We need a round table discussion."

"We'll be there," Bone said. His mother was hip. She grew up on the streets of Compton, so she was no stranger to street game.

Or street lingo.

She addressed Jo-Jo, "Call me, girl, and we'll go to church."

"I sure will. As a matter of fact, my church got a bus going to Vegas next weekend."

"Now you know I'm down for that!" Joyce declared, "Give her the new number, Willie."

"I will."

"You need some money?" Joyce knew that he just got two hundred dollars gate money, but her motherly concern blocked that out.

"I'm cool," Bone knew his answer didn't matter. She handed him the twenty her customer just gave her, and Bone just stuck it in his pocket.

"Look, Jo," Joyce said, "I'll write the number down myself for you. Come in the shop real fast."

As they walked toward the door, Bone whispered in Jo-Jo's ear, "You know nothing."

"Go get me a two-piece and biscuit," Jo-Jo said, "With a Pepsi."

Bone went into Louisiana Fried Chicken while his mother took Jo-Jo into the barber shop to drill her for information: "Between me and you." That's what she would say.

When Jo-Jo came out of the shop Bone was sitting in the car. As he got ready to open his mouth, she held up her hand. When they pulled out on the street, she said, "I told her I didn't know what was going on; that I was just dropping you off at some hotel. I made it sound kinky."

"And she told you to call her later and let her know something."

She looked over at Bone in awe. His mother had said those exact words. She wondered if her kids knew her like that. They sure did. If not, better.

"Boy, you got your mama down to a tee, huh?"

"Sometimes I wish I didn't, because if she can sense something foul…" He let his last words linger.

Bone had a cup of ice from Louisiana's. He pulled out the Remy from between the seats and poured him a shot. He fired up the joint in the ashtray and rolled the window down. He tuned the radio to The Wave, and eased the seat back to enjoy the ride.

George Benson sang on the radio as they got on the 105 East. Jo-Jo started laughing as she put her foot to the floor of her brand new Chrysler 300M. Jo-Jo kept a clean ride.

Bone did too.

***

"Why did you stuff on me, Alisha?" René was about to front Alisha off, "Let me answer that for you. You think that by holding this knot right here from me; from us," she waved the money at Brooklyn and Karin, "That you would slide Bone your own gift, huh? Face it, girl, you ran for forty months for nothin'! I take that back. You ran forty months for me!" René laughed. "I pimped your ass for almost four years without you even knowing it. I had you take care of my man while I did what I wanted to do like I always do."

Alisha and Karin just stared at her. Neither one of them expected her to say that. Brooklyn hid her head under the cover. René woke her up talking loud, and now that she heard what she had to say, she did not want to see what was coming next.

Alisha got up and went to the bathroom. She sat down on the toilet to use it, and to think about what René has just said. *Was Bone, no, was Willie that cold? Would he just lie to me just to keep me runnin' for him? No,* she thought. *Bone knew he didn't have to lie. He knew that Alisha would do for him regardless. He was the only man who took care of Alisha's kids when she was strung out, sat up all night with them and prayed with them. He even prayed with my mama,* she thought. *Nah, Bone kept it real all of the time, even if I hurt your feelings.*

Willie was a real brotha.

She got up and flushed the toilet. As she washed her hands, she looked at herself in the mirror. Her face was clear, cheeks were fat. She pulled her hair into a tight ponytail and then wrapped it in a firm bun.

Alisha came out of the bathroom and walked straight up to René. She grabbed her by her throat. With one swift motion, she swept to the left and kicked her feet out from under her. All that was heard was one loud thump.

Alisha straddled her on the floor with her hands wrapped around her neck, "Don't you ever disrespect me like that. Ever! If Bone comes here and wants to be with your sorry ass, fine. But don't you ever disrespect me again, bitch."

She got up quick so that she could be in position to defend herself. René just sat up choking. She didn't want to fight.

Alisha walked to the table and picked up the money. She counted out fifteen hundred and put the rest of it in her pocket. She handed everybody five hundred and said, "I'm going down to pay for another room along with this one for a couple more days."

Karin jumped, "I'll go with you, girlfriend. Let me pee first." She trotted into the bathroom.

"I'm hungry," Brooklyn whined.

"Order room service." Alisha looked over at René. She sat on the edge of the bed massaging her throat. "Get grand slams for me and Karin, and get René some pancakes with extra syrup and butter."

Karin came out of the bathroom and they left.

Out in the hallway Karin said, "She didn't have no business saying all that."

"Do you think Bone will come out and dis me like that?" Alisha asked.

"Bone might. Willie won't," Karin reconsidered her answer. "As a matter of fact, Bone won't even do that. Do you know what a street hustler prays for?"

"That's easy. Money. The easy come up."

"Wrong answer. I said what he *prays* for, not what he *preys* upon. A street hustler prays for a solid woman to do time with him when he falls. To make sure his *bizness* is taken care of, to make sure he don't need nothin' while he's locked down."

"Then I'm his girl!" Alisha smiled, "I was there the whole time, Karin."

"I know," Karin conceded, "And, you ain't a fat broad." She pinched Alisha's stomach. It was as flat as a washboard. Karin winked an approving eye at Alisha.

Alisha gave her a bear hug.

Chapter Eight

John was seated in the back of the Chinese restaurant. Canton' was owned by Mr. Chin. Mr. Chin was the owner of the diamonds. He had given the bag of diamonds to John, so that he could negotiate a deal with James DuVall. After he read the paper this morning, he called John. He was checking on his merchandise.

"I read in the paper this morning that your boss has expired. I hope that our deal with him was finalized before he was finalized." Mr. Chin was a man with no small talk in his conversation.

"We have a slight problem," John couldn't lie to Mr. Chin. It would just get him killed faster. "Mr. DuVall had two companions with him prior to the explosion. It seems that they picked up more than they should've before they left."

"That is not my problem!" Mr. Chin slammed his fist down on the table, "You have forty-eight hours to have my money or have my merchandise." Mr. Chin picked up his cup of tea and began to sip.

The conversation was over.

***

Jo-Jo pulled up in front of the Howard Johnson Hotel. She made no attempt to park. Bone understood. It was too much dope in the room that Bone was going to. Jo-Jo was not flirting with the game like that. Once you stop doing drugs, you don't continue to hang around where it is.

"It's room 220," she said, "Give me a call one Friday, and we'll go and get our boogie on."

"You know I will, too." Bone leaned over and kissed her on her cheek, "To hell with them, Jo-Jo, let's go get married."

She pushed him in his head. "Boy, get out of my car!"

Bone got out and headed for the lobby. When he grabbed the door, a horn blew. He turned to see Jo-Jo still sitting there.

"I love you, Willie!" She cried and drove off.

Jo-Jo had never told Bone that before, but he knew what she meant. She was afraid that she would never see him again.

"I'll be careful," he mumbled as he watched her drive off.

As Bone walked into the lobby he felt a little dizzy. With the Remy Martin in his system, and the Kush, Bone was floating on air. After being away from it for so long, he would have to slow his roll.

As he got into the elevator, he laughed to himself. The thought of dealing with four renegade hoes off of the A-line, sober, was funny. That was why he was buzzing. You have to be under the influence to deal with them.

He stepped out on the second floor and headed to the right. After passing a couple of doors, he turned back and went the other way. He should've known before stepping off of the elevator that everything involving sex and drugs was always to the left; way out in left field.

Room 220. He knocked twice.

René was the closest to the door when the knocks came. They were all sitting at the table just finishing up their breakfast. She looked at Alisha while Karin and Brooklyn busied themselves with the dishes. Alisha looked too confident.

"You gonna open the door, girl?" Alisha asked with a smirk on her face.

"How do we know who it is?" René asked a stupid question. She was scared to answer the door, too ashamed.

Alisha pushed passed her, looked in the peephole and screamed, "It's him!" She opened the door and jumped into Bone's arms.

"Hey kid!" He beamed, "Long time no see." Bone held her up by her ass while she wrapped her legs around him.

"Get the bread, daddy," she whispered, and lightly bit his ear.

He looked her in her eyes and asked, "Like that?" She winked. He set her down and looked at René. Was she about to cry? He pushed the door closed and stuck his arms out. She walked into them.

"I miss this right here," she whispered. René always felt the weight of the world leave her shoulders whenever Bone took her into his arms. She felt his strength, his determination, his courage, and his will to never lose, regardless to how the chips of life fell. In his arms, she felt secure.

She felt loved.

"Come here, Brook," he swung René to his right and gave Brooklyn a hug. "You miss me, dude?" Bone always teased her bout dressing like a man.

"Hell, yeah!" She cried, "It ain't been nothin' but hell on the streets without you."

"You shoulda took yo' butt home." Bone always told Brooklyn to go home and take care of her kids.

"Brooklyn quit getting' high, Bone," announced René.

"That's good, Brook. Now you can make you some money." He let go of her and looked over at Karin. She stood in the bathroom doorway; one hand on the door jam, and the other one on her hip.

Out of the four women in the room, Karin knew him better than them all. Alisha knew him because he opened up to her. But, Karin knew him because she opened up to him. It's not often that a woman of the streets opens up to any man. In another life, Bone would have married Karin, but nobody knew that.

Just them two.

"Can I get a piece of the Bone?" She wasn't asking.

He walked over to her as she stuck her arms out. He bent over and not only hugged her, he caressed her warm body. Karin was still in touch with her feelings. The streets had not turned her stone cold to where she never allowed a person in her space. She was a prostitute, but she was also a very caring woman, looking for her ultimate break.

Bone stepped back and appraised her, "You're looking good for an old lady."

"You ain't half bad yourself, Pops. That gray in your beard is cute." She was caressing his chin.

"Uh," René said a little curt, "I hate to break up such a warm reunion, but I got something for you, babe."

Bone walked over and sat in the windowsill. It was deep enough to sit in, plus it was the best seat in the house.

He wanted to see the whole room.

***

On Artesia Blvd. Big Lisa was getting into a black Chevy Suburban. She had to really put some effort into getting in because it sat high off the ground. When finally got in, she saw another man in the back seat.

Little Johnny.

"Oh, I don't do two at once," she said, and started to get out.

John grabbed her arm gently, "We don't want that right now. We're looking for a particular girl, and we were wondering if you knew where she was." He held out a fifty dollar bill.

Lisa closed the door and immediately grabbed the money, "Who*?" They were probably looking for some white chick out of the trailer park,* Lisa thought. She had no problem giving them up.

"René. Do you know her?" John asked as he pulled away from the curb.

Lisa knew that René was robbing tricks, so she played dumb, "Ain't no girl out here name René."

Little Johnny slapped her in the side of her head with a pistol. He thought it would knock her out, but it didn't. At six feet tall and two hundred and thirty pounds, Lisa wasn't going out that easy.

"Hey, motha fucka!" She shouted, "I said it ain't no girl out here with that name." Lisa tried to get out but the door was locked. The window was locked too. She felt the gun in her side and left the door alone.

John made a right on Coke Street and then left on Cedar. He pulled over in front of the park. He turned to face Lisa, "Do I have to ask that question again?"

Fear made her head not hurt that much. If they shot her, Lisa didn't know what would make that not hurt. "If I do know her, I don't know where she is."

John backhanded her in the mouth while Little Johnny grabbed her from behind. "Well," John whipped out his pistol and screwed in the silencer, "Until I catch up with her, street walkers are not safe." He shot Lisa in both of her knees.

Lisa bit down on Little Johnny's hand. That was the only thing that kept her from screaming. When she released him, they both screamed.

John swung the pistol upward, caught her in the chin, and she went out.

"That bitch bit me!" Little Johnny cried.

John let that statement pass. If she didn't bite him, he would've called her more than a bitch.

He unlocked the door, reached over her and opened it.

He pushed her out.

Somebody would find her real soon, and the word would be on the streets that someone was looking for René.

Looking to do no talking.

***

René went to the nightstand and pulled out the manila envelope. She strolled over to Bone, handed it to him, kissed him and said, "Welcome home, babe." She stepped back to watch his reaction.

They were all watching.

He looked around at all four faces. He could tell that they were all excited, "Ya'll look like you're waitin' on me to open up an Anthrax envelope." They all broke out laughing. "Brook, you open it for me," she started walking toward him. "Watch out kid. You won't stuff half of it one me!" The room roared with laughter. He opened the envelope and pulled out the wad of cash.

"Well, well, well, if money could wash away all the months I missed hearing from you, this stack just might clean the slate," Bone pointed out. He counted the stack. It was thirty one hundred dollar bills. "Damn," he exclaimed. "It's one for each month you were missin' in action." The laughter was kind of stiff at that remark.

Bone pulled the Remy Martin out of his pocket and said, "To René! Who came through at the right time."

"Here, here!" They all declared in unison.

Bone tipped the bottle up slightly then passed it to René. The bottle went around to everybody. When Karin got it, she poured the rest of it in a glass.

Karin winked at Bone who winked back. She turned up the glass, and Bone opened up the window. When she finished the drink, he moved out of her way. She threw the glass out of the window.

"Welcome home, Daddy," she said smoothly.

"Why thank you, Scarlet," Bone replied in a southern drawl.

Alisha stood by the door the whole time watching Bone work the room. No one was ever denied any attention when it came to dealing with Bone. He knew how to include everybody. He also knew how to check a person in a way that they weren't fully embarrassed. He had just checked René and smoothed it out all in the same breath, and he tucked the bread in his pocket. She wouldn't enjoy a dime of that.

It was no secret how he felt toward her right now. It was also still comfortable in the room. Alisha loved the way Bone operated. She went to the closet and pulled out the duffel bag. As she set it on the table, she said, "We're gonna need some of your connections to dump all of this. I know I don't wanna be on no street corner peddlin' dimes and twenties."

"How much dope is it?" Bone turned serious.

"We don't know exactly 'cause we don't have a scale," René answered him. "My guess is four or five pounds."

"First things first. Let me ask this. Are you four renegades who don't-like-to-listen-to-any-man hoes gonna listen to my instructions on this, or not?"

"Yeah sure…why wouldn't we…you know I always listen…aw, what the hell. Why not…?" That last comment was made by Karin. Bone just grinned and shook his head.

He set back for a minute and analyzed each and every one of their faces. For once, they all had a genuine look of unity; order brought about by chaos. Somebody had scared these girls real good. Regardless to how they held their composure, inside they were trembling. Good. Bone knew that they would listen.

"Okay, ladies," Bone accepted the challenge, "This is what I'll do. Since we're so close to San Fernando Valley, I'll call a kid out here I know and get a few items that we need."

Bone sat down at the table with René. The other girls went about getting the room in order. Before he picked up the phone, René grabbed his hand. He looked into her pleading eyes.

"Oh. Thanks for the bread, baby. It's way better than the chump change I got this mornin'."

"I knew you'd need it when you got out," she began, "That's the only reason why I went on..."

"We don't need to get into that right now," he cut in. "We'll talk. And stop looking like that. If I wasn't gonna fuck with you, I wouldn't be sittin' here right now."

"I know. It's just..." she trailed off. René was pouting, trying to play on his sympathy.

"If you know already, kick back and roll this up." Bone tossed her the pouch that Jo-Jo gave him and picked up the phone.

"Good morning," said a woman's voice through the phone.

"Good morning. I'd like to speak to Russell, please," Bone spoke very proper. He knew how to deal with all walks of life.

"May I ask who's calling?" Russell's wife was nosey.

"Tell him Mr. Braxton," he replied.

A couple of minutes later, "who is this?" Russell barked. "I don't know no Braxton."

"Oh, yes you do...Rash Ass.

There was only one person who called Russell that.

"Bone!" He beamed.

"What's up, Road Rash?"

"You tell me, bud," he lowered his voice and said: "Tell me you're calling me to generate some money, bro, because I'm flat ass right now."

"Do you have enough to get some baggies?"

"I got a thousand of them empty fuckers in a drawer."

"Good. Bring'em. Bring your triple beam, too. You might wanna stop off and get yourself a drink and a pack of condoms, too."

"Shhh! My wife's got ears like a hawk, you prick. Where are you?"

"The Howard Johnson Hotel by Magic Mountain: room two, two, zero.

"Old Bone," Rash chuckled. "You wasn't bullshittin' were you? Sex, drugs..."

"And rock and roll, baby! I'll see you in a minute," Bone hung up. He had been watching Brooklyn the whole time he was on the phone.

She looked a little antsy. "You alright, dude?"

He got up and sat down on the bed next to her.

"I want a flight, Bone," she muttered and started crying.

Bone put his arm around her. She leaned into him and continued to cry. He stuck his hand out and René handed him the joint. It wasn't easy resisting the urge to get high on cocaine. Everyone in the room had to fight that demon. Now it was Brooklyn's turn, and Bone would make sure that she had all of the support that she needed.

He lit the joint up and immediately started to choke. Brooklyn looked up to see if he was okay. What she saw made her fall out laughing. Bone had made his famous monkey face with the joint stuck in his mouth.

"That's what you need, Brook!" Bone declared. "Entertainment. Find other things that fill up your time and bring you enjoyment. That ya-yo is destruction, baby girl. Replace that ya-yo with something constructive.

"We're tryin' to build not tear down. Okay? Okay." He passed her the joint. "Be careful with this powerful shit, too."

Brooklyn took the joint, sniffed it, and hit it real hard. While she was passing it back, she coughed and blew snot out of her nose.

"Alisha!" Bone called, "Come and help you snotty-nose girlfriend."

Alisha came over to see what was going on and fell out laughing. They all started laughing out of control, and that was the end of that fight with cocaine for Brooklyn. All she needed now was some tissue.

Chapter Nine

Lisa woke up with gutter water running through her hair and people standing over her. Her legs were hot and screaming with pain.

"You're going to be alright, young lady. Just lay still," said the lady who lived next to the park. "My son went to get you something to lay your head on."

"My knees," Lisa groaned, "Hurt like hell."

"Yes, I know. I called the ambulance to come and get you. It looks like you scraped your knees up pretty bad." The lady didn't want to tell her that she didn't have kneecaps any longer.

"I didn't scrape them," Lisa said, "Some man shot me in my knees."

"Do you want me to call someone for you?"

Lisa tried to reach into her back pocket, but her hand was trembling.

"Don't move, honey. Is there a phone number in your pocket?"

"No, but I need you to get that stuff out for me and throw it away."

The lady stuck her hand in Lisa's pocket, pulled out a pipe, and a tiny plastic bag. She looked at the stuff in her hand then down into Lisa's eyes.

"I'm on probation," Lisa said humbly, "And if they find that one me, I'll go to jail. Please get rid of it for me." Lisa hated the position that she was in.

"I'll take care of it for you. Is this the reason why you were shot?"

"Come on, lady!" Lisa cried, "Throw the shit away and call my sister. Her name is René. 605-8409"

The ladies son came with a blanket and handed it to his mother. "Go get the phone again, Josh." He ran off again. She knelt down next to Lisa, lifted her head, and positioned the blanket under it. "You are one tough cookie," she said. "No tears, no whining."

"Ain't no room for that in the life that I lead," Lisa said flatly.

"And what kind of life if that?"

"Come on, lady!"

***

On the corner of Clark and Artesia, Shannon came out of the liquor store. She saw the black Suburban on Clark waiting for the light to change. She thought it was one of her regulars, so she waited in the parking lot. The light turned green, but as the truck drove passed her to turn into the parking lot, she could make out two heads.

Ain't him, she said to herself. She watched the truck as it pulled in. It pulled straight in front of her, and the driver waved her over. She stepped to the driver's side and the window rolled down.

"Get in, lil' mama, and come have a little fun with me," John said.

"No thank you, officer. Those hand cuffs your partner has in the back seat are not for me today," Shannon turned and walked off. "Won't get me today, sucker!"

***

Road Rash Russell had his toolbox in a duffel bag. He had a couple of beach towels stuffed around it so you couldn't see the shape through the bag. Some people called him paranoid, but everyone that called him that, they were always calling collect from jail. Road Rash had been out for two years, off of parole, and struggling like hell. He was free, though.

Room 220.

He knocked on the door three times.

"Boy, the only thing you miss...,"

Knock, knock, knock. Karin stopped in mid sentence at the sound.

"That's Road Rash, Karin," Bone said reassuringly. "Get the door."

"Road Rash? I didn't bring my nursing outfit Bone," she said as she got up to get the door. She looked through the peephole and said, "He looks like one of the Beatles."

"Please don't tell him that," Bone pleaded, "He'll start singing."

"Uh, uh…" Rash stammered.

"Uh yeah, they're real," Karin, said mocking him, "Now could you come in here?"

She grabbed his hand and led him passed the door so she could close it. Karin had on a black jersey that showed all of her white skin straight through it. With only a pair of panties on under it, it was hard for Road Rash to stop staring.

"Hey, Rash Ass," Bone tried to snap him out of the trance. "Over here kid."

"I see you, Bone head," he replied, "But she's much more sweeter to look at."

"Breath easy, big boy," Karin said smoothly, "You'll be in our company for a while. Who knows, I might let you in my jersey with me." She shook her breasts at him, pulled out a seat at the table, and offered it to him.

"Ladies, this is Road Rash," Bone announced. "I don't know how in the hell he got a name like that. You can ask that after he takes care of his bizness."

"Hi, Rash," they all said at once.

"Alisha," Bone called. She walked over to the table. "This is Alisha, Rash."

Dressed in an African two-piece skirt outfit with two long braids in her hair she looked like an Indian girl.

"Sit on this, baby girl," Bone requested, "You know I don't usually put women in my bizness, but ya'll put me in the bizness this trip."

"Call René over too, daddy 'cause..."

"That's enough daddy shit," Bone said flatly. "I ain't no pimp." Bone didn't like being called daddy. He felt that pimps beat hoes and forced them into submission. Bone just hustled with hoes because they brought money around the spot. Now, if they chose to let him manage their money, fine. If not, he was going to get his with a variety of hustles.

"Rash, this is my main squeeze," Bone pinched her cheek. "Everything else you see in this room you can play with."

"It's a pleasure meeting you, Alisha. Bone, I'm flattered, but I don't need a woman right now. I need some fucking cash. So, if it's all the same to you, let's get down to business, bro."

"René," Bone called. "Come have a seat."

René stepped to the table all business. Bone could tell she was mad, but she would not make a scene.

"Hey, Rash," she beamed. "You ready to make some bread?"

"Hell yeah, René," Rash answered. "Now this is my type of woman here. All business." He looked at Bone. "What are we working with Bone?"

Bone reached down beside him and pulled up the duffel bag. He set it on the table and pulled both ice buckets out. "We are working with coke and speed."

"Powder coke?" Rash asked.

"Yeah," Bone replied, "And, shards of glass."

Road Rash pulled his toolbox out of his duffel bag, set it on the table, and pulled out his scale. As he set up on the table he said, "Pull out that zip lock bag, Bone, and empty it out." Rash had a big zip lock bag full of small bags. "Now, dump one of those buckets in that bag."

Bone dumped the speed in first because there was more of it, "Look, Rash, I'm gonna leave you here with Karin and Brook to bag this up after we weight it. Is that cool?"

"Where the hell are you going?" Rash demanded.

"I'm just going to rent a car, and I'll be right back," Bone said defensively.

"Here, babe." René handed him a lit joint. "Don't get ahead of yourself. We got time for all of that."

"Thanks, baby girl." Bone had to watch that; moving too fast you slip up. "You sure know what will slow this ol' boy down."

"Always have," she gloated.

"Hey bro, I got a half gallon of Remy Martin in my bag."

"I thought you woulda forgotten by now, Rash."

"How could I? Every war story you told had Remy in it." Road Rash and Bone had been in the county jail together. They were in a four-man cell together so they had gotten to know each other pretty good. You bypass jailhouse rules in situations like that. See no evil, hear no evil, and speak no evil. What they did in that cell was their business. All racial garbage was dead.

Bone grabbed the bottle two glasses, and poured two shots; a drink between two men. "Here's to no sells to an undercover cop."

"Fuck Donnie Brasco!" Road Rash cried as they touched glasses. He downed his drink and said, "Welcome home, bro. This old white boy's been waiting for this day to come."

"Let's get down to bizness, then." Bone handed Rash the bag of glass.

"Okay," Rash started, "The bag weighs three grams." So, he stuck the bag on the scale and started adjusting the weights to balance it out: Forty and a half ounces. "You got forty whole plus eleven grams."

Rash dumped the speed back into the ice bucket. He picked up the bucket with the coke in it while Bone held the bag open and poured it in. "You might have more of this. You see those chunks there? Coke is a finer powder than speed so you had more packed in there than it looked like." Rash was an expert in his craft.

He balanced the scale back out, set the bag on it, and went to adjusting weights again. "See." He was still adjusting the weights. "Forty-three ounces, and ten grams. That's forty-three whole and a third."

Bone looked from René to Alisha. They sat there slack-jawed at the knowledge that they had taken over five pounds of the hottest street drugs from a dead trick. Bone looked over at Karin and Brooklyn. They looked away like they weren't paying attention but they too were in awe at the amount.

"How long you been out, Bone?" Road Rash asked casually.

"I just got out this morning."

Rash looked at Bone confused. Then it hit him, *These chicks just pulled a move.* He looked around at all of them and announced, "A toast!" Rash got up and grabbed every glass he saw, set them on the table, and filled them with Remy.

He made everybody stand around the table. Rash slid his left arm on Karin's shoulder and said, "To four of the craftiest women I have ever met, and to one lucky mother fucker named Bone."

"Here, here!"

They touched glasses.

"Thanks for the invite," Rash said.

Bone and Rash sat back down to finish their business. Karin and Brooklyn went back to the bed, and René grabbed the hotel ice bucket.

"I'm gonna get some ice," René said.

Alisha walked behind her to the door.

"I can let myself out." René stopped just short of the door.

"Girl, stop being silly. I don't want nobody in the hallway looking in here." Alisha opened the door for her and closed it right behind her.

"How do you want this, Bone?" Rash asked.

"Quarter ounce bags," Bone replied.

"Okay. Let me call my wife and have her call a few people."

"You mean doctors and shit you were tellin' me about?"

"I got those pricks lost and turned out!"

"Alisha," Bone called out, "Did you get the credit?"

"Yeah, baby. Chase sent me a card last week with a five thousand dollar limit."

"Good girl. Come here so we can talk." He got up to go toward the bathroom.

Alisha stopped him, "I got a room down the hall, baby."

"You never cease to amaze me." He kissed her and headed for the door. "Karin, help Rash Ass with whatever he needs."

"Okay, love," Karin said. She got up to let Bone and Alisha out.

"Take that bottle, Bone head," Rash said. "I brought that for you."

Bone grabbed the bottle and the half a joint in the ashtray. In the hallway, things started spinning in Bone's head. He was too high. He needed something to eat to make the high go down.

Alisha sensed it in the way he was moving and said, "We'll order you a burger and fries to soak up some of that alcohol in your stomach."

He loved her for that. She picked up on all of his needs. After all of his years in filling wants, needs, and the other desires of women, Bone was finally getting the treatment back.

They stopped in front of 202, and Bone spun Alisha around to face him. "You know," Bone wrapped his arms around her, "I feel like a high school freshman right now sneaking away from my chaperone."

"I'm nervous too, Willie," she whispered.

"Why?"

"Because I haven't had *feelings* for a man since high school. Ten years ago. Plus, me and you have never even kissed, and I'm sprung on you."

Bone pulled her in closer to him and kissed her. It felt like being behind the gym during second period Home Economics, kissing his first love. Stacey Grant.

"Wow," Alisha whispered, "You just took me way back with that one."

"Wait until we get into this room."

Alisha pulled the key out, stuck it in the door, and backed into the room. Bone slowly followed her in.

Never letting go of her hips.

***

Down the hallway in front of 220, René stood there and watched the whole scene. She wasn't accepting the fact that she had lost her man, until now. She watched Bone follow Alisha into another room. She wanted to get high. As René knocked on the door, her phone vibrated in her pocket. *Now what?*

***

Marie climbed in the Suburban at the 90/80 Club. She didn't mind two at the same time; that meant more money. And she already had a room.

"Do you have a friend for my bro here?" John tried a different approach.

"Sure," Marie said eagerly. "I have bunch of friends. What's your flavor white, black, Hispanic..."

"Black chick," Little Johnny cut in. "Not too dark." Their approach was refined. If they were going to get René, they had to be clever. René wasn't that simple-minded.

"I got one," Marie declared. "Let me call her. Turn left right here. My motel is right under the freeway."

John turned left at Clark. Right passed the freeway was the Budget Inn on the left hand side. Marie pointed to it and they pulled in.

"Pull up by the stairs," she said. They all got out and went to room 213. Once inside Marie dialed René's number. She was the only light-skinned sister on the track. Alisha had not been working that much lately. Marie didn't have her number anyway.

"Her line is busy," Marie announced. "You guys want a beer? I'll call her back in a minute. She won't be on the phone long."

"What's her name?" John chanced it.

"René," Marie said quickly. "She's a regular. You've probably seen her. She's a real cute red head."

John looked over at his son and winked. "Yes, I think a beer will be just the thing while we wait."

Chapter Ten

As Bone pushed the door closed with his foot, he dropped the bottle to the floor. He caressed her hips as they kissed with an intense passion. In the distance, you could hear cars on the roller coaster tracks, and faint screams.

Bone pulled up her skirt, and she jumped into his arms. With her legs wrapped around his waist he walked her over to the dresser. He set her down on the dresser, and she pulled his shirt over his head.

With his arms straight in the air, she undid his belt, unbuttoned his shorts, and pushed them down. He stepped out of his shorts and sandals at the same time.

"Look at my potbelly teddy bear," Alisha teased, and kissed him on his bald head.

Bone raised her skirt up all the way to her waist, and she wrapped herself around him again.

The distant roller coaster cars carried a smooth rhythm on the track; up one slope and down the next. The screams caressed the trees and floated off the leaves. Up and down, up and down; up to the top of the biggest roller coaster in California, then sliding down like a free fall. The screams trailed the last car of every ride in the park. 'Round and 'round, upside down. The heavy pantin when you go up the Superman ride - your curled toes on your way down. One ride after another. The adrenaline at an all-time high. Then the cars start to slow down and you breathe out a heavy sigh. Just like you were excited when the ride started, the ending brought about the same rush. The big splash at the end of the Log Jam.

Bone backed up away from the wall with Alisha totally wrapped around him. They were still joined at the hip. He turned and gently eased her down on the bed. He caressed her breasts and let his fingers follow a line of sweat down her body.

"You make me feel you, Willie," she whispered.

"That's my mission, baby girl," he smiled.

"No. I'm not talking about your manliness. I'm talking about you. I've never really enjoyed a man before in my life. It's always been for the money not for my pleasure. My body, my heart, and my soul are thirsty for you right now. I ain't never had it this good."

Alisha felt his warm tongue circling her nipple. She laid her legs over his shoulders.

The roller coaster cars started moving again.

***

René was back in the room fooling with her phone. She had just been disconnected and now she couldn't get a signal. She was getting frustrated. "Lost the signal. Lost my man. Shit!" She barked.

"What now, girlfriend?" Karin asked. She was at the table watching Road Rash. He didn't need any help. Karin was just doing damage control; making sure he didn't stuff.

"I lost my signal and got disconnected. I think it was Lisa on the line."

"Just pull up Incoming Calls, get the number, and call her back on my phone," Karin simply said.

"Where is your phone?"

"On the nightstand." Karin wanted her girlfriend to get her mind off of where Bone and Alisha were. *Bone was bold with that move*, Karin thought. René had it coming, but not like that.

René dialed the number.

"Hello?"

"Is Lisa there? Somebody just called me from this number and said something about Lisa."

"That was me, honey. My name is Jennifer. Are you René?"

"Yeah," René said cautiously, "What's the problem?"

"Well, don't panic, René, but your sister was shot."

"Shot!" René cried. Everybody in the room looked at her. She got up and went into the bathroom.

"She's going to live," Jennifer said calmly, "She was shot in her knee caps. Both of them were shattered. She wanted me to tell you that it was a big black truck with two white guys in it."

"How long ago was this, Jennifer?"

"About an hour ago. I've been trying to call you, but..."

"Yeah, I wasn't getting service to my phone."

"Well, the ambulance took her to Kaiser over on Clark and Rosecrans."

Lisa has Kaiser? It was so much you did and didn't know about the people you hung out with, René thought. "Thank you for being so helpful, Jen."

"Anytime hon. You girls be careful, kay?"

"Okay," René hung up. When she came out of the bathroom, she saw Brooklyn standing by the window with her phone.

"You got a signal with it over here," Brooklyn announced. René looked like she had just seen a ghost.

"What's wrong?"

"I don't know yet," René mumbled. Her phone rang. She went over to the window and answered it. "Yeah, who's this?" René's mind was on other things, so being polite when she answered the phone evaded her.

"It's Marie. How come you ain't been answerin'? I've been calling you for the last twenty minutes," she always exaggerated on time frames. "I got a double for us," she whispered. "They look like they got big money, too."

René focused as Marie talked. "What kinda car are they in, girl? And don't be talkin' so they can hear you."

"Excuse me, fellas," Marie said and turned her back to them. In the phone she whispered, "They're driving a big black Tahoe or a Suburban. Really big."

"Marie," René said firmly, "Listen to me very carefully. Please don't panic, but those two dudes are bad news. They're lookin' for me and they just shot Lisa in her knees. Get out of there as fast as you can."

"How in the hell am I going to get out of this room?" Marie was slightly shaking "René you're always...."

"Hello, René," John snatched the phone from Marie, and had his gun pointed at her head.

"What do you want, man?" She growled. "Leave Marie alone. She ain't got nothing to do with this."

"I want that black duffel bag you took off of that boat."

"That's all? You coulda been had that. You didn't have to shoot my girlfriend for that, and you ain't gotta do nothin' to Marie." She pled for her girlfriend.

"Okay," he conceded. "It's three o'clock in the afternoon. If you're not here in an hour, Marie dies." He hung up.

René set her phone down. The whole room was silent. They had heard one side of the conversation.

They heard enough.

René looked at Karin. "Call Bone and get him down here."

Karin picked up the phone on the table and punched in 202. It was busy. "Figures." Karin got up. "I'll go get him."

"No!" René barked. "What room number?"

"René, let me go..."

"What room number?" René asked through clenched teeth.

Karin let out an audible sigh, "Room 202."

***

Bone and Alisha had taken a quick shower and were now getting dressed. They didn't want to be gone that long so René wouldn't come looking. She was going to trip regardless but, not right now because they had business to take care of.

Bone was buttoning up his shirt when the two pounds came at the door. He looked through the peephole and saw René. He saw more fear than anger. He opened the door and she rushed in.

"They shot Lisa...They want the duffel bag...In Marie's room... and..."

"Hey, hey," Bone said calmly, "Slow down, baby girl. Tell me exactly what's going on. Tell me slowly, and we'll figure this out."

"You tell me what's goin' on, Bone; Willie; Mr. Braxton!" René yelled.

"Is that why you came down here?"

"No, but since I'm here, give it to me!" She was mad.

"Listen," Bone said calmly. "First of all, for you to be mad at me, you're way out of line. For thirty months you gave it to me: nothin'! You chose the streets and the dope over me. Did I act like a child and throw a fit? Nope. I kept it pushin'. You got me fucked up, kid, if you think you can leave me for dead in jail and I come home to you. Do I got snot hangin' out of my nose or somethin'? By far am I some snotty-nosed punk that will let you do any ol' thing to him. Wrong answer, HOMEGIRL!"

"Why don't you just call me what I am: a dope fiend ho," René whispered.

"Because that's not how I see you, René. You're just another black sista caught up in the street life. You ain't by yourself, and if I didn't care about your ass, I wouldn't be out here helping you in your time of need. I'm not gonna treat you no different just because your lust and desires came before me. I'm just not gonna put myself in that position again."

René dropped herself in a chair.

Bone pulled her up and hugged her, "I ain't gonna ever change my style, baby girl. I'm gonna still be that nigga that's cooler than a fan."

Alisha came around the bed and hugged René, too. Bone backed up and the two women embraced. René started crying. In spite of her movements and actions her friends, her true friends, were still there.

"You better treat him right, girl," René instructed.

"I got Bone like his clothes," Alisha stated. "All covered. You know you're always welcome wherever we end up, René. We in this shit together."

René wiped her eyes with the back of her hand. "Give me a drink and a joint."

"You got the bag," Bone reminded her. "What did you do leave it on the table?"

"Nope. It's in my pocket." René pulled out the bag and the Zig-Zags.

"See," Bone said, "You still puttin' shit in your pocket that don't belong to you." She laughed at that. "Now, what's going on in the land?" Bone grabbed the bottle off of the floor. Alisha set two cups on the table instead of three.

"Oh, yeah. Food first."

"Yeah, you lush," Alisha said. She poured René and herself a drink and went about the business of calling room service.

"Okay," René said, after she took a drink and laced a Zig-Zag with some weed. "First, Lisa was shot in her kneecaps by this guy John. John worked for the guy that died last night. John's got his son with him; the guy we tapped with a dildo earlier this morning."

"Ouch." Bone winced.

"Anyway, John and his son are now holding Marie hostage. He says that all he wants is the duffel bag that we put the dope in. We got until four o'clock to bring the bag, or he's gonna kill Marie."

"We ain't gonna make it to Bellflower by four o'clock," Bone said flatly. "People are just now getting off work. We're gonna hit traffic as soon as we get into downtown." Bone pulled out his phone to see what time it was. It read 3:15 p.m. "Where is she?"

"Karin knows," René said.

"Alisha!" Bone called out.

Alisha was just finishing up with room service. "Yes, room 202. Thank you." She hung up. "What's up, baby?"

"Hand me the phone, please," he reached out for it. "Thank you." He punched in 220

"Yes?" Karin asked.

"Karin, I need to know where Marie is."

"The Budget Inn, room 213, I believe."

"How far along is Rash?"

"Here," she handed the phone to Rash.

"Hey, bro. You need a couple of troops or what?"

"Not yet. How far along are you?"

"Yeah right! You go me baggin..."

"Don't answer that," Bone interrupted. "Keep going, and I'll be down there in a few minutes."

"Hey? Can I strip one out or what?"

"Don't ask me ask Karin," Bone said. He knew powder made Karin horny.

"I did already. She wants me to do it off of her body," Rash said.

"Then I suggest that you hurry up and finish your bizness," Bone hung up. "The Budget's number is 920-8853, right?" He asked.

"For the last seven years," Alisha replied.

Bone listened to the automated system. Finally the office picked up.

"Budget Inn."

"Amir, please."

"This is he."

"Amir, you owe me for a bottle of Absolute!" Bone said.

"Ah, my good friend Bone. It has been very long since we see you here. How is the family?"

"My wife still doesn't approve of my street life, Amir, and my daughter runs the house."

"What can I do for you, my friend?" Amir asked.

"Marie is being held against her will, Amir. I need you to..."

"You mean 213?"

"Yep."

"Hold on, I am walking over there right now." Amir started across the parking lot.

"When you get to her door tell her to come outside and talk to you," instructed Bone.

"I know what I am doing." He knocked on her door. "This is the manager. You come out right now or I call police." Amir knocked again. "You owe me money. Come out right..."

The door opened.

Marie was cursing, "I don't owe you shit, Amir!" She barked.

"Just come to the office, Marie, and we will straighten everything out." Amir closed the door for her and handed her the phone.

Clearly confused she said, "Hello?"

"Saved by the Bone!"

"Oh, thank God," Marie whispered. "They got guns and stuff, Bone." She was glad to hear his voice.

"Give Amir back his phone, Marie," Bone instructed, "And run like hell."

She handed Amir back his phone, kissed him on his cheek, and ran like hell."

"Now we are even my dear friend," Amir announced.

"One more thing, Amir. Read me the license number off of," he paused to get the make of the car they were in.

"A big black Chevy Suburban," René stated.

"A big black Chevy Suburban," Bone repeated.

Amir stood directly above it, "That will be easy. You ready?"

"Ready," Bone said.

"D-I-A-M-O-N-D. Got it, Bone?" Amir asked.

"Got it," Bone hung up. *People had personalized plates for a reason*, Bone thought.

"The license plate says diamond...odd, huh...?"

It wasn't a question.

Chapter Eleven

"What the hell was that all about?" Little Johnny asked.

"That was one clever escape. Honor among the ladies of the night," John replied. He tossed his son the keys. "Go start the truck up. I'll be there in a sec." He headed toward the restroom.

John had more than a few mixed thoughts as he used the restroom. He had to find a more clever way to get René to bring that bag. Shooting hookers in their knees wasn't the answer. Holding them in a motel wasn't working, either. Who would lead him to René?

When John flushed the toilet he saw a purse strap hanging behind the toilet. He pulled it out and dumped it on the floor: Make-up, drug paraphernalia, cell phone, cash, and condoms. He picked up the phone and left.

Down in the truck John told his son to head to Compton. Most of the people hustling on Artesia Blvd. came straight out of Compton. In Lakewood and Bellflower it was easier for them to exercise their game with the least amount of resistance. John knew a few Bloods and a few Crips in Compton. It was time to find out René's connection. If she was connected they would make her come in. If she wasn't, when John caught up with her...

She was dead.

**

"Okay, Bone," Rash said with finality, "You got 332 quarter ounce bags of dope: 160 in speed, and 172 in coke." It was just Bone and Rash in the room now. Bone sent Karin and Brooklyn down to 202.

"Here," Bone tossed Rash a bag. "Weigh this before you put the scale up."

Alisha told Bone where her portion of the weed was.

Road Rash dumped the pot on the scale, did his adjustments and said, "Twenty-three grams. A little under an ounce."

"Looks like more, huh," Bone observed.

"Yeah," Rash agreed. "It's super light. Here." He tossed Bone four baggies. He started packing the weed in them.

When Bone was finished, he tossed his buddy Road Rash one and said, "Give that to your wife. I know she likes that more than you do." Bone tossed the other three bags in the nightstand.

"Rash," Bone got back to business, "I need current prices for this area because they spend more money out here. In Bellflower and Lakewood they spend half of what they spend in San Fer."

"Glass is going for about eight hundred an ounce in Northridge and nine in Simi Valley. I got a guy in Simi that wants two right now. I make my own price up with the coke because I got a bunch of yuppies that buy powder. What you have right here I would sell for four hundred a quarter."

"Talk about a dildo in someone's ass." Bone winced.

"They got the money, bro," Rash said matter-of-factly, "And believe me it's some guys out here that will pay more."

"Okay. What's lined up right now?" Bone asked. He was ready to turn Rash loose with a hand full of bags.

Rash had called his wife after he finished bagging the dope up and she gave him a list of ready clients. "I got a doctor that wants an ounce and a stripper/actress chick that wants two."

"At sixteen hundred a piece?" Rash nodded. Bone started counting out bags. "Look. Call your boy up in Simi. Tell him to come on down for the glass. Here's the three in ya-yo. I want the grand you keep the six, and I got three ounces of your choice for your own pocket. That's for being a solid Peckerwood."

"Right on, Bone." Rash smiled. "You're alright for a black man. Hey? What about Karin?" He asked. "I'll snort a whole quarter out of her crack," he stuck his tongue out.

"You don't snort dope with your tongue you freak," Bone shook his head. "When you bring my bread back she'll be the one waitin' for you." Bone winked, and Rash nodded in return.

Bone gave Road Rash five ounces of coke and three ounces of glass: seventy-five more to go. To keep the two drugs separate, Bone put the rest of the coke in the big zip lock bag that Rash gave him, and he put the glass back in one of the ice buckets. He really didn't want to deal with dope anymore, but when it's dropped in your lap like this, what do you do?

You deal dope.

Bone wanted to go legit just like he talked about when he was locked up. You can't go legit if you come home to a situation like the one he was in right now. Prisons are full of guys who broke promises of reform.

"Oh," Bone had almost forgotten, "You still got a DMV plug?"

"Yeah. What's up?"

"Black Chevy Suburban, license plate D-I-A-M-O-N-D. I need a name and address. It ain't five o'clock yet, so call them first. I really need that info," Bone stressed.

Rash picked up the phone, called his wife and got her straight on it. She was out on stress but still employed at the DMV. Bone didn't know that Rash's plug was his wife. Some things you just don' reveal.

He hung up the phone and said, "I'll have the info for you when I come back tonight."

"I won't be here, but your girlfriend Karin will," Bone said slyly. As an after thought he said, "If you run across anybody that buys nine ounces or better of the glass, six fifty a piece."

"What about the coke?"

"No deals. I want a grand an ounce. Everything else over that is yours. Karin will be here to handle bizness. I'm going to see my mama."

Bone and Rash went about the business of cleaning up and putting the dope in a concealed place. After everything was put away Bone walked Rash to the elevator. "Let's get the bread, Rash Ass, and never turn back. We've both been looking for light at the end of this tunnel they call The Street Life."

"I see a little light," Rash responded.

"Stick with me, kid, and I'm gonna light this whole tunnel up like Dodger Stadium!" Bone slapped his buddy on the back when the elevator door opened, and he walked on down to 202.

The Ultimate Break 110. Rio Jonz

He stuck the key in and opened the door. The girls were laid out on the bed, giggling and passing joints. The whole room was cloudy. Bone had never seen them so relaxed, really enjoying themselves. Bone sat at the table and bit the burger from room service. He sat back and watched his crew of renegades. They were really tired of the streets, so this time out right here they were enjoying to the fullest. In the back of their minds though, they were dreading the day they had to pound that pavement again.

Bone wouldn't let that happen. They had enough dope to make the money needed for his full-scale hair salon; men, women, and children - manicures, pedicures, and massages. He would turn street prostitutes into massage therapists and manicurists. Karin already did nails; owned her own shop at one time. Drugs led her all the way to a wicked life she had never dreamed of. Bone would help her, because she had some know-how to help him. The big picture was coming into focus as he ate. He just had to get that dude John off of the girls' back. Then everybody could breathe easy.

A street hustler's dream.

Alisha came over to the table. "We need to talk."

"I'm all for that, baby girl," he wiped his mouth,. "Tell your girlfriends to get on, and I'll play under your skirt while you talk."

"They don't gotta to leave," she flashed him, "We can go in the bathroom."

"Nah, I don't want it like that. You're a cold freak, though."

"I got something to show you," she nodded her head toward the bathroom. "Seriously."

So she did stuff somethin! *Now I get to see the real bizness*, thought Bone as he followed her to the bathroom. Before he closed the bathroom door, he peaked around it to see if the rest of the girls were paying attention. They were all staring at him shaking their heads.

"It's not what you think," Bone said shyly.

"Boy, close the door!" Karin said.

Alisha sat up on the counter tossing a small black velvet bag in the air.

"What's that you got there, kiddo?" Bone asked.

"Open your hands like the Allstate Insurance commercial," she said coolly.

Bone stood in front of Alisha and cupped his hands. She untied the top, opened the pouch, and poured it out in his hands. As the stones fell into Bone's hands his eyes got wider, his mouth dropped open. When they were all in his hands he looked at them and her, in awe. He couldn't talk. He had never seen so many diamonds like that before in his life. In the movies, yeah. On the streets? Hell no! He once saw an Asian lady in the pawn shop with a few loose diamonds. That was it. Never on the streets.

"I can see why dude is chasin' ya'll," Bone said after a minute. "I would be too. These are worth millions, Alisha." She just sat there smiling and swinging her feet.

"Who, besides John, knows you got these?"

"Brooklyn," she answered cautiously.

"Barbara Walters?" Bone frowned. "You told the news ho of the streets. That's your little girlfriend, huh?"

"She needs a break too, Bone," she said matter-of-factly. "We all do."

"Then why did you stuff on René? Don't answer that," he said quickly. "'Cause I already know. Nobody knows what to really do with them, so I'll tuck them so they don't get fucked off."

"Exactly," she agreed.

Bone took the pouch from Alisha and put the diamonds back in it. This was the ultimate break for a street hustler. You always talk about the one move that puts you over the top; you retire from the life and go legit. This was the one move. All five of them would be all right now. Hanging on Artesia Blvd. had finally paid off. All of those stressful days when the money was slow, and those nights when the drugs were priority over a motel room were gone.

Bone dropped the pouch in his pocket and hugged Alisha. He hugged and kissed her all over her face. "This is it, Alisha! The hair salon, the house, mama's house, cars, and some mo' shit. You did it!" He cried. "This is the ultimate break!"

"We gotta get John off our back," she reminded him.

"Baby girl, nothin' will stop this show. I refuse to crap out this time. This doesn't happen to everybody in the life, and I ain't gonna let no trick stand in the way of fulfilling dreams. We almost stopped even dreamin'. Oh, hell nah!"

"I trust you, Willie," Alisha said and kissed him on the forehead. "Now get out, 'cause I gotta pee."

He pulled his phone out and handed it to her. "Call Hertz and have them bring us an Escalade. We got a dinner date at my mama's."

"Okay," she said as she pushed him toward the door. "Now get out so I can pee."

Bone walked out. His thoughts were not on the diamonds anymore but on keeping everybody safe. He didn't want other girls on the track to get hurt behind what René and Alisha did, and he really didn't want the immediate crew to get hurt. Dinner at Ms. J's would have to be fast. He dare not miss, but he couldn't stay long. Things had to be done.

Traps set.

Karin snapped him out of his thoughts. "Are your nuts out of the pawn shop yet?" She smiled.

"It wasn't even like that, home girl. I woulda just told ya'll to get on, or I woulda just got naked out here!" He was being a smart ass.

"I don't think you got that much heart, Bone." Karin was testing the water. What happened next almost made her blow snot out of her nose.

"I'm too old to be bashful," Bone unbuckled his belt, and with one swift push, down came his shorts and underwear. He stood straight up with his hands on his hips and shook his waist from left to right.

With their eyes bulging out of their heads, Karin and Brooklyn fell out laughing. René got off of the bed and walked up on Bone. She grabbed his hips, and he stopped moving; she slowly descended to the floor. *It was too late to turn back now*, thought Bone. He was committed with his shorts at his ankles. What he expected didn't happen.

René grabbed his boxer briefs and pulled them up around his waist, then she pulled up his shorts, unzipped them, tucked his shirt in, and zipped them back. She buckled his belt and stepped back to inspect him: perfect.

"You're way too smooth for all that, babe," she whispered.

Bone breathed a sigh of relief and said, "Thanks, baby girl." He looked over at Karin who was actually blushing. "We're gonna step out for a while. Rash will be back later. He should have forty-eight hundred. Any other cash serve him. Glass is two twenty-five a quarter; ya-yo is four a quarter. I'll show you where it is before we leave."

"I like the cash flow out here," Karin said. "How you gettin' around? You know you can't drive my car."

"I got Hertz bringing me a Cadillac Escalade." Bone stuck his tongue out at Karin. Back to René he said, "We're gonna go see my mama, so let's run and get us a couple of outfits."

René lit up. "They got a cute little shop down in the lobby. That's where Alisha got her outfit."

"Okay cool."

Alisha came out of the bathroom. "What did I miss?" She heard all of the laughter, but she was still sitting on the toilet.

"Oh that." Karin said off handedly. "I finally got to see why they call him, what is he girls?"

"A man!" Yelled René and Brooklyn.

"I finally got to see why they call this man, Bone."

Alisha looked at him in shock. "You didn't?"

Bone smiled. "She dared me."

At the elevator Bone said, "Alisha, you and René go on down to the gift shop, and I'll be there in a minute." He walked on with Karin and Brooklyn to 220.

Karin opened the door and said, "Burr, it's cold in here." She went to cut the air down.

"If you had some damn clothes on, you wouldn't be cold," Bone said.

"You know you like my jersey, boy," she shook her ass at him.

"I sure do," Bone replied as he grabbed a hand full of her ass. "Listen." He was all business, "I'm gonna get rid of all this dope and use the bread for the shop." He watched Karin's face light up. They had been talking along those same lines before he got busted.

"You think we'll have enough cash?" She asked.

"We got eighty ounces, Karin. That's enough seed money for what I want to do. We can go to a bank for a loan with that kind of up-front cash," he was talking reasonable like that because he didn't want to let on about the diamonds just yet. "Even so, the conventional ways of getting money wouldn't be hard to get with fifty thousand of your own to start with."

"I'm ready, Bone. To hell with these streets. I'm ready to play with some hands and feet again."

"What about Brook?" Bone turned to her. "You ready to do something different?"

Brooklyn stood there crying.

"Why are you crying, love," Karin asked warmly.

"I thought…you…guys were…" She stopped to blow her nose, "Gonna drop me off after this was all over. I never thought you would include me in the better plan," she blew her nose again, "I thought I would be stuck on Artesia Blvd. for the rest of my life."

"Brook, I couldn't leave you or Karin out. We're all in this together. You know that. Was I ever any different?" Bone looked at her expectedly.

"No," Brook mumbled.

"Well then," Bone beamed, "It ain't no different now. You might have to suck on my toes the rest of your life, though." He smiled.

Brooklyn dropped to the floor and was trying to take his sandal off.

"Stop, girl!" Bone cried. He was trying to get away from her. "I ain't never seen a bunch of sentimental hoes before in all my life. I'm going down to the gift shop and fool with these other two emotional broads." He stomped his foot at Brooklyn who was still playing around his feet. "Stop girl!"

As he got to the door he stopped. "Oh, the glass is in that ice bucket at the bottom of the nightstand, and the ya-yo is in the nightstand drawer. We'll be back later on."

"I got it covered, Willie." Karin gave him a warm thank-you smile. "Go on."

***

Down in the gift shop the girls were acting like teenagers. "Look at this right here, girl...ooh, with these sandals bitch...and these earrings."

"I guess you found something, huh?" Bone asked.

"Yep," answered René And we found something for you, too." She pulled a shirt and shorts off of the rack.

"All I need is a hat and I'll look like I'm going on a safari." He looked at Alisha as she pulled a hat from behind her back and stuck it on his head.

"We'll all look like Nigerians," Alisha said.

"Shiiit," Bone laughed. "I ain't never seen no light skinned Nigerians." They all started laughing as they walked to the counter to pay. "How much is this?"

The clerk started scanning price tags. "Your total is $194.74, sir."

"I thought you were gonna say about five hundred." Bone went into his pocket. "You know how gift shops are."

"These items are on sale," René said. "They probably woulda been about five, babe."

"Here," Alisha stepped to the cashier, "I got it." She pulled out her knot of cash and paid for the items. "Stop thinking cheap, baby," she whispered as she patted his pocket with the diamonds in it.

"You're right," he said. "How long did Hertz say they would be?"

"They'll be here at six," Alisha announced. "As a matter-of-fact," she looked down in the display case, "Pick one."

In the case were a variety of men and women's watches. He immediately picked out a flat Tag Heuer; silver with a black face and a black leather band. It was as thin as a fifty-cent piece. The price tag said $2,675.00.

"I know this is a sale price," Bone said matter-of-factly. "I like it."

"That fits your character baby: mysterious."

"Can we go now?" René asked, curtly. She was getting upset at herself more than them. It would take her more than a few hours to get over losing like she did.

Alisha paid for the watch, too. Bone grabbed the bag off of the counter. Alisha held his face in her hands. "Anything for my baby." She was performing in front of René. She kissed him. When they started to walk out of the gift shop René was already stepping on the elevator.

"Come on!" She cried.

Chapter Twelve

They were going west on Alondra toward the Compton Airport. John was caught up in his thoughts until a ragtop '63 Impala pulled up beside them at Long Beach Blvd.

Popeye.

He still had a big peanut head, John thought. He rolled his window down. "You want to sell that piece of shit?" John asked sarcastically.

Popeye looked up to see an old friend. "They take trucks like that from white boys in Compton." Popeye knew if John was in Compton these days it was strictly business. "What chu' needm John?"

John jumped out of the truck and into the ragtop. "I need some info. Who do you know from The Hub working down by Lakewood Blvd. on Artesia?"

The light turned green and Popeye tiptoed across the intersection. This was his part of The Hub and he loved to show off the all-original honey-gold Impala, with the peanut butter top down on a sunny Friday afternoon - just another summer day in the lovely City of Compton.

"John," Popeye looked at him like he was stupid, "information?"

"No not information, Popeye. Info!" John returned the look.

"Who's affiliated with Compton Crips out there hustling with the prostitutes?"

"You let a ho in your game and she got chu'. Typical white boy shit. Ha!" He paused, "I got a homeboy who just touched down this mornin' that knows every ho it is out there. I don't think he went straight out there, though."

"Here," John reached into his coat pocket and pulled out a card. He wrote his son Tino's cell number on the back and circled his on the front. "I need to talk to him, bad. Call me or my son when you locate your boy."

"Was she white or black?"

"Black. Why?" John looked confused.

"Once you go black, you never go back!" Popeye smiled as he elbowed John in his arm.

"Whatever. Pull over before somebody starts shooting."

Popeye pulled to the curb to let John out.

"Hey!" John cried, "What's your homeboy's name so I'll know?"

"When the man named Bone calls you have your checkbook ready."

"Hoes and "info" ain't free." Popeye stuck his hand out.

John shook his hand and said, "Thanks, cuz!"

***

The phone rang. Alisha picked it up and listened. Her eyes got wide and René said, "What?"

"Hold on Karin," she said into the phone. To René she said, "Get a pen out the nightstand." Back into the phone, "Okay. Read it to me. John Forrest: one, five, six, zero, six, Downey Avenue. Damn! That fool stays right in the spot...alright." She hung up.

"Whose address is that?" René asked but she already knew.

"Stop askin' stupid questions," Alisha looked at René crazy, "It's John's. Road Rash just called and gave it to Karin. He got that shit fast, huh?"

"Bone knows some cold people in the game," René stated.

"15606," Alisha thought for a moment, "That's down passed Alondra, huh?"

"Yep. Right by that park," said René.

Bone was coming out of the bathroom after a nice hot bath. "Whew!" He cried, "I ain't never taking a shower again. After forty months of hard water showers, I'm cool. I'm gonna get me a big ol' tub like Scarface: 'Who do I truss? Me, das who!'" He looked at Alisha and René but they didn't look in a joking mood. "Now what?"

"Road Rash just called and gave Karin the name and address to the black truck." Alisha was all business. "John Forrest,15606 Downey Avenue."

"They never stay too far from the track," Bone said casually.

"What do you plan on doing, Bone?" René asked.

"Well," he simply said, "Since he wants the bag so bad, I'm going to hang it on his front door. Just to let him know that he ain't hard to find, either. All he wants is the bag, right?"

"That's what he says," René said.

"What better way to get it? Like picking up the morning paper off your porch." Bone walked over to the bed and started getting dressed. He sensed them staring at him, so he turned around.

"What now?"

The girls were stuck in a trance by how casually he was dealing with the situation. Bone snapped his fingers. "You are now coming out of your hypnotic state. When I snap my fingers again, you will start purring like kittens."

"Boy, shut up...yeah, you cornball."

"Okay," Bone clapped his hands, "Let's get dressed for Ms. J's famous spaghetti."

"How do you know your mama's gonna cook spaghetti?" Alisha asked.

"It's Friday, she's been standing on her feet all day, and it's a one course meal. Spaghetti and bread. Make your own salad."

The girls looked at each other and giggled. They both had children, and when they didn't feel like cooking, that's what they would whip up real quick. The phone rang, and Alisha picked it up.

"Mrs. Braxton?" asked the Hertz clerk.

"Yes, this is Mrs. Braxton," Alisha beamed.

"Our driver is down in the lobby waiting with your vehicle."

"Thank you," she hung up. "The caddie's here." She announced.

René looked confused, "You said a truck, Bone."

"A Cadillac Escalade is a truck, baby girl. That's cool to float in for the weekend, right?"

René was stunned. Not at what kind of truck really, but how did Alisha rent it? You had to have a credit card to…wait a minute. Mrs. Braxton?

"How did you rent that truck?" René asked.

"With this," Alisha handed René her Chase credit card. It read Alisha Braxton.

"Does Bone know about this?" René asked as she tried to suppress her anger.

"He's the one who told me to do it," Alisha grabbed the credit card back and stuck it in her purse.

"Uh-huh," René said flatly.

On the way out the door Bone grabbed René. "On the way to my mama's I need you to tell me the bizness about this dead trick and his goon, kay?"

René wasn't listening. She had something of her own to say. "You told her to use your last name to get credit?"

"Don't start, René," he said calmly. "You were out of pocket." Bone closed the door behind him.

"I coulda did for you, Bone. It's just that..."

"Don't have no pity party, baby girl," he said smoothly. "You're doing for me right now. Three grand and eighty ounces of dope is the bizness, baby girl, for a guy fresh out of prison. Put your mind on that, and stop worrying about Alisha." Bone had to calm René down. "Everybody's got a position to fill, woman. You're doing an excellent job." He kissed her on her forehead, put his arm around her, and continued down the hall.

"Are we gonna stop to holla at Karin and Brook?" Alisha asked.

"Nope," Bone answered. "If we do they'll wanna go." They stepped into the elevator and descended. When the elevator deposited the three into the lobby, Alisha broke away to deal with the Hertz employee at the counter. Bone and René kept going outside.

Parked right at the door was a pearl white 2005 Cadillac Escalade. It had twenty-four inch chrome rims on it and a moon roof. Alisha walked up next to them and said, "Wow! We gotta get one of these."

"No shit, huh," Bone was smiling like a fat cat. Alisha handed him the keys. He hit the alarm switch (chirp-chirp) and opened the front door. He opened up the back door for René. While she was getting in, he helped her by caressing her ass with both of his hands. She looked over her shoulder at him and smiled. He winked at her and closed the door.

Had to keep everybody happy, he thought.

Bone swung around the front of the truck to the driver's side. When he got in he said, "Wow! I gotta have this." He stuck the key in and started it up. Bone started adjusting the seat and got familiar with the controls around the steering wheel and then the radio; 94.7 The Wave. He adjusted the mirrors, looked at his passengers and said, "This is the bizness."

Bone pulled the Cadillac out of the parking lot and headed for the freeway. Outside of the Escalade you could hear screams from Magic Mountain.

***

"Hello."

"Hey, Ms. J. This is Darren. Is Willie home yet?"

"Yes, Popeye," Joyce knew real names and nicknames. "He'll be over here at about seven thirty."

"Could you have him call me when he gets there?" He asked.

"You tryin' to get my boy in the street already?"

"Oh, no," Popeye said quickly. "I'm tryin' to keep him out of 'em, if I can. If I can't, I want him to know the bizness, Ms. J."

"At least you're honest, Popeye. I'll tell him to call you as soon as he gets here."

"Thanks, Ms. J."

"Bye, Darren," she hung up.

"Everything okay?" Barry asked. He had been engaged to Joyce for ten years: scared to get married again.

"Get that shoe box out that boy left you."

"Already?" Barry sounded anxious.

"I sure the hell hope not," she put on her sweater. "We're gonna need some more bread. I'll be right back." Joyce was out of the door.

She wasn't headed toward the store.

***

"So then the fool told me to burn him with the pipe," explained René. She was giving Bone the run down about Adam/James DuVall. She had a cold blank stare on her face while she told the story. No remorse whatsoever.

"So, you burned him in more ways than one," Bone conceded. He was dealing with some cold women. If you set out to hurt one of them, and they caught up with you later, bye-bye, Mr. Trick. You could not get away with doing these hoes wrong, and then date one of their friends. You were asking for trouble.

"This is what I don't get," continued René, "Why John wants this duffel bag? There's nothin' in it but straps that Alisha cut off the trick. Does it have sentimental value enough for him to shoot Lisa, and try to hold Marie hostage? Come on, Bone. I ain't that stupid, and you ain't that stupid." She looked around the seat at Alisha. Then she sat backwards on the armrest to look her in her eyes.

Alisha looked around René over at Bone. She was giving him the okay to reveal their secret.

"I knew you stuffed on me, bitch!" René hauled off and slapped Alisha.

"René!" Bone said angrily. "Sit yo' ass back!"

"Bone, she took off on me in the room before you got there," René said defensively.

"You deserved that." Alisha said, with finality in her voice.

"Okay," Bone said firmly, "You two are even. We're all still together, so you ain't left out on nothin', René. Do you really think that I would conspire to leave you out?"

"I don't know," René said flatly.

"I'm not like you, René," Bone declared.

She felt as if he had just slapped her in the mouth with that statement. René had left Bone out of eighty percent of the time, but this was the first time he had ever said anything about it.

"Let me out," René barked. "Pull this mothafucka over and let me the fuck out!"

Bone put the pedal to the medal. He looked in the side view mirror, and from the fast lane he dipped through traffic all the way to the shoulder. René knew Bone was dead serious almost all of the time. Why would she push him right now? He put the truck in park and cut the hazards on.

"Get your punk ass out," Bone got out first. He swung around the front of the truck and met her at the back door.

"Ms. Shepherd," he said through clenched teeth, "How dare you push me to a state of mind that neither one of us want. You hit a cool lick. Alisha stuffed for a good reason. Everything ain't always gonna happen the way you want it. You ain't comin' up short in this, so don't try to blend your other short comings in life with this. You gotta be held accountable for your own actions, and you can't make everybody else help you pay." Bone knew when she acted out like she did it was really because of other issues in her life. "How dare you force your misery on me, on Alisha, and on every trick you run into. You the one being irresponsible, punk," he hated to check her like this, but some people are more hard headed than others.

René was one of them.

Bone strolled back around to the driver's side and got in. He cut the hazards off, put the truck in drive, and slammed the gas pedal to the floor; he didn't bother to see if René got in or not.

She did.

As they merged back into the flow of freeway traffic Rick James was on the radio talking about how he used to love them and leave them. Bone turned it up and darted through traffic back to the fast lane. Alisha reached over and grabbed his hand. She felt a small tremor in his hand. He was beyond upset. He didn't need to feel like that his first night home. Alisha would ease all of that tension when they got back to the room.

Bone's anger eased up as they got closer to his mom's house. As he got ready to get off of the freeway, he kissed Alisha's hand and let her go. "We are now on our final approach to Ms. J's. Could you please fire up a joint?" He reached his right hand in the back seat and René set a joint between his fingers.

"I'm sorry, babe," René cried.

"Don't be sorry, kid!" Bone beamed. "Stand up and be counted."

"Speaking of being counted. Can you count out my half of what she stuffed?"

Bone pulled up in his mother's driveway and parked. He reached in his pocket and pulled out the velvet pouch. "Come sit right here," he patted the armrest. "Open your hands." Bone poured the diamonds in her hands. René screamed.

"That's why he wants this bag back," she kicked the duffel bag. "For these."

"And he ain't gonna get them," Alisha said defiantly. "After what his boss did to Shelley, to hell with both of them."

René looked from Alisha to Bone. A tear rolled down her cheek, "This is our ticket out Bone."

"Yeah," he agreed as he wiped her face. "I'm just here to make sure we don't pay dearly for this ticket. No crappin' out this time." He put the diamonds back in the pouch and stuck them in his pocket. He tried to pass the joint, but they didn't want it, "You'll wish you hit it after we get in there."

They all got out and walked up on the porch.

The   door   was   already   open.

Chapter Thirteen

"Little Johnny, go to your house and get some rest," John instructed, "And I'll call you when I need you."

He was cool with that. Little Johnny was tired of running around on this dumb mission, anyway. He made a left on Alameda and headed for the 91 freeway. He was tired of traveling the streets looking for some chick that stole some dumb bag. *I don't even know what's in the bag*, he thought, *so why did he have to help, anyway?* Let Tino drift around town with pops. Oh, this isn't a pleasure mission; so take the most unwanted son on this mission. At that thought, he speeded up. He was in a hurry to get home.

Little Johnny got off the freeway on Downey Avenue and made a right. Across Artesia Boulevard down two streets, he made a right on 64th Street and parked. He stayed on Johnson Street, but he wanted a drink from the store he was parked next to.

"I'll walk from here," he told John. "I need a cold one."

"Not too many," John said firmly, "I might need you tonight."

Little Johnny didn't respond. He jumped down out of the Suburban and walked into the store.

"Pissant," John muttered. He slid over into the driver's seat, picked up his phone, and called Tino.

"What's up, Pops?" Tino asked.

"If a guy by the name of Bone calls you let me know. Fast! I'm on my way to Jans, I mean, Mrs. DuVall's place. This Bone hustles on Artesia and he knows all of the hookers. Call me as soon as you hear from him."

"Is he gonna make these hoes give up the goods?" Tino asked.

"All hustler's got a price."

"Why is he gonna be calling me?" Tino already knew the answer to that question.

"He'll get your number along with mine if my source pays off. As of right now, I'm going to voicemail. This situation is giving me a migraine," he hung up.

Tino knew his dad was lying with Mrs. DuVall. John never outright said he was. Tino knew that if his dad's voicemail was on that nine times out of ten he had Mrs. DuVall's knees touching her ears.

***

Bone let the girls go in before him. It was a small living room for a four-bedroom house. This wasn't the hood so there was no need for enough space for a let out couch when you didn't have enough rooms to accommodate your family.

The living room was in oriental design: futon, small tables, throw rugs, hardwood floor, and Buddha sitting on a Jade stand in the corner. There was a string of oriental lights down the hallway hanging from the ceiling; three bedrooms on the left side of the hallway, the den/bedroom, and kitchen on the right.

Joyce came out of a bathroom at the end of the hall on the right and stopped short. "Boy, you scared me."

"The front door was open," he explained.

"Yeah," she agreed. "I burnt some of the bread, and I was letting that smell out." Joyce stuck her arms out. "Alisha, come here and give me some suga."

"Hey, Ms. J," Alisha said as she walked into her arms. "I meant to come by yesterday, but I got tied up."

"Yeah. You got tied up with this one here. Come give me some suga, René," Joyce was ready to read her the riot act but she already looked whipped. "Where you been hiding, girl?"

"I've been around, Ms. J. How are you feelin?" René asked.

"Younger than you," she said matter-of-factly. "You need to come by and let me introduce you to these teas I be drinkin'."

"Mama, you always got somethin' going on, huh," Bone stated.

"Boy, please. Who you think taught you how to hustle? You coulda been rich," Joyce stated, "If you woulda stuck to hustling legal shit. Excuse me ladies, I didn't mean to say shit. I think that's the only language this boy understands." Joyce looked at Bone, shook her head, and said, "Go on in the back and talk to Barry while me and your "girls" get this food ready."

Bone walked to the master bedroom all the way in the back of the house. At the door he could see through patio doors to the pool deck. On the deck Barry was seated under a big umbrella. As he slid back the patio door to come out, he saw a figure in the pool. Bone squinted under the descending sun and froze: Imani. His daughter was floating on her back with her eyes closed. Bone eased the door shut, quietly slid onto the deck, and emptied his pockets. He took off his sandals and shirt and jumped in. "Aaah!" He screamed, and splashed down behind her.

"Daddy!" She cried. Imani hadn't seen her father in over forty months. Bone and her mother were at odds before he got locked up, so she played games with letting him see his daughter.

"What's going on, stinky booty?" he asked, and splashed her in the face.

"Da-Dee," she beamed as she swam to him. "I missed you so, so, so, much!" She squeezed him around his neck.

Bone had been in and out of jail since she was born, but she still loved him. That was her daddy and nobody could say anything bad about him. He brought a joy and energy to her that no other human being could. Imani knew that her daddy had a problem with letting go of the street life. He never hid that from her. She also knew deep down in her heart that he loved her. She knew he would let go of the streets and then they would really have some fun.

"Where's your mama?" Bone asked.

"She's at home. Mama Joyce came down to get me.

"We moved down the hill last month, daddy," Imani explained. "You didn't know?"

Nobody told Bone anything. He hadn't even heard from her mother his last month to the house. Kristene could be stubborn to a point of real frustration for Bone and he didn't need that a month to the house. He was focused on more positive relationships; Willie and Imani, minus Kristene.

"No, I didn't know you lived down the hill, baby."

"Yeah," she said off handedly. "Let's go to Magic Mountain, daddy!" Imani quickly changed the subject. "I go some coupons from the supermarket."

"It's funny you said Magic Mountain, Imani. I was thinking of the same place. We'll go Sunday, kay?"

"Kay. Can Mr. Barry come, too?"

"If Mr. Barry wants to he can."

"Mr. Barry," Imani started in her properly funny way, "I am formally inviting you on a trip to Magic Mountain. Do you accept?"

"I would love to, Ms. Imani," Barry replied, "But I'm afraid Ms. J has me tied up this Sunday. Maybe some other time."

"I shall pray for you, Mr. Barry," she bowed her head and broke out laughing. Imani knew that a Sunday with her grandmother meant church from sun-up to sundown.

"I'm gonna talk to Mr. Barry," Bone said as he treaded water to the edge, "You just keep swimming and I'll be back."

"Kay, daddy," she released his neck.

Imani was a very respectful seven-year old. With Carmel colored skin; with red undertones and high cheekbones, she was the spitting image of her daddy. With her long silky hair down her back, and her slightly pointed chin, she had Kristene written all over her. She had her own persona, though. It was like God had tossed Bone and Kristene in a cup, shook them up like dice and poured out Imani.

All of their imperfections made perfect.

Bone climbed out of the pool and sat down next to Barry. "Mom's pulled out all stops, huh?"

"She just wants you to stay home, dad," Barry replied. Barry was a short version of Cedric the Entertainer. The only difference was Barry's pencil-thin mustache.

"I got something I want to show you," Bone was all business.

"Already?" Barry asked. "Oh, them hoes had it ready for you," he answered his own question. "How many you got with you?"

"Two right now. There's two more back at the room."

"Four hoes," he chuckled. "That sure is a lot of street walkers to have around for a guy who says he ain't pimpin'. Let me see what your hoes laced you with your first day out."

Bone got up and picked up the pouch out of his sandals and handed it to Barry. He untied it and looked in. Barry couldn't really see in so he dumped it out on the table.

"Wow!" He whispered intensely. "They came through in more ways than one this time."

"Yeah, but how do I dump them? I thought about downtown, but..."

"You gotta know somebody," Barry finished.

"You know somebody, dad?"

Barry smiled. "You know me. The kid I buy all of my suits from is downtown. His daddy owns a jewelry store two blocks from his store."

"By you just looking at these right now, how much do you think is here?" Bone asked.

"Over ten million, easy. I'm no expert but these aren't chips. These are..." Barry's last statement trailed off. He looked at Bone slack-jawed.

"DuVall," He looked astonished. "I just read about him in the paper this morning."

"Don't look at me," Bone said with his arms up like he was surrendering. "I was in prison last night."

"The less I know the better." Barry changed the subject. "You need something out of your box?"

"One item. What I really need is for you to set up a meeting with those kids downtown. Can you do that tomorrow?"

"I already got a meeting with one of them tomorrow. I was gonna take you down to get fitted."

"Let's postpone that and get with his pops. We close a deal with pops and his kid will fit both of us on me."

"The food is re..." Alisha froze in mid-sentence. She was stuck looking at the little girl in the water.

Barry slid the diamonds back into the pouch, and Bone jumped back in the water.

"Hold onto daddy's neck, and I'll tow you in." He swam toward Imani.

She grabbed him. "Let's go around twice before we got out, kay?" Imani wasn't asking.

"Okay," Bone swam toward Alisha. He wanted to give her a good look at his daughter since she was staring.

As they turned left in the water Alisha stared at Imani and Imani stared at her. *Bone's twin,* she thought. The only difference was their gender, and Imani had hair.

"Who is that, daddy?" Imani whispered in his ear.

"Why that there lil' filly be Ah-Lee-Sha," Bone said like a cowboy.

"Da-Dee!" Imani cried, "For real?"

"Why don't you introduce yourself? You ain't shy."

Imani stuck her hands on her daddy's head and pushed him under water. After she did that, Imani swam as fast as she could to the edge and got out. She went to the deck and grabbed her towel.

"I owe you one and you know," he switched voices, "That I'll get chu', my pretty!"

Imani laughed as she strolled over to Alisha. She looked up at her and said, "Hello, lady. My name is Imani. My daddy gave me permission to introduce myself. So, who are you?"

Alisha squatted down to Imani's level. "My name is Alisha, and it is a pleasure meeting you, Imani."

"You look like Pocahontas. You know who she is?" Imani asked.

"She's a little Indian girl just like me," Alisha replied.

"You're not a cartoon," Imani said matter-of-factly.

"No, but I am Indian.

"Daddy," Imani called over her shoulder, "Did you find Ms. Alisha in a tent?"

"A tent called the Motel 6," Bone replied.

"Da-Dee!" She cried.

Bone got out of the pool. "Go inside with Alisha, baby. Daddy and Mr. Barry are right behind you."

Imani trailed Alisha into the house shaking her head. "A tent called the Motel 6."

"That little girl is just like you, Willie."

"How?" I ain't even been around that much."

"She comes from you, dad," Barry said. "On another note: where did you find <u>that</u> <u>one</u>?"

"She bad, huh?" Bone was smiling. "That's the one that's been hangin' with me these last forty months."

"She's a keeper," Barry paused. "Where's René?"

"You remember her?"

"She makes a lasting impression just like this one's doing."

"That punk is in there."

"She must not be that much of a punk if she's in my house," Barry said as he got up. "Let me put these in the safe, and get you your box." He walked into his room and into the closet. He emerged a couple of minutes later with the box in his hand. He set it on the table.

Bone looked at the dusty Nike show box. He had memories in there. He didn't feel like stirring up those memories but he had to get his heat. He flipped it open. Right on the top was an ultrasound picture dated December 1997 labeled: Imani growing in Kristene. Bone eased the top down on the box and looked up at Barry. Barry shrugged his shoulders and grabbed Bone's shoulder. "Let's go see how the big girls are handling your little girl." They strolled on into the den.

***

"Like I was saying, Imani," Joyce was saying, "Your daddy didn't mean a Motel 6 made like a tent, baby, he..."

"Meant a Motel 6 made like an upside down ice cream cone," Bone finished.

"A tent," Imani said with finality. "See. I told you, Mama J."

Joyce sighed, "I guess you're right, baby."

"Willie, where have you been hiding this cute little girl?" René asked.

Bone leaned into René and whispered in her ear, "The hell away from Artesia Blvd. You thought I was supposed to bring her out there to meet and greet?"

"No, not like that," René said uneasily, "It's just, just..."

"Here she is now. Enjoy her energy, take a couple of flicks, and let's finish this John bizness, so that we can enjoy more evenings like this."

"Okay, babe."

Bone could feel René. She was sulking. He pulled her into the hallway. "You alright? I don't want you upset at the chain of events. You forced my hand with Alisha, and if I seem stand-offish with you, you're right. I don't take too kindly to being lied to. Now, I see how my daughter's Mother felt by all of my broken promises. I've lied unintentionally to love one's myself. That's the only reason why I'm still dealing with you."

"I'm gonna tighten up, Willie, okay? Just don't throw nothin' up in my face," she said pleadingly.

The table was live with conversation. Bone was grateful to his mother for going to get his daughter. In more ways than one, Imani's presence brought a sense of belonging to his life. He had to make responsible moves to ensure his longevity in the streets, her safety from *any* of his moves, and her financial security. He would not place in jeopardy his relationship with his daughter anymore. All he had to do was clean up this mess that these girls made and they would be home free.

How many times had Bone said that?

"Ladies," Joyce announced, "Please clear the table while I talk to my son."

"René said, "Sure Ms. J."

Alisha said, "Get him to slow down."

Imani said, "Don't hurt my daddy, Mama J."

"I won't baby," she told Imani. "Show them ladies how to work the dishwasher, kay."

"Okay. Come on ladies. This will be fun," she declared. Imani liked the dishwasher because it talked.

Joyce walked Bone out onto the pool deck and set him down. She went into her room, got the cordless phone, and came back to sit down.

"Popeye called before you came tonight so call him back," she handed him the phone.

Bone scanned through Caller ID until he saw Popeye's number and pressed Dial.

Popeye answered on the second ring, "'Bout time you called me, Bone."

"My mama said you tried to hit on her."

"You stupid for that one, boy!" Popeye cried. They always played the dozens.

"What's up, Popeye! Boy, it sure is good to hear your voice. Where you at?"

"My house, fool. That's how I stay free," he turned serious. "Look, this ain't no social call."

"I figured that much. You never call me as soon as I get out. "What's the bizness?"

"White boy stopped me by Jack Rabbit's today talkin' 'bout some ho beat him on Artesia Blvd. He's a heavyweight, Bone, and for him to come lookin' for some help in The Hub to locate this broad, means that the ho got over real decent."

"Did you give him my name?" Bone asked.

"Yeah. He gave me a couple of numbers for you to reach him," Popeye said.

Bone waved at his mother for a pen and paper. She had it in her hand already. "Give me the numbers, my pretty," Bone teased.

Popeye read them off to him.

"Let me guess the name: John."

Popeye paused for a second, "The first number is his son Tino. How did you know his name is John?"

"All tricks are named John," Bone said off handedly.

Popeye was not going for it. "For real, Bone. How did you know his name is John?" He pressed.

"Because the ho he's lookin' for is with me," he whispered. Bone gave him the answer he was looking for.

"Wow!" Popeye's wheels started turning, "Bone, check it..."

"Bye Darren," he hung up. Bone set the phone down on the table and looked at his mother. He sure hoped that she wouldn't demand an explanation because he wouldn't give it up this time.

"Listen. No long speeches, no Sermon on the Mount. I went and got that little lady in there for a reason. Before you make any moves tonight, tomorrow, and everyday after that, you think about Imani; will this help or will this hurt my daughter? You ask yourself that question before you make a move, and I promise you, I promise you, you'll make the right move every single time," Joyce finished. If she said anymore, it would lead her into doing something that she was too old to participate in: going on the mission with her son.

"Is she staying here tonight?" Bone asked.

"Only if you're staying," she said flatly.

Bone sighed. His mother didn't want to see him back in prison anymore. She used every trick she could think of to make him see what he was missing. All she could do now is pray that he followed through on what she said to him.

"I'll take her home," Bone said. He got up and started towards the patio door.

"Don't you start nothin' with her mama, boy!"

***

"System overload, system overload," the dishwasher was repeating itself.

"See?" Imani overloaded the machine so it could repeat itself. "I told you it talked." She had René and Alisha laughing so hard they were crying.

"You ready to go home, stinky booty?" Bone asked her. He could see her whole body sag.

"I thought I was staying with you," she whined.

Bone squatted down in front of her and said warmly, "Not tonight, stinky. I'll come and get you Sunday for Magic Mountain. Then, if your mama says okay, you can stay all week."

"All week?" She eyed him suspiciously.

Bone smiled. She was just like him. Everybody was suspect if things didn't come out of their mouth right.

"All week," he said brightly. "Me and you? Promise."

Imani searched his eyes for a moment, "Okay, daddy. Now let's go and see if mommy approves."

"You work on her tonight, and I'll call her tomorrow and work on her. We'll team up on her, kay?"

"Deal!" Imani declared as she shook her daddy's hand.

Alisha and René sat back and watched Willie, not Bone, being a father to his daughter. They had never seen this side of him before. They were used to the hard-as-nails hustler of the streets, not a loving, caring, struggling-to-get-it-right father. Struggling mentally to leave the street life alone and just be a father to his daughter. Leave it alone after he got the bread - a street hustler's curse.

Refusing to retire broke.

"Come give me some suga, baby," Joyce said as she walked into the kitchen.

"Bye, Mama J," Imani said and gave her grandmother a big hug and kiss.

Outside in the driveway Bone lifted his daughter into the front seat then helped René and Alisha into the back. Joyce and Barry stood on the porch as they backed out of the driveway and pulled off. Joyce turned toward Barry and was about to question him.

"He didn't take nothing out of the box," he informed her before she could ask.

"Good for him." A smile spread across her face. "Good for him."

***

"Right here, daddy," Imani pointed to a house on the right. Bone pulled into the driveway of a two-story Spanish-style home.

It looked like it was made of clay with a brick porch. As they approached the front door, the porch light came on and the door opened.

"Your mother just called and told me you were on your way," Kristene stood behind the screen door.

"So you decided to meet me at the door instead of inviting me in." Bone shot the first lug. "How did you get this place?"

"Not with your help," she shot back. "Come in Imani and get ready for bed."

"Bye, daddy," Imani said sadly. She kissed him on his cheek.

Bone picked her up, gave her a big kiss and whispered in her ear, "Don't forget we're a team, kay?"

"Kay." Bone set her down. "See you Sunday, daddy," Imani said as she walked into the house.

Bone held the screen door open, "How did you get this house?" He pressed.

Kristene sighed, "The house your mom and Barry are in was owned by the same man that owned this one. They did the deal. You satisfied?" Kristene suppressed her fluttering heart with a veil of annoyance.

Barely.

Bone dug in his pocket and peeled off fifteen hundred dollars. He handed it to her. "Imani wants to go to Magic Mountain Sunday. I'll call you tomorrow about it."

"What's the money for?" She asked.

"Go get your feet done," Bone said and walked off. Before he got in the truck, Kristene called out to him.

"Willie! Wait!"

"We'll talk tomorrow," he said over his shoulder. He waved his hand at her but never turned around. He didn't want her to see the big kool-aid grin plastered on his face. It was way too soon for that.

Chapter Fourteen

"Okay, this is the bizness," Bone said firmly. "We go drop this bag off on this fool's front door. We call the fools..."

"Call him!" Alisha cried from the back seat.

Bone looked in the rearview mirror at René and Alisha. "I feel like I'm driving Ms. Daisy and her bridge partner."

Alisha sat on the armrest and swung into the passenger's seat. "How did you get his phone number?" She asked.

"He went into Compton today lookin' for hustler's on Artesia Blvd. He ran into one of my homeboys left some numbers and now I have them."

"Why would he go to Compton lookin' for people hustlin' in Lakewood and Bellflower?" René asked.

"Because half of the people on Artesia are from Compton," Alisha answered. She looked back at René. "Look at the three of us."

René thought about it for a moment. Actually, she was doing a mental head count of everybody that was from Compton out there. "Try like eighty percent of us out there," she admitted.

"So this trick ain't that game goofy," Bone observed. "He's just up against the wrong, or should I say, the right crew from Compton. We're about the only one's sharp enough to get away clean," Bone declared. "So, we ruffle this fool's feathers by giving him the duffel bag he wants; delivering it to his front door. Then we call his son to relay the message to him."

Alisha changed the subject. "Your daughter is really smart and cute."

"She's got your sense of humor that's for sure," René added.

"We all got cute kids," Bone conceded. Then he brought them back to the business at hand. "Let's finish what ya'll started so that we can enjoy our kids, and vice versa." With that said he cut up the music, pulled the joint out of the ashtray, and jumped into the fast lane.

They floated down the Harbor Freeway South soon to be merging onto the 91 East. They were going to duck in and out of the land that crushed dreams separated families, and yet offered so much to a hustler's itch. They were going to Artesia Boulevard.

***

Bone got off of the freeway at Paramount. He made a right and got in the far left lane to turn onto Artesia. The light turned green and he swung onto The Blvd The light at Orizaba caught him. Shop-n-Go was on the corner. The store had normal activity for a Friday.

Jam-packed.

Young hustler's were in and out of the store hollering at each other about the kind of money they were making, the fly broad in the car with them, and the promise to connect one day and get paid together.

Bone pushed on when the light changed. When he got the F&M Bank Alisha grabbed his arm.

"There's that fool's son!" She cried, as she pointed at a man staggering across the street.

"Yep," she confirmed. "That's him."

Bone pulled into the Rally Burger's parking lot on the corner. He went through the alley to come up into the K.F.C. parking lot. He saw Little Johnny staggering down the street. He was going home. When he passed the parking lot Bone pulled out on the street.

"What street is this, Alisha?" Bone asked.

"I don't know..."

"Johnson," René answered. "You think he lives over here?"

"Look!" Alisha pointed again. One house before the next corner a big white Chevy Blazer sat in the driveway. "That's the truck he was in," she looked at René for confirmation.

"Yep. That's it," René agreed. "Look at this fool." Little Johnny wasn't paying attention to the slow-moving Escalade in the middle of the street. He walked across his neighbors grass straight to his front door. He stuck his hand in his pocket, pulled out his keys and fumbled with them at the front door until he opened it. He finally staggered in and slammed the door.

He left the keys in the door.

Bone hit the brakes, threw the Cadillac in park and jumped out. He ran to the door, snatched the keys out and ran back to the truck. He threw it in drive and turned left at the corner like any other normal citizen.

"Wow!" Alisha cried. "He just really slipped."

"No shit, girl. Did you see that?" Rene cried. "Yeah John, the tables are startin' to turn."

"Yeah!" Alisha said excitedly. "Let me hang the bag on that fools door."

"Don't get too cocky," Bone said coolly, "Or we'll start to slip like they are. Remember, we got kids to look after, and I ain't quite ready to be looking after them from above." Bone sounded like Ms. J. He looked at Alisha reprovingly. He reached in the ashtray and handed her the joint.

"How did you know I wanted that?" Alisha asked as she pushed the lighter in.

"Cause it's his job to know," René said matter-of-factly.

They drove down Downey Ave. toward Alondra Blvd. Bone was driving slowly while Alisha and René checked addresses. The fifteen thousand block started at Alondra. The house was just a few yards passed Alondra on the right side. Since they were traveling north they were on the same side of the street as the house.

The girls said that John had a big black Suburban. It would be easy to spot if he was home because all of the driveways were on Downey. There was no alley running behind the houses. There was an old gas station on the corner and two businesses before the houses. As Bone drove passed the last storefront Alisha cried out.

"That's it right there," she pointed at a two-story house. The bottom floor had been converted into a business: DuVall Diamonds.

Bone made a right at the first street and parked. He turned in his seat so he could look at both of them while he talked. Bone had already made up his mind. He was going to take the bag to the door himself. They were just a little too excited to do it. Excited women make too much noise. Especially street women.

"Hand me that bag, René," he instructed. Bone flattened it out on the armrest and started rolling it up. "Real simple, ladies. I'm guessin' that he lives on top of the store. I'm gonna get out and see if my guess is correct. I want ya'll to drive back to the corner and wait for me in the 7-Eleven parking lot."

"What if he's there, Bone?" René sounded worried.

"If he's there," Bone said calmly, "He's not expecting me. Besides, I didn't see the truck ya'll describe. It's real simple. I go to the door, drop the bag on his doorknob, walk to 7-Eleven, buy me a handful of Bingo tickets and we're outta here. I call his snotty-nose son, he calls pops, and they sit around and scratch their heads tryin' to figure out their next move.

"Be careful, baby," Alisha said and kissed him.

Bone got out of the truck, stuffed the bag down the back of his shorts, lifted his shirt over it and stepped on around the corner. The building was only a hundred feet from the corner. He strolled along casually. When he got to the front of the building he saw empty display cases in the window of the diamond store. There was a staircase on the right side of the building. It was pitch black. Bone looked around for the Suburban but didn't see it. There was no car in the driveway and the garage was way too small for a Suburban.

As he got ready to go up the stairs Bone looked around one more time and saw the girls drive by him. They were both looking over at him. *Too excited*, he thought. He stepped lightly on the first two steps. The third step creaked real loud: the alarm step. He froze in place and listened. All he could hear were cars driving by. He took the next two steps quick. They made even more noise.

"To hell with this shit," Bone said to himself. He ran up the stairs to the landing and stopped. He sighed real easy and stuck his ear to the door. Nothing. He pulled the bag out of his back and hung it on John's doorknob.

On his way down the stairs Bone pulled the piece of paper with the phone numbers on it out of his pocket. He pulled out his phone and dialed John's son.

Tino answered on the first ring. "Who is this?"

"Wow, kid. Is that the way you answer your phone all the time? I would hate to do business with your rude ass. I take that back. I wouldn't do business with you. Didn't your daddy tell you to be expecting a call from a stranger?" Bone was reprimanding the youngster.

"Bone?"

"Mr. Bone to you, kid. Where's your pops?"

"I can reach him," Tino said flatly. He didn't like Bone.

"You're stale, kid. Maybe this will put some salt on your cracker. Tell your dear ol' dad that the bag he's been missing has been found. I just hung it on his front door."

"You what?" Tino asked excitedly.

"Now you got some flava to yourself, kid. You heard what I said. Run and tell that." Bone pressed end. He walked through the 7-Eleven parking lot. Right before he got to the door Alisha yelled out. "I got the Bingo tickets already."

"What color?" If she didn't know what color he played then Bone was giving her too much credit.

"Orange, baby. I got orange!" Alisha declared.

Bone gave her a thumbs-up and she knew that she got it right. "Thanks, girl."

"No problem," René replied.

Bone jumped in the passenger's seat. He wanted to scratch his tickets. Alisha bought ten of them. He would get those thirty bucks back, and then some with ten tickets. It had been almost four years since Bone tuned out the world, took a dime and scratched some Bingo tickets. No, he wouldn't be driving for the rest of the night.

"Where to, baby?" Alisha was going down Downey Ave. headed toward the 91 freeway.

"Huh?" Bone was already caught up in his first ticket. "Oh, go back by my mama's house." He pulled his phone out and dialed her number.

"Hey, boy!" Joyce beamed.

"You finally got caller ID, huh?" He teased. Leave it up to Joyce and she would still be using a rotary phone.

"What do you want smarty drawz?" She fired back.

"Put my sweatshirt jeans and a pair of black tennis shoes in a bag. I'll be by in a few to get it," he answered.

"What for, boy?" She sounded upset.

"It's cold woman!" Bone said defensively. "Just put the bag on the porch for me."

"You watch who you talk to like that," she said evenly.

"My bad. I'll be there in ten. Bye." Bone hung up before his mother got started.

"We need to go see Lisa, babe," René stated. "Oh, did you call John?"

"I called his son and shook him straight out of his boots. He's probably talking to daddy right now," Bone said.

"We need to go see Lisa," René repeated.

"You gonna take the ya-yo in to her?" Bone asked.

"Hell nah!" She cried.

"For what, Bone?" Alisha asked.

"Because, if she's still getting high that is what she'll want. If we ain't got no ya, we get cussed out," Bone declared. The statement rang so true in their ears at the same time, Alisha and René nodded in agreement. "So, how do we deal with that situation?"

"Boss Hogs," they said at once. He was the closest to the hospital with dope.

Bone was barely paying attention. "Go then." He was back scratching tickets.

At the thought of taking Lisa some crack René wanted some herself. "Damn." she muttered.

***

John laid next to Jan in her king-size sleigh bed. He had one arm behind his head, the other one was around her. He had given her a little of what was going on, because if he failed to get the diamonds back he would need her help.

Or die.

"You say Jimmy was going to give up to ten million for the diamonds?" She asked.

"They're worth at least thirty, Jan." John said. "This Chin guy knows nothing about diamonds. His son pulled a job in Orange County that Chin set up. It was really a payback. He wasn't expecting to come up with a bag of diamonds."

"What was he after?"

"Ten kilos of China white," John said casually. "And the guys left hand."

"His left hand?" she cried.

"The guy stuck a needle in Chin's daughter's arm. Got her hooked on dope," He informed her. "He stuck her with his left hand. The point is, Jan, I need to get those diamonds back. No telling what he'll cut off of me."

Jan's phone rang.

She reached behind herself, blindly searching the nightstand for the phone. "Hello."

"Mrs. DuVall, how are you feeling?" Tino asked. This was his first time talking to her since he blew her husband up.

"I'm fine, Tino. I'm a tough ol' cookie. I'll get through this." Jan had fantasies about Tino. He was very handsome at twenty-two. Besides, John was starting to bore her.

"Is my pops still there?" He asked.

Jan handed John the phone.

"He called you?" John asked.

"Oh, yeah, he called," Tino announced. "He hung the bag on your front door."

"What!" Pillow talk was over. "Get over here," John demanded through his teeth. He reached over Jan, hung the phone up and grabbed her bottle of gin.

John sat on the edge of the bed and drank straight out of the bottle. *How did he find out where I lived?* he thought. Popeye didn't tell him because he didn't know. This Bone guy must be one of the more clever ones out of Compton. As long as the diamonds are in the bag, who cares? Who am I kidding?

He got up to get dressed. He wasn't worried about Jan anymore. He wanted to get to his house and get the duffel bag.

"You're leaving, huh?" Jan asked.

"I've got to go by my house, but I'll be back later."

Jan was fed up with John. "Don't bother, dear. Could you pour me a glass of gin before you leave?"

"Don't bother?" The way she said that made John angry. "Would you like for me to send Tino back?" The second he said it he knew that he would regret it.

"If you won't need him, that would be just lovely." Jan reached out for the drink he poured her. He stopped short so that she couldn't reach it. Jan looked up into John's awe struck face.

"Oh, I must have given the wrong answer."

***

Alisha pulled onto Ms. J's street. All was quiet. She lived in a more settled neighborhood. More older couples and fewer families with small children. At eleven o'clock on a Friday night, all was still.

"Cut the lights out," Bone ordered, "And don't pull in the driveway."

René laughed at him. "Babe, you are thirty-six years old. You don't have to creep in the house no more."

"Shut up!" He growled. René embarrassed him by exposing that he was acting like a teenager.

"Don't be talking to her like that, little Willie," teased Alisha. She laughed at him while he shrunk down in the seat.

"Both of ya'll got jokes," he said weakly. "That's cool. Get out and get the bag, René."

"I ain't goin' up there," she laughed harder. "Ms. J ain't gonna catch me on her porch and drill me with a bunch of questions."

"Oh, so you feel a little childish yourself now, huh?" Bone teased her back. "A thirty-eight year old kid."

"I'll go get it," Alisha announced. She parked in front of the house got out and ran up the grass to the porch. All of the lights were out, so she didn't see Joyce sitting on the porch. As she reached down to grab the bag, Joyce grabbed her arm.

Alisha screamed. "Help!"

"Be quiet, girl," Joyce whispered. "My neighbors ain't used to all that kinda noise."

"You scared the hell out of me," Alisha said as she tried to control her breathing.

"Willie sent you up here because he knew I'd be waitin' for his ass. Now you listen. That boy just came home this morning. I like you, Alisha. Don't get me wrong. But, if you are leadin' him into somethin' that will get him locked up again, you're gonna need more than the po-lease to keep me off yo' ass. Do you hear me?"

"Yes ma'am," Alisha said quietly.

"Now you take that bag, and you tell that boy I said come here."

Alisha picked up the bag with a trembling right hand and ran back down to the truck. She got in and closed the door.

"Whew," Alisha let out a long sigh.

Bone and René just looked at her. They heard her scream but didn't dare try to get out and help her. She had to deal with Ms. J on her own.

"What did she say?" Bone asked.

"You knew she was on the porch?" Alisha asked. Bone nodded. Alisha looked in the back seat at René; she nodded too. "Ya'll ain't right!" Alisha cried. "That wasn't even right."

"You the one that jumped out, Ms. Helpful," Bone said, and René fell out laughing. He looked at Alisha shrugging his shoulders as a smile stretched across his face, and she smiled back. They both joined René in a good laugh.

When they calmed down Alisha said, "She told me to tell you to come here." She jabbed Bone in his arm.

They all got quiet and looked at the porch. It was still dark, but you could barely see the cherry from a cigarette.

"Pull off, baby girl," Bone said calmly.

"She wants to talk to you, Bone," Alisha insisted. She wanted him to get the same treatment she just got.

"That's why I didn't go in the first place, Ms. Rocket Scientist," Bone growled. "Now put this motha fucka in drive and let's go."

Alisha put the truck in drive and drove off real slow. They were all still looking at the porch. A light came on in the house and they could see Ms. J's silhouette in the doorway.

"Let's roll," Bone said. "René, reached in that bag and give me that envelope with my name on it." She handed it to him, and he handed it to Alisha.

"What's this?" She asked clearly confused.

He took it back from her, glanced at what the note said inside, and stuck it in his pocket. "Something that would hurt your feelings."

"She already did that on the porch," Alisha muttered. She looked in the rearview mirror at René.

"I already know, girlfriend." René sympathized with her. "I can't find the Zig-Zags. Cut the dome light on."

Chapter Fifteen

John pulled up in his driveway and threw his truck in park. He looked over at his son and said, "Go up and grab that bag."

Tino jumped down and ran up the steps. He unhooked the bag and came back down. Inside the truck he handed the bag to his dad. John cut the dome light on, unzipped the side pocket, and looked inside.

Nothing.

He unzipped the main compartment and started pulling out leather straps.

"What are those?" Tino asked.

"They come off of the pool table on the boat you blew up," John said bitterly.

He turned the bag inside out. No diamonds. Who was he kidding? He should've known it wasn't going to be that easy when it came to dealing with street trash.

"Do you have Bone's number saved in your phone?"

"When he called me my Caller ID said, "Private." Tino replied. "We gotta wait until he calls back."

"Shit!" John said through clenched teeth. "Call your brother." He threw the truck in reverse and backed out all the way to the other side of the street. He slammed the gearshift into drive and burned rubber about twenty yards down the street.

Headed to Little Johnny's.

All was quiet inside the truck until they reached Artesia Blvd. John's phone rang. He looked at the display screen: "Private."

***

Bone sat in the front seat In between changing his clothes and scratching a Bingo ticket, Bone slipped out of his shorts and his shirt.

"Bingo!" He cried, "B-I-N-G-O. I got an 'X' in the top square for a nifty fifty," he beamed. "That's a good sign, ladies. I hit on the first ticket. Let's take that as a good sign for the mission we're on." He threw the ticket up on the dashboard. "Now, I feel like a pervert ridin' like this, so stop rambling through bags and hand me some pants, René."

"You're a mama's boy, Bone," René said. "Do you know what's in this bag, Alisha?"

"Tell me girl," Alisha smiled at Bone.

"A toothbrush, toothpaste, mouthwash, a beard trimmer, two pair of underwear, two pairs of pants, a sling shot T-shirt, sweatshirt, and get this, girl, a manicure kit!" René started laughing.

"It better be a bowl of spaghetti in there, too," Bone stated.

René set a plastic bowl on the armrest, with a knife, spoon, and fork wrapped up in a napkin.

Alisha broke out laughing. "The big bad street hustler..."

"Gotta mama that still loves him," Bone finished. He reached behind him, and René handed him a pair of black jeans and the sling shot T-shirt. "You didn't say it was socks and shoes in there, René."

René took the bowl off of the armrest and replaced it with the socks and shoes. While he was putting on his clothes, Bone could hear René in the back seat smacking away. He just smiled to himself. Bone's mother didn't send that bowl just for him. Everybody he dealt with in the streets felt her love.

Bone pulled all of the stuff out of his shorts, put his money in his pocket, and set his phone on the dashboard. He had the paper with the numbers on it. Bone decided to call John. He answered on the first ring.

"Yes, this is John."

"Did you get that bag you asked for, kid?"

"Listen up, Bone. I don't know whom you think you're fucking with. I am not the one to fuck with!" John could barely contain his anger.

"If I wanted to really fuck with you," Bone said coolly, "I woulda tied your drunk ass son up to that tree in his front yard."

There was silence on the other end of the line. John felt like he had been punched in his gut. How in the hell did he know where Little Johnny lived?"

"Are you still there?" Bone asked.

"I'm here," John finally muttered.

"This is one thing that I know, John," Bone stated. "Everybody buyin' ass on Artesia Blvd. lives relatively close. I put a few feelers out, ask a few questions, and wow, I'm knockin' at your door. Chalk this bag of stones up as a loss, kid. You live on top of diamonds. You won't miss these."

"Those aren't mine," John let that slip. He had not regained his composure yet. "Shit," he muttered.

"Shit is right, kid," Bone replied. "Now you have to come up with a lot of cash to pay back the owner because I'm keepin' these. This will be sufficient enough for all the girls your boss abused while he was still livin'. Oh, and if you shoot another one on the track, I will return to Johnson Street." Bone hung up.

"That white boy pissed his pants when you mentioned his son," Alisha said. She was excited. They could sell the diamonds and move on without any problems.

She hoped.

"Come on. Let's go see Lisa," René said. She would go into Boss Hogs herself and get the dope. She would buy enough for two people.

"Make this quick, René," Bone said. "I'm too loaded and I'm sleepy." He leaned the seat back a little more.

Alisha was in the fast lane on the 105 East. They were headed to the dope man for Lisa. *It was crazy bringing her dope while she was in the hospital*, Alisha thought. *I guess after being shot in both knees any dope fiend would want to get high*, she mused.

"Boss Hog, here we come!" Alisha announced.

"Step on it," René said, a little too anxiously.

Alisha eyed her suspiciously in the rearview mirror.

***

Karin could tell that Brooklyn was antsy. Ever since Road Rash had come to drop off the money she had been antsy. He had dumped some coke out on the table and snorted it. He said that he was too busy to stay and party but promised to call later; something about his wife following him around.

"You wanna smoke another joint, Brook?" Karin asked. They had been drinking and smoking all night. Brooklyn would not pass out. Karin knew she was waiting for her chance to get a bag and split.

"Nah," Brooklyn replied, "I'm too high as it is, girl." Brooklyn knew that Karin was trying to drink and smoke her under the table. It wouldn't work. Brooklyn's mind was locked on smoking cocaine. She didn't care how long it would take. One slip from Karin, and she would get a bag and split.

"I gotta use the bathroom," Karin announced. She was tired of watching Brooklyn. If she wanted to dip a bag and go, Karin would give her a chance. Besides, she was ready to pass out herself.

She got up and went into the bathroom. She closed the door, slammed the toilet seat down, and went back to the door. She eased it open just a hair.

Karin watched as Brooklyn eased the drawer open, cracked the zip lock bag just a little, and pulled a bag out. Brooklyn was so nervous she just closed the drawer; zip lock bag still open, hanging out of the drawer.

Brooklyn tiptoed out of the room. When the door was closed behind her, Karin came out and pulled the drawer out. She closed the zip lock bag and tucked it down in the drawer. She lain back on the bed and said a silent prayer for Brooklyn. A minute later she was snoring.

Outside in front of the hotel sat a couple of taxis. Brooklyn jumped in the closest one to her. She was too afraid to go back to Artesia Blvd., so when the cabbie asked her where to, Brooklyn said, "Sepulveda and Roscoe." She would find Dark and Lovely.

***

"He ain't answering his phone," Tino said.

John had pulled up in the liquor store parking lot on Downey and Artesia. He went in and bought a pint of gin. He needed to think. Bone had came into the picture and created a stir.

A man amongst a crew of renegade street women meant that he was just a little more cunning than they were. If he has the diamonds in his possession they respect his game enough to trust him with them. Can he sell them? John's mind was running. Maybe he could use him to sell the diamonds. What the hell am I thinking? He's just a street hustler that just got released from prison. What the hell did he know about diamonds? "Bling, bling, baby!" he said aloud.

"What?" Tino asked.

"Nothing," he answered. "What did your brother say?"

"I just told you he didn't answer."

"He's drunk that's why. He's probably passed out on his damn porch." John started the truck up and headed to Little Johnny's. He lived less than fifty yards away from the store.

He pulled out of the parking lot by the cleaners so that he could just shoot straight across Artesia onto Johnson Street. John pulled up in his son's driveway and got out.

"Go around back," he instructed Tino, "And I'll try knocking on the front. One of us will get him up." Tino walked down the driveway while John went to the front door.

John banged on the door and rang the doorbell at the same time. He went to the bedroom window in front and knocked. Nothing. He went back to the front door and tried the knob. It was unlocked.

His heart skipped a beat. John pulled his pistol out and eased the door open. The street lights shone through on a figure lying on the couch face down. Little Johnny. John's heart started racing. *Was he dead or alive? Did Bone already repay me for the whore that I shot in the knees?* With that thought in mind, John didn't care if someone was in the house. He rushed in, bent down next to the couch, and started shaking his son.

"Hey!" He cried, "Little Johnny!" John shook him furiously, "Get up, son."

He stirred.

"Wassup, popzz?" Little Johnny was wasted. "You neber ta' me." He let his emotions go. "You tink I'm stu, thupid." He started crying. "I hate chu'!"

John let out a heavy sigh. Bone had him too much on edge. First his own house then his son's place. Too close for comfort. He got up and walked to the back door and let Tino in.

As Tino walked in he could hear his brother rambling on. "How did you know he was in here drunk, pops?" Tino asked.

"Our friend Bone told me. My guess is that they spotted him up on the corner and followed him home."

Tino was in shock. "But how did he…"

"I don't know, son," John said through clenched teeth. "I'll put on some coffee. You get your brother in the shower." As John started going through the cabinets looking for the coffee he could hear Little Johnny mocking him.

"Pissant! You lil' puissant!" Little Johnny repeated over and over again.

***

Bone had nodded off on the freeway. When they pulled up in front of Boss Hog's he woke up to the door behind him slamming.

"Where we at?"

"Boss Hog's," Alisha answered. "I told René I was gonna get out to get the ya-yo, but before I could park good she had jumped out."

"Is she still gettin' high?" Bone asked.

"Nope." Alisha answered too quickly.

"You said that too fast," Bone stated. He sighed. "When's the last time she got high that you know of? And before you answer that question, look at me." He turned so that they were face-to-face. He flared his nose at her. "Do I have boogers in my nose?"

"No. Why you ask that?" Alisha looked confused.

"'Cause I don't want you to answer me like I'm game goofy."

"Don't do me like that," she pleaded. "Ask her that."

"Don't do me like that!" Bone yelled. "Okay," he said more calmly. "Would you leave your kids with her? Can she be trusted to baby sit?"

"No," she muttered.

He looked deep into her eyes. "Can you be trusted to baby sit?"

"Hell, yeah!" She cried defensively.

"Then don't stick up for no faulty broad with me. I know she's slippin'. I just don't know how bad. I don't deal with no half-steppin' ho, and if I do, it's on a limited basis. And, she ain't in my immediate circle."

"I know that."

"Then don't try to cover up flaws and gaps in this immediate circle. Expose them to me so I can deal with them properly. Flaws and gaps get filled in by the po-lease and the undertaker in this game if you don't deal with them yourself. Got it?"

"Got it!" Alisha gave him a thumbs-up.

René came running down the driveway and jumped in. "Let's go see my crazy ass girlfriend."

As Alisha pulled off Bone asked, "Did you tell Hog I was out here?"

"I forgot. I was tryin' to trick some girl he had in there out of her pipe," René replied.

"Did you get it?" Bone already knew the answer.

"What kinda question is that?" René said sarcastically. "Don't I always get what I want?"

Bone didn't answer her back. He got the answer he wanted, though. If she didn't tell Boss Hog that she was with Bone, she was preoccupied.

René wanted to smoke.

***

Alisha swung into the hospital parking lot and parked. They all jumped out and walked in. At the receptionist desk they let René do the talking.

"Excuse me. My sister was shot in both of her knees today, and I'm just now getting the news. Could you please tell me what room she's in?"

"What's her name?" asked the receptionist.

"Lisa King."

The lady typed in her name, waited for a few seconds and said, "She's in 324A, but visiting hours are over."

René went into her act. "Listen, Ms.," she looked at her nametag, "Ms. Woods. My sister has been living on the streets for the last two years. I'm the only somebody that cares about her. If you don't let me up there, who knows what she'll do when she gets released from here. If she sees me right now, I might, just might, convince her to come home so I can help her get her life together. I don't want my sister to die in the streets." René let a tear drop.

Ms. Woods was a chubby white lady in her late fifties with a salt and pepper ponytail and green eyes. Eyes that had seen a whole lot. She had lost a sister in the streets twenty years ago. She had fought her tooth and nail to stay off of the streets, but her drug addiction won the fight. They found her sister dead in a dumpster on Downey and Artesia. Some psycho was killing prostitutes.

Ms. Woods looked them all in their face, one by one. "I'll give you ten minutes," she pointed at René, "By yourself."

René looked at Alisha and Bone.

"We'll be across the street at Denny's," Bone said. "I need a cup of coffee, anyway."

He and Alisha walked out and René walked over to the elevator.

Up on the third floor the nurse at the counter was on the phone. She held her hand over the mouthpiece and said, "You're looking for Ms. King?" Ms. Woods was the phone.

"Yes," René answered.

"The second-to-the-last door on the left," she pointed down the hall.

"Thank you," René said warmly. She walked down to the room, took a deep breath, and walked in.

Lisa was in the room by herself. She looked so peaceful in her sleep. Someone had brushed her hair back and put it in a ponytail for her. Her chocolate skin was a little ashen, but she didn't look that bad. A blanket covered her legs, so you couldn't see her knees. René didn't want to see anyway.

She sat down next to Lisa and just stared at her. Lisa had been a victim of René's street activity. Now that she didn't do wild things herself. Lisa did her fair share. This time though, it was all René's fault, and the guilt weighed heavy on her heart.

She pulled the dope out of her pocket. René had all of the paraphernalia wrapped in a napkin. She unwrapped it, stuck a piece on the pipe and hit it. She looked up at the ceiling when she was about to blow the smoke out and saw the smoke alarm. She covered the dope and pipe with the napkin on the nightstand and ran into the bathroom. She leaned over the toilet, blew the smoke in it, and flushed at the same time.

René came back out and sat down. Her heart was pounding like crazy. She started looking for shadows under the door.

She was paranoid.

"What the hell are you doin'?" Lisa woke up.

René almost jumped out of her skin at the sound of Lisa's voice. "Shhh. I thought I heard somebody comin'."

Lisa let out a heavy sigh. "You just now comin' to see me, and you got the nerve to take a hit before me? You a greedy ho!"

"You don't sound hurt, girl," René said after she regained her composure.

"Let's not talk about that right now," Lisa squirmed around on the bed. "Unstrap me and give me that pipe."

"Why did they strap you down?" René asked.

"Girl, I slapped two doctors and bite a nurse," Lisa declared. "I thought that they was gonna call the po-lease on me."

René started laughing. In spite of her injury Lisa was still being Lisa --stand-offish and rude. René unstrapped her and handed her the stuff.

"Go into the bathroom and wet that towel," Lisa pointed at a towel on the chair in the room.

"For what?" René was confused.

"The wet towel will absorb the smoke, dumb ass."

René went into the bathroom and wet the towel. When she came back out, Lisa looked like she was about to explode. René ran over to the bed and Lisa snatched the towel from her. She blew the smoke into the towel.

Lisa leaned back and said, "Now that was a red-eye flight." She looked like she was on cloud nine.

She came down fast though.

"You owe me, bitch," she stated. "I took a blow to my head and two bullets in my knees for you today. For you out there being scandalous I coulda got smoked. That ain't cool, René."

"I know, Lisa," René muttered. "I'll make it..."

"No!" Lisa barked. "You're gonna do whatever it takes to get me back right or I'm gonna hunt you down myself and kill you. I make my money on my knees, bitch. Fix my knees."

"I got chu', girlfriend," René tried to change the subject. "Bone is out."

"Good," Lisa said flatly. "You get his red ass to help you."

Getting high didn't do nothing but piss Lisa off. She was high, stuck in a hospital bed with her kneecaps blown off, and couldn't move around like she used to. That really pissed her off. René knew it was time to leave, so she got up. She left the dope sitting on the nightstand.

"Take that shit with you," Lisa mumbled. "I can't enjoy it like this anyway."

René picked the stuff up and walked out. That didn't go like she thought it would. She thought that two girlfriends were going to get together, get high, and forget all about life's current problems. The dope wasn't relieving the stress anymore. It was adding to her stressful issues, and yet, she still felt the need to smoke some more dope. The more René smoked the less she felt. She had to shake Alisha and Bone.

René walked over to Denny's to meet up with Alisha and Bone. When she got ready to walk in, she stopped short. She observed them sitting at the counter; laughing and pushing each other back and forth. She felt out of place. She didn't have to give them an excuse to leave. She could just walk off now. She turned away from the door and left. She pulled out her phone and dialed Marie's number.

Chapter Sixteen

John was in his son's kitchen still looking for coffee then he thought, *what nineteen year old that wasn't in college drinks coffee?* As he walked back into the living room a strange vibrating started in his pocket. He reached his hand in his pocket and pulled out a phone.

That hooker's phone from the motel.

Caller ID said, "René."

He answered it.

"Hello."

"Who the fuck is this?" René asked. She knew that she had the right number.

"Where are my diamonds?" John hissed.

"Oops," René hung up.

John stared at the phone for a second. He was thinking that René had to be close. She wanted to hook up with her girlfriend for whatever reason. *Maybe I can catch her slipping*, John thought. If he could catch a stray cat in his cage it just might be enough bait to draw Bone out.

"Tino!" He yelled, "Let's go. Now!"

Tino came out of the bathroom and asked, "What do I do with Little Johnny?"

"Do you think he'll drown?" John asked.

"No," Tino answered. "He's coming around."

"Leave him. Let's see if we can catch us a broad that just might be," he paused, "Just might be slippin'." He smiled.

"Now that's ghetto slang, Pops," Tino exclaimed. "There's hope for you yet."

***

After René hung up on John she stopped to think; John has Marie's phone, so where would she be at making calls? Back at the Budget Inn. She was that stubborn.

Marie would drift around for a while but without her phone? Back to her room she would go. *And, she would be pissed off at me because John has her phone*, René thought. She dialed the Budget Inn. The automated system started and she pressed 213.

"Who is this?" Marie asked as she picked the phone up on the first ring.

Why did you go back, stupid?" René asked.

"You owe me a phone. That trick took my phone," Marie stated. "You be doin' too much in these streets, girl. And what do you mean why did I come back? My purse is in here my car is in the parking lot, and my dope is here," Marie talked fast. "Tricks don't scare me off that easy."

René tuned Marie out until her last statement. "How much dope you got?" She asked.

"How much money you got?" Marie asked.

"'Bout five hundred," René said casually.

"Where you at, girl?" Marie asked quickly. She loved money. Especially if she didn't have to hook for it.

"I'm on Rosecrans in between Clark and Lakewood. I'm closer to Lakewood, though." She didn't want Marie to tell her to wait at Denny's.

"I'm on my way," Marie announced. "Meet me in front of Food-4-Less." She hung up.

René stuck the phone in her pocket and started jogging toward Lakewood Blvd.

***

"You think I'm crazy?! Road Rash screams, and grabbed the youngster through the bars and pulled him into them. He banged the boy's head against the bars about four more times, then let him go; all because the youngster wouldn't give up the bottom bunk." Bone told Alisha how he first met Road Rash Russell. "When they finally opened the cell door he came in picked the youngster up, sat him down on the toilet, cleaned him up, and then moved the kid's stuff to the top bunk."

"Wow," Alisha said, "Rash doesn't even look like that kinda guy." She sipped her coffee. "So the youngster didn't want to fight him?"

"With his nose already touching his cheek? Please." They both started laughing.

The waitress came to the counter for the third time to refill their coffee cups. Bone stuck his hand over the top of his waving her off. He looked at his watch and said, "We've been here way longer than ten minutes."

"More like almost thirty," Alisha declared. "Where is René?"

"She tip-toes away, baby girl." Bone was no stranger to René's moves. "She went upstairs, flighted with Lisa, and ducked us. Sound familiar?" He eyed her suspiciously.

"Shut up, boy!" Alisha cried. She smiled when she said it because that was a routine move if you wanted to shake somebody, "What we do now?"

"We go back to the Ho-Jo and get naked. I damn sure ain't gonna waste the rest of the night looking for René. She's on a mission, and she's grown. She was gonna do it eventually, Alisha. We just got her back to familiar ground so she can maneuver." Bone was getting up off of the stool.

"Let me pee first," Alisha said as she walked toward the restroom.

Bone walked to the cashier and paid for two coffees. He went back to the counter where they were sitting and stuck a five-dollar bill under his cup.

When Alisha came out of the restroom they strolled back over to the hospital. Alisha hesitated at the truck. She was looking at the hospital entrance.

"Go on and see," Bone said. "I'll pull up by the door."

Alisha tossed him the keys and said, "You bet not back door me."

"You better hurry up."

Bone jumped in the Escalade and pulled up to the front door. Alisha was already walking out. She got in and said, "She left about fifteen minutes ago."

They pulled out of the parking lot, made a right onto Clark and a left on Rosecrans. Right before they got to Lakewood Bone pointed at a figure running on the left side of the street.

"René."

"Pull over, Bone," Alisha pleaded.

"Nope!" he said firmly. "She shook us for the night, baby girl. Let her go unless, you want to share me with her. Hey that sounds like a good idea," he started to slow down.

"Oh, no you don't," Alisha countered. She looked at René as they passed her. She said a silent prayer for her girl.

***

Karin was in a fog of weed and alcohol, but she could hear a phone in there somewhere. She rolled over and picked it up.

"What?" She whispered.

"Uh, I didn't mean to wake you, Karin," Rash said. "This is Road Rash. Uh, I need to come up."

"Business, or pleasure?" Karin asked. She thought about Brooklyn and welcomed the distraction.

"Uh, a little of both," he replied shyly.

"How long, love?" Karin asked in her best seductively drunk voice.

"Two minutes." Rash was calling from the lobby.

"Give me five so that I can freshen up," she hung up. Karin got up and stuffed the dope in Brooklyn's bag. She didn't know Road Rash like Bone did. *He might want to try me*, she thought. She pulled her gun out of her purse and stuck it under her pillow.

Better safe than sorry.

Karin went into the bathroom and sat down on the toilet. While she used it she cut on the cold water in the shower. She got up flushed the toilet and stuck her head under the shower.

"Oh, yeah!" she cried. "That'll make anybody's nipples hard." As she brushed her teeth, she heard a knock at the door. She spit the toothpaste out wiped her face and went to the door. Through the peephole Karin could see Rash standing there smoothing out his eyebrows, holding a single red rose in his hands. She opened the door.

"For you Karin," he said coolly as he handed her the rose.

"Oh how lovely, Rash," she whispered. "Come on in."

He came in and sat down at the table. He was visibly nervous, shaking his legs and drumming his fingers on the table.

"Bizness first, love," Karin said.

"Okay," Rash said. He was glad for some direction. "I got nine hundred for some glass," he stated firmly, "And I got two hundred for you." He said that a lot softer and smiled.

Karin came over to where he sat and straddled his legs. She sat down on his lap and said, "Put the nine in my cleavage." She put her breasts in his face. "And put the two in my panties." She raised up her jersey slightly.

She got off of him so she could get the dope and he could get the money out of his pocket. When she came back he was ready. Rash stuck the nine hundred up top as she sat down. As he was sticking the two hundred in her panties she stuck her hand into his pants and grabbed him.

He jumped.

"Wait," he grabbed the dope from her. "I got this." He lifted her off of him and got up. He tucked the glass in his pocket and pulled a small bag of coke out. He waved it at her.

Karin pulled her jersey up over her head and laid back on the bed. Road Rash pulled off his shirt and shoes and laid them in the chair.

"Where do you want me to start?" He asked.

Karin pulled him onto the bed and said, "Start at my neck and work your way all the way down," she whispered. She felt him sprinkling powder down her body and shuddered. Karin hadn't had this done to her in a long time; get paid to thoroughly be stimulated. This was the part of her job that she loved.

**

Brooklyn got out of the cab on Sepulveda and Parthenia. The cab pulled a little passed the corner to let her out. She looked at the meter and it read $53.27. She slid the cabbie a hundred dollar bill, and he gave her back a fifty.

"You've been the quietest fare I've had all night. I'll eat the change for you," he said and smiled at her.

"Thank you, sir," Brooklyn got out. The cab pulled off and she just stood there. Brooklyn didn't know where to go.

Across the street were a laundry mat and a liquor store. She needed some baking soda to rock up her powder and some more stuff so she crossed the street.

Brooklyn drifted around the store looking for the baking soda but it wasn't on any shelf. What liquor store in a drug/prostitution area didn't sell baking soda?

It was behind the counter.

She walked up to the counter and before she could ask the clerk any questions she heard someone screaming outside. "Tipi!" She looked toward the door and saw Dark and Lovely coming through the door.

"Tipi!" She cried again. "I've been thinking about you all day long!" She was actually having wild fantasies about her.

"I came out here looking for you!" Brooklyn said excitedly. To the store clerk she said, "I need a pack of Newport's and a box of baking soda."

"Don't get the soda, girl," D.L. said. "I got a whole box in my room."

"No soda," she told the clerk. "You got a room, D.L.?"

"Hell yeah! And I got a bunch of money," she whispered. "That stuff ya'll gave me? They do that stuff out here like crazy."

Brooklyn paid for her cigarettes. As they were getting ready to leave she stopped. "I need to buy a pipe."

"I got about four of them in my room." Dark and Lovely grabbed her arm. "Come on, girl." She was eager to get Brooklyn to her room so that she could show Tipi a good time. Pay her to fulfill her fantasy.

If she had to.

"Tipi?" She couldn't wait. She had to know if she would get a chance to make Tipi feel good in more ways than one. "Have you ever been intimate with a woman before? There. I asked."

"No, but I hear some blow down below ain't no joke!"
Brooklyn knew that Dark and Lovely liked her from the beginning.
"I got enough blow to last us till' the sun comes up."

"Call me Tish from now on, kay?"

"Why is that?" Brooklyn was confused.

"'Cause I'm getting ready to show you the real me." Tish
grabbed Brooklyn's hand and led her across the street. She was
going to do whatever it took to make her Tipi enjoy the night and
maybe some more nights to come.

***

Bone lay back on the bed flipping through the TV channels.
Alisha was in the bathroom changing her clothes with the door
open so that they could talk.

"So now what do we do, baby?" She was talking about
selling the diamonds. Bone didn't answer right away so she
repeated her question a little louder. "Baby! Now what do we do?"

Bone was dozing off to sleep when he heard her ask the
first time. It had been a long day. Now, at a little after twelve the
next morning, he was fading fast. The second time she asked woke
him up.

"Now we try to make a connection downtown to dump the
diamonds. I was hollerin' at Barry about it at the house..."

"Barry knows?" She asked. "I didn't know he was hip to
stuff like that."

"In more ways than one. The only square I mess with is
you." Bone started laughing. "We're going downtown tomorrow
to do a little networking."

"What about the other stuff?" Alisha wanted to know just
how interested he was in the dope game.

"I'm gonna let Road Rash handle *all* of that. I don't have a
need for that in my game anymore. You put me so heavy in the
game with these stones, baby girl. I don't need no nickel and dime
dope sack."

That's what Alisha wanted to hear: no more wild street life.

As she unbraided her hair to comb through it she had only
one vision in her mind: getting her daughter's Angela and Ale'sha

from her mother. It was still early in their life. At two and four the traumatic issues they had gone through with their mother were severe, but not beyond repair. In time they would forget all about it. In no time at all it would all be erased from their little minds.

She hoped.

"Baby, I can't wait to go get the girls from my ma..." she was walking out of the bathroom while she was talking. When she got to the bed she stopped and smiled. Bone was asleep with a smile on his face.

***

John stuck to the back streets from Little Johnny's to Jan's. If René was around Artesia Blvd., he didn't want her to see his truck. They were going to get Tino's car. The Lexus was a more common-looking car so they could blend in with the traffic better.

When they surfaced on Artesia the traffic wasn't that heavy at midnight, but it wasn't that light either. After all, it was a prostitution/drug-zone on a Saturday night.

It was pretty easy to drift up and down Artesia with only the more eager prostitutes noticing them. John thought about picking one up but decided against it. One less Woman of the Night he would have to hurt.

"Pull in this motel," John said. He was returning to where he first picked René up. Like a dog she might return to her own vomit. If she did he would drop his net over her head.

***

"Why are you pullin' in here, Marie?" René was agitated. Marie had pulled up into The Royalty Inn; the place René and Karin had shared a room - the motel where John had picked her up.

"Somebody wanted somethin' for fifty down here. They called me right before I came to get you." Marie turned down no money. "This will be quick, girl. Stop being so paranoid."

René didn't feel like going back and forth with Marie so she held her tongue. She eased all the way down in the seat as far as she could. Marie pulled all the way around in front of room 105 where some guy stood. He walked up on the driver's window stuck his money inside, and she dropped something in his hand. They went back and forth about how short it was and Marie backed out with a promise of more next time.

As they pulled around to leave, a black Lexus pulled in front of them. It was blocking them from pulling out, so Marie pulled up on the walkway and went around them.

"Asshole!" She yelled when she got next to them. René was leaning into Marie so she couldn't be seen. She wasn't sure if that was the same car that she saw John in out in the valley, but she wasn't taking a chance on being seen.

As they pulled out on Artesia René said, "I need some beer before we go to your room, Marie."

"You do too many different kinds of drugs," Marie complained. "Coke, weed and alcohol? You need some treatment, girlfriend."

René looked at Marie in shock. Marie looked back at her and started laughing.

"You liked that one, huh?" Marie said as she elbowed René in her side. "Hey! How's my main man Bone lookin? I hope he don't come out here tryin' to run my program."

René didn't want to talk about Bone. She wanted to get high. Plus, she knew that Marie really did want him in her program. Marie thought that she could have every hustler that she chose. "Bone don't want your pink ass, girl. He likes brown ass."

"Just not your brown ass," Marie teased as she pulled into the liquor store on Clark and Artesia.

***

As Tino rounded the corner in the motel parking lot he found himself nose-to-nose with a Silver Dodge Intrepid trying to come out. Two cars couldn't fit in the space, but before he could back up his dad stopped him.

"That looks like that chick that slipped through the cracks on us at the motel."

"Slipped through the cracks?" Tino was confused.

"She got away from me and your brother, Mr. Hip." John scooted up in his seat to get a better look. "Is that somebody in there with her?"

"Yeah, but they're ducking," Tino answered.

"That might be René." John was trying to get a good look. He thought he got a glimpse of some gold hair as they went around them. "If it is René I know where the driver's room is. Go to the Budget Inn on Clark and Park."

"You don't want to follow them?"

John let out a heavy sigh. "Don't start acting like your brother."

Tino pulled out of the motel, and instead of going up to Clark he made a left onto Lakewood. As they passed under the freeway they came up on Park Street and made a right. When they got close to Clark John told him to slow down. On the right was the motel parking lot, but the gate was locked. John instructed his son to back into a driveway on the left hand side of the street. It was a vacant house. They waited there until Marie and René pulled into the motel.

Marie swung into a parking slot close to the stairs. They got out of the car and ran up to the door. It was René all right. Dressed up like she was coming from a party.

John looked over at Tino and smiled. "We're going to an after party, son."

Chapter Seventeen

As usual René was in the bathroom--stuck. The dope was too powerful. She sat on the side of the bathtub with her head in her hands. She felt that if she held her head she could control the paranoia. It wasn't working. She got up went to the sink and splashed cold water in her face. That brought her around slightly. She thought, *I need a beer.* As she was getting ready to come out of the bathroom she heard two voices in the room. One was a male voice. Marie had let someone in.

René peeked out of the bathroom and saw what looked like a half black/half white boy with a long wavy ponytail over tanned skin, and high cheekbones. You could tell that he had some cut in him. He was dressed like he was coming from the club; cream colored silk shirt, blue slacks, cream loafers with no socks, and black gloves.

Black gloves?

Why would he be wearing black leather gloves? She closed the bathroom door and looked in the mirror. "Snap out of it!" She growled at herself. As she bent over the sink to splash more water in her face she felt something hard in her waistband.

Her pistol.

She was carrying the pistol that Karin had given her. "Thanks, girlfriend," she whispered. She came out of the bathroom.

"You look so sexy this evening..."

"Who in the hell are you?" René cut Marie off in mid sentence. She had the pistol pointed at Tino.

"René!" Marie cried. "Put that thing away. Young sexy here brought me a rose."

"Is that why he's wearing those leather gloves? Didn't want to stick himself?" They sounded like questions. René was not looking for answers to them, though. Marie didn't notice the gloves until René said something.

"Hey," Tino said casually, "I knocked on the wrong door and she let me in." It was the right door. Tino just wasn't expecting all of this.

"You damn right you knocked on the wrong door," René said in agreement. "Put your damn hands up and stand up." She was a good distance so he couldn't rush her and get the gun. He would get shot.

Tino raised his arms up, stood up, and moved away from the table.

"Search this clown, Marie," René ordered.

Marie got up and rubbed around his waist, Nothing. She slid down his right leg. Nothing. She slid down his left leg and stopped at his ankle. She felt it. Marie raised his pant leg up to reveal a Velcro holster holding a .380. She ripped it off of his leg and backed away from him.

"I should shoot you, punk!" Marie barked at him. "You came in here to do something to me, and you don't even know me!"

"Not you, Marie," René said flatly. "He came here for me."

Marie looked confused. "You? Damn, René!" She cried, "You be doin' way too much out here. Two different guys in one day try to get me because of you. Yeah, you need treatment, girlfriend." Marie was looking at the stranger standing before her. He looked familiar for some reason. Long wavy hair. Overly tanned skin. He looked just like that other youngster who was with that other guy.

"Your brother was here earlier, huh?" Marie asked. Tino was hesitating so she pulled his own gun on him. "Answer me!" She yelled.

"Look, lady," Tino started, "This ain't got nothing to do..."

"I said, *ANSWER ME!*" She waved the pistol at him.

Tino nodded.

"Where's yo' daddy?" René asked.

The girls were making him real nervous. "He's in the parking lot waiting for my signal."

"You sure gave that up easy," Marie observed.

"He don't want nothin' stuck in his ass like we did his brother," René stated.

Marie looked at Tino. He nodded in agreement. She looked over at René who just smiled. Marie shook her head. *She was in too deep*, she thought to herself, and it was too late to turn back. She shrugged her shoulders and asked, "So what's the signal?"

"I'm supposed to flash the lights on and off two times and open the door halfway," Tino explained.

"And what was we supposed to do, just let you hold us down with no problems?" René laughed at him. "Your daddy has more goofy plans than we do," she paused. "I got a better plan. Take your clothes off."

Tino flashed a look of anger and fear across his face.

"Don't worry. I ain't gonna stick nothin' in you," René reassured him. She waved the pistol up and down at him to get undressed.

Marie walked over to René and whispered, "What are we gonna do, girl?"

"We're gonna tie this fool up and use him to get down into your car and get the hell out of here," René answered. "Can you shoot real good?"

"I grew up huntin' with my daddy, girlfriend." Marie said proudly.

"Good."

***

John was backed in under a tree. He could see the room perfectly from his vantage point, but he was hidden from view. He looked at his watch. It read 12:47 a.m. His son had been in the room too long. The plan was to hold them at gunpoint, flash the lights two times and open the door. How hard was that? Every woman was scared of a gun pointed at them.

The door opened, but the lights didn't go on and off. René backed out of the room, looked around the parking lot, spotted the Lexus, and pointed a gun back into the room.

"What the..."

John cut his own self short when he saw his son emerge from the room stripped down to his underwear. Marie came out behind him with a gun pointed at his back. They all walked down the steps. They stuffed Tino into the back seat of Marie's car and tied his ankles and knees; tied him with strips of his own clothes, and closed the door.

As John got ready to get out and help his son the phone in his pocket vibrated again. He pulled it out and answered. "If you hurt my boy I will kill you two and every fucking whore on this street!"

"Slow down, cowboy," Marie said. "First, I want my phone back. Second, you'll get your boy back, and he won't be harmed. We'll drop him off at his brother's house. Now," she took a breath, "Get out of the car and set my phone on that car next to yours. Just put it on the bumper then get back into your fine automobile and relax. We'll be out of your hair shortly." Marie hung up on him.

John got out and set the phone on the car's bumper. He got back in the Lexus and pulled out his pistol. Any chance he saw he would take them both out. They weren't dumb broads, though. René got in the back seat with Tino.

Marie backed up all the way until she was in front of the Lexus. She got out with the gun pointed at John's head the whole time. She picked her phone up stuck it in her pocket, and fired. She fired again.

Marie got back in her car and drove off, "Where to?"

"To the alley on the side of Rally Burger's," René announced.

Marie drove down Park Street all the way to Downey Ave. She made a left on Downey, crossed Artesia Blvd., and turned right into the alley. She drove through until they were behind KFC and stopped.

René dragged Tino out of the back seat and propped him up next to the building. "You should be able to make it to your brother's from here." She got back in the car and they pulled off.

"Now where do we go?" Marie asked wearily.

René knew that Marie was too involved now to be left out on Artesia floating around. "Magic Mountain."

On Artesia and Clark John was getting into the back of a cab. He was beyond upset. They stuck one of his son's in the ass with a dildo, and now they had the other one in the back seat of a car. Stripped down and tied up. On top of all that, they had just shot out two of the tires on the Lexus. All of this and still no diamonds. Oh yeah, John was beyond mad. René was causing him too many problems, and it was evident that she did not want to cough up the diamonds. "Bitch."

"What?" asked the Cabbie.

"Downey and Artesia."

Chapter Eighteen

Bone woke with a start. He thought that he was in a cell and a fly was buzzing around his nose. What he saw made him smile: hair. Alisha's hair was all in his face. He was home. No more smelling another man's gas; no ten-minute showers. No more bland food and no more strip searches. He was finally free. He eased up closer to Alisha, put his arms around her body, and started squeezing…kissing…rubbing. Bone caressed her body. He loved being in bed with a woman, instead of just a pillow.

"You went to sleep on me, party pooper." Alisha turned over to face him.

Bone looked over at the window and saw sunlight shining through the curtain; Saturday morning on the streets--a lovely morning to get rich. He kissed Alisha on her forehead, on her chin; he licked around her ear then kissed her neck. Moving down to her breasts was Bone's next move. He was a horny toad. After forty months, who wouldn't be?

"Baby…I gotta…ooh…mmm…baby stop…let me pee." Alisha didn't want to get out of bed but nature called.

"I…gotta go…too," Bone said in between kisses. He let her get up and they both went into the bathroom.

Alisha used it first while Bone brushed his teeth. All of the cosmetics that were in his bag were laid out on the counter.

"I wonder if Rash Ass came back last night for Karin."

"The way she was shakin' them big ol' balloons on her chest at him? You know he did." Alisha got up and flushed the toilet then she cut on the shower.

Bone watched her as she bent over the tub. She had on his T-shirt with no panties on. He was instantly aroused at the sight of her.

"Move, girl, so I can piss." Bone said as he bumped her hip with his hip. As he stood over the toilet Alisha grabbed his dick and aimed it for him. He pissed on the seat, the back, and the floor before she got it right.

"Damn!" That was harder than I thought."

Bone laughed at her. When he finished, she still held onto him. "What chu' gonna do with him?" He asked.

"Get in the shower and I'll show you," she whispered.

Bone pulled the T-shirt over her head and tossed it on the counter. "Wow!" He cried. He was amazed at how perfect her shape was. She had a body like a young Tina Turner, with a Ki-Toy bottom.

Alisha pulled off his underwear and they got into the shower. Like a king being fed grapes and fanned with big palm tree leaves, Bone was being served. He held on to the curtain rod and the wall until her task was completed. She washed every inch of his body and licked half of it. When he emerged twenty minutes later he stood in front of the mirror and laughed.

"What's so funny?" Alisha asked. She was still in the shower.

"I told myself I wasn't gonna take showers anymore but after that shower..."

"You've had a change of heart!" She finished.

"Oh yeah," Bone said smoothly. He wrapped a towel around himself and walked to the phone to call Karin. When she answered he yelled, "It's the golden-shower-hour!"

"I've been up down here," Karin said bitterly. "New twist, Bone. Brooklyn took a bag of ya-yo last night and ran off. René showed up at around three this morning with Marie."

Bone was silent for a minute absorbing the information. He was more concerned about Brooklyn. "What did René do?" He asked flatly.

"She ran into dude and his son at Marie's room again. This time they took the boy hostage to get out of there, and shot the tires out on their car. She dragged Marie right into this mess," Karin said angrily.

"Calm down, baby girl," Bone said calmly. "Are they gettin' high?"

"They're going in the bathroom a lot, Bone," Karin whispered. "They say they ain't getting high but I can smell it."

"Put Marie on the phone," Bone said.

A few seconds later, "Hey, Bone!" Marie cried. "Welcome home, baby. Your girl René down here needs drug treatment. She almost got me killed this morning." Marie was talking a mile a minute.

"Listen, Marie," Bone started, "We'll get a chance to chit-chat some other time. Right now I need for you to go rent another room to play in. That room right there is for bizness."

"You're always tryin' to run so..."

"Hey!" He barked. "Do what I say or get your pink ass on."

"Chill out, bro," Marie said, mocking him for calling her pink.

"You're right," he said smoothly. "René shouldn't have involved you, Marie. It's not your fault. I just can't have you down there takin' flight. It's too much going on to get caught slippin' like that."

"You just want me in another room so you can do something to me." Marie hoped that was what it was but she knew better--not right now anyway.

Bone knew that she wanted to brag and say that they slept together, so he played along. "If you want my bone to fill up some holes on your body then you'll go down and get a room on the fifth floor. And, if you want a slice of this pie we got you'll go right now."

Marie hung up on him.

Bone called back.

"Yes," Karin said.

"Did Rash Ass come back through last night?" He changed the subject.

"Boy did he!" Karin beamed. "He gave me two hundred to snort lines off of my body. That man is a cold freak and...."

"And that's enough bizness over this phone. I'll be down there in a minute. Is Marie and René leaving?"

"Marie is," Karin laughed. "You must've lied to her again. She's a slow learner. I told her about you stringing her along."

"Ouch!" Bone cried. "The salt is melting me," he turned serious. "Let me talk to René.

After a long moment René said, "What's up?" She was on the defense.

"You alright?" He asked disarming her. "Tell me what happened at the Budget." He knew she would listen better is she wasn't on the defense.

"Marie's dumb ass pulled into the Royalty first and they spotted us there. I guess they followed us back to the Budget. John sent his son up to the room. I was in the bathroom..."

"Takin' flight," Bone broke in.

"Anyway. I hear a male voice so I peek out and see this kid sitting in the room with leather gloves on. I pulled the heat on him, used him to get us out of there, and here we are."

"Still takin' flight." Bone was not going to let up. "René, I can't...we can't have you down there flighting with all that stuff down there. You know better than that. Now, Marie is going to get a room upstairs. Take that game goofy shit up there." Bone was talking as calm as he could, hoping that she would listen to reason.

"So you really don't care if I get high now, huh?" It wasn't a question. "You got what chu' want so to hell with me?"

"I can't force you to stop. I'm trying to show you a different side of the game in hopes that it looks more appealing than a straight shooter." Bone was walking a tight rope in the conversation.

"What are you gonna do about John?" René asked. She was starting to breakdown mentally. She was scared.

"You let me deal with that," Bone replied calmly.

"Brooklyn ran off too." The walls were closing in on René. Now she was looking at all of the issues critically. "I should've came back with ya'll. She would've stayed if I was here."

"Brook was gone before we came back so don't blame yourself. Mount up and go find that kid, and bring her back." Bone tried to give her something, one thing to focus on. "Show her that somebody cares about her. I'm going downtown today to see what's really going on with these stones."

"You comin' down here first?"

"Yes, René. We'll be down there," Bone sighed. "Calm down and order some breakfast for everybody." He hung up.

Alisha stood in the bathroom doorway listening to one side of the conversation. She admired how Bone dealt with all of them. He shared his energy with five women now. That made her jealous. She walked toward him with her lip poked out. He saw her drab look, and before she could say anything he grabbed her and guided her to the bed.

"Let me Rick James you baby," Bone said as he rubbed his hands together. "Tie you up and super freak you."

"I'm up for the latter part of that," Alisha whispered.

Surprised at her choice of words, Bone asked, "Where did you learn that word?" He laughed. "Latter."

"I sure didn't learn it from you, Boo-boo," she said as she poked him in his nose.

"Okay, Ms. Yogi." Bone slung his towel to the floor and slowly guided his manliness inside of her.

Alisha received a part of Bone that the other four in the fold would not get.

His bone before breakfast.

***

Brooklyn came out of the liquor store. Inside of her bag she had a pint of Belvedere Vodka a bar of lye soap, and a scrub pad. She felt dirty. She was mad at herself for allowing a drug to twist her mind into compromising her body. First, she was selling it, and now she was laying with women? Brooklyn was going to scrub her body until it bled. *I gotta get back to my friends*, she thought. Nobody out in the streets really cared about her, and the ones that did she had stolen from. *Will they let me back in?*

She walked back up to the motel room where Dark and no…Tish was asleep. *Hopefully, I can take a bath and just leave without her lusting over my body*, she thought. Brooklyn opened up the door and there she was sitting at the table. Damn!

"Hi, Tipi," Tish said cheerfully.

"Look Dark and…"

"Call me Tish."

Brooklyn sighed. "Tish, about last night."

"I know, Tipi. You're not into women, but you did it anyway just to please me. And for that, I love you. Thanks, girlfriend." She knew Brooklyn didn't want to do it and that she was using dope to keep her mind off of it. That's what the dope was for: to keep your mind off of the evil that you were involved in when you lived in the streets.

"I just want to take a bath and go," Brooklyn said. She felt like her skin was crawling. She was glad that Tish understood her position, though. "Does your phone work?"

"Ten dollars for a deposit and I only get four calls? That manager is out of his mind," Tish stated. "Don't trip, Tipi. Take your bath and we'll go call at the store. You'll let me buy you breakfast, right?"

"I guess," she muttered. Brooklyn pulled out her bottle of vodka and downed half of it.

She went into the bathroom and decided to take a shower. She wasn't ready to sit in her own filthy water. Brooklyn cut the water on as hot as she could stand it.

She came out thirty minutes later feeling much better. Her body was a little tender in some spots from the scrub pad but she was clean again. The vodka eased the pain.

They went over to the store to use the phone. Alisha was her real girlfriend, but René was more understanding in situations like she found herself in: outcast by choice.

"Hello," René said.

"René, this is Brooklyn."

"Where you at, girl?" René cried. "We're worried sick around here."

Brooklyn felt a surge of heat run through her body. *They were worried about me?* That meant that they cared. "I'm on Sepulveda with Dark and...with Tish."

"What motel is it?" René asked. "Me and Marie are gonna come and get you."

"Marie? What's she doing out there?"

"Don't trip on all that," René said firmly. "You just tell me where you are."

"I'm at the Traveler's Inn on Sepulveda and Parthenia. Room 224."

"Two twenty-four," René repeated. "Stay right there. We're on our way."

Brooklyn hung up the phone feeling more excited than she ever felt in her whole life. Help was on the way. Somebody really cared about her. She looked around and saw Tish across the street waving for her to come on. Brooklyn was so excited that she just took off running. She never saw the Jaguar pulling out of the parking lot. The car caught Brooklyn in her left knee and propelled her into the air. She landed in the bed of a truck parked on the street. Tish screamed as she ran across the street toward the scene. She looked in the back of the truck at Brooklyn. She was bleeding from a gash on her head.

Unconscious.

***

"Your breakfast is getting cold," Karin said. She had been trying to get through for the last fifteen minutes. She knew what was going on.

"How long," Bone caught his breath, "Has it been sittin' down there?"

"It just got here two minutes ago," Karin replied. "I'm just disturbing the groove." She laughed.

Bone handed the phone to Alisha and got up. "You cock-blockin'?" She cried.

"If I can't have none, you can't have none!" Karin teased. "I'm lonely down here. Come down here." She whined.

"Any word from Brook?" Alisha asked. Bone had told her about her girlfriend running off.

"She called René just now. Her and Marie are going to get her."

"Damn!" Alisha cried. "Five money makers out here. We'll take over this Ho-Jo. They need some entertainment around here anyway."

Karin laughed. "Girl, I went to get some ice last night and turned down some money. She paused. "Just think about it for second, girl. It's nine more floors to travel."

"Shake that money maker, girlfriend!"

"We'll be down there," Alisha said and hung up. She looked over at Bone getting dressed. "What chu' doing? We ain't done yet."

"My mind is on the bread now, baby girl," Bone replied. "Thank Karin for the interruption."

"Oooh!" Alisha fumed. "We need to find them hookers some men."

"It's nine more floors to explore," Bone said matter-of-factly.

Alisha stood there in awe at what Bone just said to her. Karin had just said the same thing. The hustle never stops.

Bone tossed her the skirt she had on and said, "We got bizness to take care of."

When they got down to the other room, Karin immediately got the cash out. She handed Bone sixty-six hundred dollars. He took the six grand and left the six hundred on the table.

"I'm going downtown today. Ya'll go shopping. Go to the Northridge Mall or something. Put this bread," he pointed to the table, "With yours and shop for us three. When the stray cats come in, we'll go again." He picked up the phone and call Road Rash.

"What!" Rash yelled.

"Hey, man," Bone said calmly, "You alright over there?"

"Bone, would you tell my wife that I..."

"Where did you take my husband last night?" Rash's wife had snatched the phone from him.

Bone didn't have no idea what Rash told his wife. "I took him with me to see my mother." There was silence on the other end. "Hello?"

"I thought he was lying to me, Bone," she calmed down.

"Raina, right?" Bone asked. He was relieved that he had told the right lie.

"Yes," she answered. "And when do I get to meet you in person?"

"Maybe this evening. I'm super busy this morning."

"You guys always are when you first get out. Trying to do everything in one day."

Rash took the phone from her. "We got big biz this morning, bro," Rash stated.

"Be here in ten, then." Bone hung up. He started in on his breakfast and stopped. Karin and Alisha were staring at him. "Now what?"

"You just told Rash's wife that he was with us last night," Alisha said accusingly.

"Yeah, and I don't look nothing like your mother, Willie," Karin pranced around.

"Things must be done to protect the innocent," Bone confessed as he shrugged his shoulders. The all broke out laughing.

**

In front of the Traveler's Inn René spotted Tish sitting on the curb. "Pull over, Marie!" She cried. She jumped out of the car and ran over to her. René knew something was wrong, "Tish, where's Brooklyn?"

"Who's Brooklyn?" Tish was confused. "All I know is that Tipi got hit by a car right after she called you. They took her to a hospital on Roscoe."

"Who is Tipi?" Marie asked.

"Tipi Lorraine," Tish stated.

"Her name is Brooklyn, Tish," René said. "Take us to the hospital."

"Okay." They all got into the car and Tish pointed toward Roscoe Blvd. "What's your name?" She asked Marie seductively.

"I'm Marie."

"My name is Tish, but you can call me Dark and..."

"Damn, girl," René cut in. "Do you hit on every woman you see? Calm your freaky butt down and tell us where to go."

Embarrassed and upset, Tish said, "Make a right at the light."

Marie was at a loss in that conversation, so she looked at René for some clarity. What she got back from her friend made her turn red in the face.

René licked her tongue out at her.

***

Bone and Road Rash were seated at the table with a bag of dope sitting between them; ten ounces of glass and ten ounces of coke. Bone was about to set his friend on his feet the right way. If you're dedicated to the underworld, this is a necessity: getting money through drug sales. It's like cooking chicken at El Pollo Loco: It's always in heavy rotation.

"This is it, Rash Ass," Bone declared. "I'm kicking you out of the nest. You can fly on your own from here. If you don't bring my bread back I'm gonna fill your little pink ass with some little copper pellets and let the dogs fight over your body."

"That don't even sound like you, bro," Rash said, as he looked at Bone with a sideways glance. He knew that Bone was easy like Sunday morning.

"This is Hollywood, Rash," Bone smiled. "Everything is dramatic, and I'm about to set you in the center of the stage with this here." He pointed at the dope. "With no holds barred. At the prices out here you'll make a killin'."

"Cut the shit, bro," Rash was all business, "And tell me how much you got here, and how much you want back."

"Right here is ten and ten," Bone stated in his all business tone. "I want ten grand from you. Is that fair?"

"More than," Rash replied quickly. "When do you want it?"

"When you get it, dipshit." Bone wasn't putting any pressure on his friend. Too much pressure in the game can cause anybody to slip. Besides, there was no need for pressure with a bag of diamonds in your safe.

"Cool," Rash sighed. "Raina's got some people lined up in Santa Barbara. She's going out there tonight to see her folks. Her dad hates my guts, so I'm staying home."

"Staying at home or staying at the Ho-Jo with Karin?" Bone knew the business.

Mind *your* bizness, not mine." Rash said slyly.

"Karin is *my* bizness, pinky. For that matter, you are too." Bone stood up to stretch. He looked around the room at Karin, then at Alisha. When it was all said and done, those were the two solid ones in the crew. Two renegades ready for a real change, and patient enough to watch it play out. Everything in life had a process to it. They were ready to go through the whole process and receive their crown in the end.

"Alisha, Karin, I'm outta here!" Bone stated. They turned to look at him, waiting for further instructions, "Spend some money today in the mall. Enjoy yourselves. Oh, make sure this wanna-be Beatle keeps his shorts on while he's here. I'm gone."

Alisha slid over to Bone and wrapped her arms around his head. Looking him square in his eyes she said, "Go get the bread, baby." While they kissed Karin slid up behind Bone and grabbed his ass.

"Give those kids downtown hell, big boy."

***

In Ramona Park two teenagers were playing catch with a baseball. One stood at the edge of the grass by the parking lot. His friend was about twenty yards into the park. The ball got passed to the youngster by the parking lot and went through the back window of a taxicab.

"Oooh!" Kevin cried. "You broke that window, Tre'.

"Man, shut up and get the ball so we can leave." Tre' walked over to where Kevin stood. They walked to the back of the cab and looked in.

The baseball was wedged in between the dashboard and the windshield. As they walked around to the passenger's side to peek in they saw a body on the floor.

"Whoa," Kevin muttered. He stared at the back of the Cabbie's head. He could see a small bullet hole with a streak of blood that had ran out of it and dried up. "We need to forget about gettin' that ball and go call the cops." He didn't get any response out of Tre' so he looked to his left where Tre' stood.

Tre' was no longer standing there.

He ran top speed across the park toward his house. He didn't care about that baseball anymore. He didn't care about Kevin standing there looking at a dead guy in a cab, either. Tre' was out of there.

Chapter Nineteen

Barry and Bone stepped into Rashad's Apparel. They were greeted by a young Arab dressed like he just stepped out of an old Mafia movie. He had on a green silk button down shirt with a butterfly collar and some green slacks. His shirt was open at the top revealing his hairy chest and about ten pounds of gold chains. With tan socks olive green loafers and straight black hair slicked down on his head, Rashad was the Tony Montana of the new millennium.

"Barry!" He cried, "Where have you been? I got suits in my store with your name on them and you never come and pick them up."

"I'm waiting for your delivery lady to bring them by my office," Barry replied slyly.

"Ah," said Rashad, "If you requested a delivery lady to bring your suits to you, you wanted other services out of her, too. You are trying to get me killed. Ms. J is down here too much doing her shopping. No, my friend, you don't get delivery service."

Barry shrugged. "I tried." He looked over at Bone. "I'll take them suits with me today after you take measurement on my man right here."

"Ah," Rashad said again. "This must be William." He looked Bone over.

"Just call me Willie," Bone said as they shook hands. "I really didn't come to be..."

"Size him up," Barry interrupted. When Rashad went to get his measuring tape Barry said, "Let me hand this. Don't be so anxious."

Rashad came back with the tape. "Stand up over her, Willie, and let's get your numbers." As Rashad went around his waist down his legs and across his shoulders, he made idle conversation. "I got a new shipment in last week from Stacey Adams. I think you will like their new line, Willie."

"I like this kid, Barry," Bone beamed. "He chose the right designer for a guy like me."

"Yeah," Barry agreed. "He stumbles up on the right thing sometimes. Just as long as you don't wear Stacey Adams with some three-liner jeans, and a Monte Carlo shirt."

"Boy, what chu' know about them days?" Bone laughed. "That outfit right there will get plenty women sweatin' your zipper."

"Yeah, it will get your old ass shot at, too," Barry reminded Bone. To Rashad he asked, "How's your dad doing?"

"Ah. He is making all of the money in the world, as usual. You should go see him. Get a few new pieces to go with your new suits."

"You never stop advertising do you?" Barry asked. "Why don't you call him before we leave and see if he's available today."

"Don't have to." Rashad pointed at the door.

Coming through the front door was Rashad's twin, or an older version of him. The only difference between father and son was age and outfit color. What Rashad wore was green. His father Hassan had on Burgundy.

Barry stood up to prepare himself for the hug that was coming. They not only loved him as a person, they loved him for the money that he shared with them. *It was time that they gave back a little now*, they thought. A whole lot as a matter of fact.

"My brotha," Hassan said warmly and extended his arms. He hugged Barry and said, "You need to come around *my* store more often."

"Your store costs me more money," Barry said with a smile. "It just so happens that today I was coming to see you too, though."

"I have some new pieces in there that Ms. J will love." Hassan pointed at Bone standing on a stool with his arms extended at his sides and said, "And this must be her handsome son."

"Nah," Bone said. "That's my sister. You better not tell her she's old enough to have a son as old as me."

They all started laughing.

"You two come down when my son is finished and I will show you some fine jewelry at discount prices." Hassan sounded like a guy in a TV commercial.

"You sound like that beeper salesman that says he's the King of Beepers," Barry said. That brought out more laughter. He leaned over and whispered to Hassan. "I got something to show you."

Hassan looked at Barry greedily and said, "Come." He led Barry to the back behind a curtain to an office. Inside, he gestured toward a fold-out chair for Barry to sit in. He walked behind the desk and sat down.

"Brotha Barry, what do you have for me?"

Barry stood up and pulled the pouch out of his pocket. He tossed it over to Hassan. He caught the pouch in mid-air with a look of confusion on his face until he opened it up.

As Hassan's eyes widened Barry said, "I thought about you as soon as I saw them."

"And I am grateful for that," Hassan stated. "Where did you get these?"

"Come on, Hassan. You don't ask where. You examine the merchandise and say 'yes' or 'hell yes'."

Hassan poured out the diamonds on the desk and very carefully pulled out his loop and tweezers and began examining the stones. He picked up each and every one of them before he commented.

"Well, they are all E.G.L. certified with thirty-two facets or more. These diamonds come out of the Golconda mines, a legendary mine; beautiful stones, very expensive. You and I can retire very wealthy men with these." Hassan was really excited about the diamonds but didn't want to reveal his emotions.

"That's the idea I had myself, Hassan," Barry agreed. "How much are they worth?" Barry knew that his question would start a mental pissing contest. He was ready.

"Well now that depends," Hassan started. "Do you want the wholesale price or the retail value?" He knew Barry wanted black market prices. He just didn't know if Barry knew that he could get at least thirty million for the diamonds on the desk.

Barry sighed, "I don't want to pen up a jewelry store, Hassan. I'm into too many other things." He looked Hassan straight into his eyes. "I don't know a thing about diamonds, but I do know that you're *very* interested. It's millions sitting between us right now."

"Cut to the chase, huh?" Hassan asked.

"Cut to the chase," Barry agreed. "We both know business and I don't have time to wrestle mentally with you today."

Hassan had much respect for Barry. He would give him the street value for a man of his caliber—and still turn a double-up profit. "There is fifteen million dollars in diamonds on this desk right now."

"So you can make between forty to fifty million, Hassan?" It wasn't a question. "Let's go out here and discuss this with Willie."

Hassan looked confused. "You mean Ms. J's son? These are his?" He was clearly surprised.

"Don't sound like that, Hassan." Barry smiled. "My boy's far more clever than he looks."

"Clever is not the word, my brotha," Hassan declared. He scooped the diamonds back into the bag and held on to them.

They were his now.

It was just a matter of getting the money together. Hassan was even willing to go as far as twenty million, but he couldn't reveal that.

They walked back into the store from the office to see Bone draped in a three-quarter-length leather coat. He stood in front of the mirror admiring the way that it fit him. Out of the corner of his eye he watched them come from behind the curtain.

"This kid wants five hundred for this, Barry!" Bone cried "I could see if his store was in the Lakewood Mall or something. Downtown? I can go down three stores and cut a deal for two hundred for the same coat."

"I was going to include my delivery service too, Willie." Rashad said proudly.

Barry started laughing to the point of tears. Rashad didn't know that his delivery ladies/hookers were no match for the illustrious ghetto game that Bone exercised on women.

After Barry regained his composure he said, "Don't share that service with..."

Ssshh!" Bone hissed. "Let me wake him up in my own way, Barry.

Rashad looked back and forth between Bone and Barry totally confused. His father interrupted the fun.

"Willie, right? I am Hassan," he paused. "I'm going to let you have that coast as a gift from my son and myself. You let me know what you want for these in the bag." Hassan wanted to see if Bone knew what he had.

Bone was no dummy when it came to diamonds. He knew a jewel thief doing time in Folsom. That's all that they would talk about when they walked the yard.

Diamonds.

"How many carats are they a piece?" Bone asked quickly.

"Three."

"Are they certified?"

"They each have a laser inscription – E.G.L," Hassan stated.

"And what kind of cut, Mr. Hassan?" Bone gave him a bonus smirk.

"Marquise," Hassan answered. "You know a little about diamonds, huh? Well, these diamonds come out of the Golconda mines."

"No nitrogen in their atomic structure. Damn, Hassan! Tell me how many facets per stone."

Hassan was thoroughly impressed. He liked the way that Willie had done his homework. "I'd say the average is thirty-two per stone."

Bone didn't waste any time quoting a price. "You give me two diamonds back and fifteen million cash and we got a deal."

"I'm curious, Willie," Hassan said. "How did you come up with that figure?"

"Easy. At my level of the game those stone are worth a quarter of a million a piece. Sixty stones is fifteen million. I take two back, make my mama and my daughter a ring and live life like never before."

Hassan just smiled and nodded his head. He liked Bone's style. He knew his position in the game and he was okay with it. He also knew how to play at a high-tech level, and remove himself when his business was complete.

Get in, get paid, and get out.

At the front door an Asian man yelled, "Hey Bone! Hey Bone!"

Bone looked over at the door and saw Daniel Chin walking in. "Hey there, Danny Boy!" Bone cried. "Long time no see." They embraced like brothers.

"When did you come home?" Danny asked.

"Yesterday, kid," Bone replied.

"You were supposed to be in the restaurant last night, then," Danny declared. "You know Papasan will not like this."

Danny Chin and Willie Braxton were like brothers. They had known each other for over twenty years. Danny's family had a restaurant next to Willie's family's barber shop for over two decades. They had survived robbery attempts leaky roofs, and the '92 riots together. Their two families were as one.

"Buy me this coat, Danny." Bone tried to change the subject.

"I ain't buyin' you shit until you go see Papasan," Danny declared.

Bone leaned over and whispered in his ear. "I'm about to be a millionaire, kid. You better be nice to me." Bone leaned back and winked.

Danny looked around casually at the faces in the store. He knew Rashad from buying suits from him, but the other two faces were foreign to him. *The brother was with Bone*, he thought, *and the other Arab could be Rashad's father.* They were both dressed alike. Like father like son. You could tell that something was brewing. Danny looked back at Bone.

"Step outside for a second," Bone instructed. To the rest he said, "Excuse us for one second."

Once they stepped outside Danny said, "Okay, what do you mean a millionaire? You robbing banks already?"

"Nope. I came up on a bag of diamonds from some girls I be hustlin' with." Bone confided in Danny like he was his brother.

"You still hanging out with them silly ass prostitutes on Artesia Blvd.?" Danny cried. "You sure they didn't give you a bag of Zurc's?" Danny smiled, but he could see that Bone was dead serious.

"A bag of zurc's worth fifteen million, kid," Bone stated.

"Who? How? Where? Are they cute?" Danny fired a volley of questions at Bone. He was excited.

"Not now," Bone said calmly. "I'll be through for lunch today. Now, let me go back in here and take care of my bizness." He winked at Danny as they strolled back into the store.

As they walked in Bone asked, "What are you doing down here?"

"Oh, I was supposed to have some suits delivered."

"Still buyin' pussy, huh? I should tell Natalie." Bone patted Danny on his back.

"You should see the delivery girls before you tell," Danny spun away from Bone to talk to Rashad about his service.

Bone approached Barry and Hassan. It was time to close this deal out.

Hassan led the two into the back office. "You want all of the money in cash?" He asked.

"That's all I know, man," Bone replied. "In my line of bizness I don't accept checks money orders or credit cards. Big face dead ass crackers on green paper. That's all I know."

"That is going to take some time to get together," Hassan said.

Bone reached out and grabbed the pouch of diamonds from Hassan. "You're an Arab, man. You're not puttin' your money in no banks. You got safes full of bread. Separate mines from yours and give me a call." Bone grabbed a pen and a piece of paper off of the desk. He wrote his number down and handed it to Hassan.

Hassan looked at Barry for some help. He did not want those diamonds to get away from him. *What if he finds another buyer?* he thought. Every jeweler in downtown Los Angeles had safes full of cash. No one Hassan knew used any bank, and he knew eighty percent of the dealers.

Barry sighed audibly. "Why don't you leave them with Hassan so you don't have to have them on you? Anything could happen." That was all that Barry would say.

"I don't want the devil to tempt Hassan into thinking that I'm a chump, Barry." Bone said casually. "I like Hassan, so let's keep our bizness with him straight across the board. Besides," Bone added at the right time, "We might come across a better offer down the way."

"No!" Hassan cried. "I will have the money together for you by tonight."

Bone smiled at that statement. All Hassan needed was a little push, and the thought of another buyer was just enough.

"Now *that* is the bizness!" Bone declared. "Give me a call when you're ready, and we'll meet up." They both nodded in agreement and walked out of the office.

Danny grabbed Bone by his arm when they all came out. "Lunch will be served at eleven-thirty, dude. Don't be late. I already called Papasan and told him that you would be there."

"Don't *you* be late waiting on your suits to be delivered," Bone said and walked out of Rashad's Apparel.

On the street Bone turned to Barry and asked, "Does Rashad's delivery girls have dots in their foreheads?"

"No, but they deliver in coats like the one you have on with nothing on underneath it." Barry smiled.

"*That's* the bizness!"

***

Back in the Escalade Bone headed toward Canton's. Mr. Chin would be expecting him for lunch, so he went in that direction. No hesitation. There were no excuses used when Papasan was expecting you. Jail and death were the only two passes he allowed.

Bone picked up his phone and dialed his mom's number. He forgot to get Kristene's new number before he left last night. He had to keep his word and call. *Imani would be fully expecting to hear from her daddy this morning*, he thought. And Kristene would be praying that he wouldn't let her down.

"Hello," Joyce answered.

"Ms. J, what's Kristene's number?"

"She didn't change her number. She wanted to keep it so you wouldn't have a problem getting in touch with her."

"Come on mama," Bone sighed. He didn't want to hear the reunite-with-your-family speech. Bone and Kristene had too many ill years between them for that right now. It was going to take way more than twenty-four hours of freedom for them to get that conversation.

"I'll get around to talking to Kristene," he finally said.

"You need to be with your family, *boy*!" Joyce barked.

"Don't get me started," she stated. "If I didn't love you I wouldn't say nothin'."

"Okay. Finish getting ready for work," Bone said and hung up. He looked over at Barry who was acting like he wasn't paying attention to the conversation. He dialed Kristene's number.

"Daddy…"

"Hello."

Imani and Kristene answered the phone at the same time on the first ring.

"What did I tell you about answering my phone, Imani?" Kristene was in a scolding mood and she didn't care who was on the line listening.

"Do you always ride down on her in front of people calling you?" Bone asked quickly to cut off the verbal assault awaiting his daughter.

"Daddy!" Imani beamed.

"She's been picking the phone up all morning thinking it was you," Kristene said with a slight whine and relief in her voice. "What took you so long to call?"

"Bizness," Bone said flatly. "Hang up, baby, and let me talk to your mama for a minute," he said to Imani. "Maybe she'll let me take you out to lunch."

"I'm going to get dressed, daddy," Imani said, and dropped the receiver on the floor. She didn't waste time hanging it up.

"Why did you do that?" Kristene said with frustration in her voice.

"You can go, too. It's evident that you want to talk. Plus, this call is costing for air time."

"You get free nights and weekends, Willie," Kristene countered.

"I'm five minutes from you, so I suggest that you get dressed to impress."

"I'm already dressed," Kristene said matter-of-factly. Kristene was glad that Bone didn't let his daughter down by not calling. Now she had a chance to talk to him. Let him know that the door that was previously closed and locked was now ajar. The time had come for them both to grow up and let go of the past.

Grow *out* of the past.

Imani needed her father in the same house not down the street. Imani needed her mother and father as one, to teach her all that was needed to live life to the fullest. And let the truth be told, she wanted her husband back. Kristene hated to fail, and she would not let her marriage fail due to some wild hair in her husband's ass. She would pull that hair. No, she would have it lasered off so that it couldn't grow back. Kristene wanted to be a wife again.

Bone was taken aback by her declaration. No fussing or nothing. "I'm already dressed," is what she said. She was waiting on him more than her daughter was. Wow, could the door be open to daddy/husband again?

"I'll be there in a minute. Hey? What chu' wearin'?"

"Don't talk extra ghetto, boy," she knew her answer would get him. "I'm wearing a pair of tight jeans."

"And I'm on your street," Bone hung up. He looked over at Barry and said, "I'm droppin' you off, kid, so I can see what this woman wants."

"You mean so you can see what your *wife* wants," Barry corrects him.

"Don't cash that check yet."

Chapter Twenty

With Little Johnny and Tino were sitting in the truck. John stepped into Canton's. Mr. Chin called him early in the morning to see what kind of progress was made in getting him straightened out. He wanted his money or his diamonds back. Twenty-four hours had gone by with no word. The next twenty-four would be more productive, or else.

Mr. Chin was seated at his normal table. Only this morning two goons stood behind him. When John approached the table he hesitated, but Mr. Chin waved toward a seat for him to take. When John sat down, the goons came around to stand behind him.

"You don't look like you have a positive progress report for me," Mr. Chin stated.

"The bag was dropped off at my place, but it was empty." John tried not to sound nervous. "I got a line on where they are," he lied, "And I should have the diamonds back tonight."

Mr. Chin knew a lie when he heard one. He would not tolerate John lying to him about ten million dollars of his money. He nodded to his goons. One of the goons slipped a thin rope over John's head and began choking him. He instantly stood up. His reflexes demanded that his body fight for dear life. That fire was quickly extinguished by the sight of the other goon pointing a 9mm at his head. John was no fool. He was not about to fight a gun. Two hundred and eighty pounds was no match to a bullet to the head. He eased his back down into the seat.

"Who is this girl with my diamonds?" Mr. Chin asked. "I will send my own people out to find her, and for your sake I hope that they find her with my diamonds."

"Her name...is...René." John tried to talk with a rope extremely tight around his neck. He looked at Mr. Chin with pleading eyes. Chin nodded and the goon that was choking John eased up a little.

"Her name is René," John repeated. "She's got red hair, tall, and thin. She's with another girl with long dark hair. She looks Indian." John was not holding back on given them up. "I guess her dude just got out of prison and now he's involved. They call him Bone. From what I gather, he's well known on Artesia Blvd. Anything that goes on with the prostitutes out there he's involved with it somehow."

At the mention of Bone, Mr. Chin showed a small hint of recognition and relief.

There was only one Bone hustling on Artesia Blvd. with the prostitutes. Willie Braxton. If Willie was involved in this Mr. Chin had a good chance at getting his merchandise back. He had known Willie and his family for many years. Their history and mutual respect for each other would make this ugly situation work out just fine. For John's sake it had better work out. Chin would find out over lunch.

"You continue to look, John," Mr. Chin said after a long pause. "If you find them before my people do bring them to me." He waved his hand at John like he was fanning a fly away.

The goon holding the gun on him put it away, and the other one took the rope from around his neck. He had to find René. Even if she didn't have the diamonds she would take a bullet along with him for this slip up. He was not going to die by himself.

Inside the truck his sons looked at him like two little worried children. They knew by the look on his face that it was down to the wire.

Find the diamonds or die.

John put on his sunglasses, and without looking at either one of his sons he said, "We are going to the valley to look around. We are going to find this red headed black chick," he spoke through clenched teeth. "I don't care if she's with the fucking mayor of Los Angeles. I want that bitch."

At the sound of their father calling her a bitch both of their eyes got as big as silver dollars. They had never in their whole entire life heard him call a woman a bitch. He was beyond mad.

"Let's all go and rent a car, dad," Little Johnny suggested, "So they don't spot us before we spot them."

"Good idea, son," John said flatly.

Little Johnny suddenly felt cold. The summer sun in Los Angeles couldn't penetrate the chill that he felt. For his pop's to agree with anything *he* said, meant that his pop's was so nervous about the situation that he would go for just about anything. Like all other ideas to rectify the situation were futile. Little Johnny shuddered at that thought.

"You want a stiff drink, Pops?" Little Johnny asked.

With no hesitation John replied, "Good idea son."

Oh yeah, Little Johnny thought, *My pops is scared to death.*

***

In the hospital waiting room René, Marie and Tish were all caught up in their own thoughts. Whenever something bad happened to another working girl in the streets the rest of the girls went deep into thought about their own situation; sorry for the hurt girl's situation, and real glad that it wasn't them.

Brooklyn's left leg was broken, and she had a mild concussion. With ten stitches across a gash on her right temple, and a cast on her left leg from her hip to her ankle, the doctor said that she would be fine. They were waiting for the doctor to let them in to see her.

"Ladies," the doctor started, "You can see your friend for about ten minutes. She'll probably be asleep before then, but my guess is that she will hang on about that long. She's a little scared right now so some familiar faces is healthy. Oh, she's registered in under Tipi Lorraine, but she does *not* like that name. Could one of you *please* tell me what to call that woman?"

René giggled at the doctor's pleading manner. "Her name is Brooklyn. We call her Brook for short, though."

"Brooklyn it is," he sighed. "I'm Doctor Stein. Joseph Stein." Looking from face-to-face, Doctor Stein knew that these ladies were a part of a world that right society looked down upon, but often used for pleasure. Prostitution got a worldwide frown by day; cash, check or charge by night. Doctor Stein knew from experience. He had motel receipts as proof.

"When can she leave, Doctor Stein?" Tish asked. She wanted to nurse Brooklyn/Tipi back to health.

"We'll just keep her overnight for observation and release her in the morning."

"Let's go see her before she goes to sleep," Marie said. She wanted to get out of the hospital as fast as she could. The last time she was in a hospital her son had died from a car crash. A drunk driver slammed into his car head on. That's what led her to drugs.

"Ten minutes, ladies," Doctor Stein reminded them.

They walked down to her room and stepped in. Brooklyn's leg was elevated by a hoist, and her head was wrapped up like a mummy. Her right eye was black and her skin was ashen; a black woman's version of being pale.

She opened her eyes at the sound of the door. Relief swept over her face at the sight of her friends. "Hey ya'll," she moaned. "Did anybody get the license plate of the truck that hit me?" She smiled wearily at her own joke.

"I got a plate number, but it wasn't a truck." Tish didn't get the joke.

"Good," Brooklyn stated. "Call Larry H. Parker so I can get about eighty thousand for this broken leg." They all broke out laughing at that.

"It's good to see you're okay, Brook," Marie said quickly. "I guess we'll be back to get you in the morning." With that said, Marie was ready to go.

"Yeah," René added. "We just wanted to make sure that you were okay and let you know that you are not alone." René knew that Marie was uncomfortable, so she was doing her hi and bye fast. "Don't get hooked on that pain medication in that tube."

"What is that stuff, René?" Brooklyn asked.

"Morphine," Tish stated. "I broke my left leg twice stepping into traffic, and both time I had to detox off of that shit. Liquid heroin."

"Take the bottle and sell it, René," Brooklyn teased. If morphine was liquid heroin she knew a lot of people who shot dope. They would love to be in her position right now, or would they? A dose every ten minutes if she wanted it. Instant addiction. *I'll just have to deal with the pain*, she thought.

René faked like she was taking the bottle off. "I know just the right bitch to sell it to, girl." More laughter.

"We'll see you tomorrow, Brook," Marie said firmly. She looked over at René who nodded in agreement.

Getting the hint that the hospital was eating away at Marie's sanity, Brooklyn nodded, too, "See ya'll tomorrow."

Tish was the last one to walk out of the room. Before the door closed she turned around and blew Brooklyn a kiss. "Bye, Tipi."
When the door closed Brooklyn leaned over the edge of the bed and vomited.

***

Outside at the car Marie said, "You drive, René." Marie got in the back seat and let Tish ride shotgun. Before they pulled out of the parking lot Marie had her pipe loaded and smoking. She was not over her son's death, and after that brief visit she didn't see any closure in her near future.

As soon as they pulled on to Roscoe Blvd. Marie blew smoke everywhere. "Pull into the first liquor store, René, and drop this chick off as soon as possible." She wanted to get high and drunk and cry on her girlfriend's shoulder. No stranger allowed.

Tish didn't take offense to Marie's words. She had seen the change in her at the hospital. It was none of Tish's business. She had work to do.

Tipi/Brooklyn would be out of the hospital tomorrow morning. Her friends would be there to pick her up. Tish would be there, too. Be there with a breast full of money and a motel room paid up for a week. She was not going to give up on having Tipi in her life. Maybe her injury would soften her up.

René pulled up into the liquor store. Tish jumped out of the car fast. "I'm gonna go from here, ya'll. I got bizness to take care of." She looked at herself in the tint on the car window, made some adjustments to her clothes and hair, and walked off.

Marie and René stood in the parking lot watching. No more than ten yards away from the store Tish climbed into a Toyota

Tundra; her first date of many more to come before the day was over.

"She's fast," Marie observed.

"She's determined," René stated. "She's gonna flatback and jaw-jack all day and all night. She's on a mission. Call it, 'Brooklyn's Bread'."

"Brooklyn's Bread?" Marie was confused. Then it dawned on her. "She's chasing Brook?"

"Choosin' fees, Marie." René smiled. "Choosin' fees."

***

Bone pulled up in the driveway and got out. He climbed the steps and rang the doorbell. He heard someone running. Imani.

She stopped at the door but didn't open it. Bone could hear Kristene yelling something about not answering her door. If she did she was going to beat the brakes off of her, or something. Imani looked through the window and waved. She mouthed something about her mommy wouldn't let her answer the door as she swirled her finger next to her ear. An indication that she thought her mother was crazy at the time.

Kristene finally opened the door. Bone was stuck on the porch with his mouth wide open. She was stunning. All that Tai-Bo that she was doing paid off. Bone had known Kristene for years, and he had never before seen her wear anything remotely close to showing her stomach. Yet now, she stood in the doorway in Apple Button Jeans and a sports bra.

With a washboard stomach and firm hips, long black hair down to her waist, with a hint of gray in the front, she looked like a young version of Jane Kennedy. The sports bra was a little too ghetto for her taste, but she knew that Bone liked a little ghetto fabulous every now and then.

"Stop staring at me like I'm a piece of meat."

"Girl, please," Bone said. "Dressed like that you want my tongue hangin' outta my mouth."

"I won't tease you no more," Kristene smiled. "I was just showing off what you can't have anymore." That was a lie. She was showing her body off to her husband to let him see that what was in the streets didn't compare to what was available to him at home.

Bone continued to stare at Kristene. It had been a long time since he had held her in his arms. He would give anything to just caress her like the days of old; holding her secure in his arms and feeling her release her independence to him.

"You gonna come in or what?" She asked as she backed up.

As he stepped in he saw Imani standing there crying. She had been there the whole time watching her mother and father eye each other. Admire each other. She wanted them to get back together.

"What's wrong, baby?" Bone asked as he knelt down in front of her. She was the spitting image of her mother to him. With her Baby Phat pink shirt on, her dark blue jeans with pink seams and pink sandals, Imani looked like a kid model. The tears didn't fit, though.

"I want you to come home, daddy!" She cried. "I need you here every morning and every night."

Bone was speechless. He looked from Imani to Kristene. They both had long looks on their faces; a subtle request for the main man in their life to stand up for his family, instead of the underworld. A pleading look for Willie to stand up.

And for Bone to step down.

"Okay, ladies," Bone beamed as he picked up Imani, "Let's go have some lunch, and we'll discuss a solution to these long faces. You know I don't like long faces, so whatever I gotta do to fix them, that I will do."

Kristene had heard that tired line before, but she held her sarcastic comment to herself. This time she would give him the benefit of the doubt. She wasn't going to crush him right from the start. *Maybe that was a reason for his half-hearted attempts at reform*, she thought. He was looking at the home as a battlefield instead of a safe haven.

"The way you fix our long faces is to feed us," Kristene said. "Right, Imani?"

"Right!" She replied with a great big smile on her face.

Kristene went upstairs to get her purse. When she came back down she had on a three-tone Fubu Jersey that Bone recognized to be his own.

"I thought you told me that you took all of my clothes to my mama's house when I got busted," He said accusingly.

"You can have this thing back when you're ready for it," she lied.

"Do I get to take it off of you myself?" Bone shot the best line he could think of.

"Don't be talking like that in front of your daughter."

Bone looked at Imani perched in his left arm. She had her hands over her ears. He looked Kristene over once more and said, "Let's go before I get hungry for something else." He let his daughter down and they all walked out of the house.

When they were all in the truck Kristene asked, "Whose truck is this?"

"This is Cadillac's truck," Bone replied sarcastically.

"When does Cadillac want their truck back, smart butt?" Kristene didn't curse.

"If everything goes right, I might buy it."

She suddenly had a flash of Bone lying in the middle of the street on his stomach with the police surrounding him. They were taking him to jail on a stolen vehicle charge.

"Willie, you haven't been out a good twenty-four hours."

"It's a rental Kristene," he said calmly. The keys had a Hertz key chain that he flashed her. "I got it until Monday, kay?"

It took a moment before her fear subsided, but she managed a weak okay as they pulled off. Once she fully recovered she asked, "Where are we going to eat?"

"Mr. Chin's Canton," Bone announced.

"Good," Kristene sighed. "Maybe he will talk some sense into your fat head." She pushed his head slightly as she said it.

Kristene looked in the backseat at Imani and winked. In return, Imani gave her a thumbs up. The door was open for daddy to come home.

***

René knew that Marie was running from her past. It was hard for her dealing with her son's death. Her answer to the memory was cocaine, alcohol, and the streets. After about ten hours of abusing her body, then she would slow down and cry. She would cry for her son. She would cry for her lack of a relationship with him. She would cry hateful tears for that drunk driver who killed him. Although he got ten years in prison, and lost his right leg, Marie wanted him dead and her son alive. René didn't understand her way of dealing with her issue, but as her friend, she would ride the episode out with her.

"Let's go make some money, René," Marie said, "Let's hit the track out here and see what kinda money these tricks got out here."

"You load that pipe up first," René ordered. "I ain't workin' with you and I ain't high." Marie was more aggressive when it came to chasing cars. René was more cunning, sneakier.

"Don't even trip," Marie said excitedly, "I got enough dope for us to burn this whole track up!" Marie was getting into her zone.

"You just make sure you're burnt out before the sun goes down," René said firmly.

Marie stuffed a whole twenty-dollar piece on the pipe. She knew that René was reluctant to hang with her when she was feeling the way she was. Enough coke in the pipe would numb her thoughts. Marie melted it down and passed it to René.

"Before nightfall, girlfriend," Marie lied as she passed the pipe. She held the steering wheel so René could take a hit.

René took a full pull, looked over at Marie, and smiled.

That was the last smile she would show Marie for a long time.

Chapter Twenty-one

"Ladies and gentlemen, this is a stick up!" Bone announced as he stepped into Canton's. His daughter looked up at him with a curious look on her face.

"Da-Dee!" She cried. "I thought your bad boy days were over with."

"Just this last one, baby," Bone pleaded. "This man right here has been robbing me for the past twenty years." He pointed at Mr. Chin as he approached.

"Your father is a very funny man, young lady," Mr. Chin beamed. "Kristene, how do you put up with this kind of behavior?" He had his arms stretched out toward her.

They hugged each other and she replied, "With your help, Papasan. I am hoping to curve his appetite for foolishness."

"Such an appetite calls for too many different dishes, but a loss of the main dish might bring about a change." Mr. Chin kissed her hand. "Leave him and marry me. Let's see if that will bring about a change."

"Oh it will. But you two won't like that change." Bone laughed, but his face told a serious story. He meant what he said.

Mr. Chin put his hands on Bone's shoulder. He looked him up and down. *Could Willie already be involved in the street life so soon?* He thought. Don't kid yourself, Chin. A bag full of diamonds would make any man get involved some kind of way.

Especially a man like Bone.

He lived for the ultimate break in the game. That final score that tells you that you won. You beat the odds. You made it out with enough cash to live above ghetto fabulous.
Tax-free street hustling bread was Bone's goal; to stack money in the underworld without the white man getting a dime. However much prison time it cost him, if the street game paid enough in the end to live forever, it was all worth it to Bone. *Foolishness!* Thought Mr. Chin.

"You look like you mother, son," Chin said after he looked Bone over. "Make her proud of you and stay home this time."

"That just might happen this time, Papasan." Bone lowered his voice. "I finally got that *one*." He knew Mr. Chin knew what that meant: The ultimate break in the game.

So he is involved, Mr. Chin thought. Relief swept across his face at that knowledge. "Come," Mr. Chin waved toward his table. "Let us sit down for tea until the food is ready." He looked down at Imani and asked, "Do you like video games?"

"Yes, Mr. Chin," Imani answered politely.

"How did you remember my name? The last time I saw you was almost five years ago. You were only two."

"My daddy said your name before we got here today," she replied offhandedly.

Mr. Chin smiled. "Well, Imani, I'm glad your father brought you today." He shocked her by calling her name.

"How do you know my name?" She asked.

"I knew your name before you were born." Mr. Chin was the only man that had slowed Bone down enough for him to be there for Kristene when she was pregnant. "That lady at the counter is going to give you all the quarters that you need for the games."

Imani ran to the counter and started a conversation with the young lady at the counter. They both looked toward Mr. Chin, who nodded his approval, and then they headed toward the video games.

"Come." Once again Mr. Chin led the way to his table in the back. When they were seated another young lady brought out a tray with a small tea kettle, cups and a bowl of cookies.

"So," Mr. Chin started, "How does it feel to be free again?"

Bone thought about that for a moment. With the package that he received upon his release he could solidify a real position in society. Like he was going to be there for a minute. "It feels permanent this time, Papasan. If I can get you to convince Kristene of that feeling, then we'll be in bizness."

"In time, son," Mr. Chin said warmly, "In due time. You cannot rush her into believing you. This is your fourth time coming home with almost the same feeling. Then your money gets low and you go back out into the streets with this get rich scheme."

"Okay, let's change this conversation," Bone said quickly. "You sound like her."

"Maybe you need to hear it, Willie," Kristene added. "For your own good as well as your family."

"Oh," Bone said proudly, "Trust and believe me when I say that we are gonna be alright this time around." Nobody at the table knew that he had just closed a deal for fifteen million dollars today. The street game was over for Bone once that bread came in for him. He hoped.

Mr. Chin studied Bone before he spoke again. He was judging him to see if he would receive what he had to say. He decided to tell him after they ate. He raised his hand and out came three waiters with bowls on top of bowls.

They cleared away the tea and cookies and set out fried rice, steamed rice, beef broccoli, orange chicken, sweet and sour port, and barbecue beef on a stick.

Bone looked over at Imani playing the video game. She was too caught up at the moment, and he didn't want to ruin her fun.

"Imani," Kristene called out.

"We'll make her a plate to go," Bone said as he held Kristene from getting up. "Let her enjoy herself."

"I'll take care of that plate," Mr. Chin added.

"Thanks, Papasan," Bone replied. "Now pass that orange chicken before I poke you with these chop sticks."

They enjoyed a peaceful lunch. There was no more talk about do-right-by-your-family, stay-away-from-street people, or grow-up-and-be-a-man. Those topics were on the back burner for now.

They talked about gas prices and an increase in seafood prices. Mr. Chin explained how the vendors he bought his products from were robbing him blind, but business was flowing enough to overlook them. He wanted to open another restaurant and offered Bone a job.

"Papasan," Bone said proudly, "I'm gonna start looking for a building to buy so I can open up a full scale hair salon."

"And with what money do you plan on using?" Mr. Chin asked. He saw his opportunity to hit Bone with the news about whose diamonds he was playing with.

"Oh, I stumbled across a good bizness deal," Bone replied casually.

"Explain," Mr. Chin encouraged him.

"Some friends of mine gave me a few trinkets that are worth a pretty penny."

"Willie!" Kristene cried. "You dealing drugs already? You just got out yesterday."

"Willie is not dealing drugs, Kristene," Mr. Chin said coolly. "He has 'trinkets' of far greater value."

Bone looked confused for a second then he remembered that he had told Danny about the diamonds when they were downtown.

"Danny told you, huh, Papasan?" It was a question.

"No son, I'm afraid he didn't tell me this time."

"Tell you what?" Kristene asked.

Mr. Chin looked Bone straight in his eyes. "I had a business deal go bad this weekend, son. I'm afraid those trinkets, as you call them, are mine."

Bone's jaw dropped in his plate. He looked into Mr. Chin's eyes looking for a sign that he was lying. There was no sign.

"Would somebody please tell me what is going on here," Kristene insisted.

Bone sighed. He couldn't lie to Mr. Chin. The code that he lived by demanded that he keep it real. Staying true to the game had to be maintained in his life. "Bring that tea back, Papasan," Bone said humbly, "Because this is gonna take a minute."

***

John, Tino, and Little Johnny hit Sepulveda Blvd. in a three-car caravan; a Dodge Magnum, Neon, and a PT Cruiser. They were swerving in and out of traffic and making U-turns like a team of vice unit cops. They pulled side-by-side at Roscoe and

Sepulveda. Little Johnny rolled his window down to talk to his pops. He was going to tell him that they should pull up into the donut shop at the next light. His best suggestion of the day.

"Follow me, pops," he said. "I saw some hookers hanging at this donut shop the last time I was out here."

"Is that where you got that dildo stuck in your ass?" John couldn't resist that sarcastic remark.

Little Johnny hated the way his father threw his faults back in his face. He just nodded this time though. because there was no room for his attitude with his pops right now. Right now they had to locate some hookers with enough diamonds to finance a motion picture.

The light turned green and Little Johnny shot out in front. John motioned for Tino to follow and they fell in behind Little Johnny. At the next light he pulled into the donut shop, followed by Tino, but John pulled to the curb next to the donut shop. As he got ready to get out, he checked his side mirror so a car wouldn't tear the door off of the rental. What he saw made his heart skip a beat. Silver Dodge Intrepid was pulling into the donut shop. It was René and her girlfriend that shot the tires out on Tino's Lexus. He started the Magnum up and waited for them to pull all the way in. Once they were in he backed up and pulled in behind them. It was three parking slots in front of the donut shop. Tino and Little Johnny occupied two spaces and the car in between them was backing out. The girls were waiting for the slot to be available.

They pulled in and John pulled up behind them. His prey was blocked in. He jumped out with his pistol drawn and stuck it through the window to the side of René head.

"Please scream so I can blow your head off!" John's voice was filled with pure fury. He looked through the car at this son as he rolled his window down. Little Johnny had his gun trained on René's girlfriend.

"Good boy."

René kept her cool. She had plenty of guns and knives pulled on her in the streets. She was scared, but she knew that her fear was not going to keep her alive.

"Now, if you shoot me, John," she said calmly, "You'll never know how to get your diamonds back."

She had a point, but John didn't let her know that. "At this point, I could care less about them diamonds. You've made this little adventure a little too personal." He pointed over at Little Johnny.

René looked over at Little Johnny and waved.

He flipped her off.

"If he wants to pay me back for that dildo experience I don't take checks or credit cards," René said as she cracked a smile at John.

That slight sarcasm sent him over the edge. With one swift motion John backhanded René in her mouth with his pistol. He saw her friend wince at his act of aggression. At the same time he saw her easing her hand down the side of the seat. He pointed his pistol at her.

"Don't even think about it. As a matter of fact, get out." John motioned behind him for Tino to come around and join the action.

As Marie was getting out slowly, she was met by Tino grabbing her right arm.

"Tino," John said, "Put her in the Magnum and make sure she doesn't have a gun on her," John looked back at René. "What's the matter? Cat got your tongue?"

René didn't make a noise when he slapped her with his pistol. She was too stunned to scream. She felt her whole mouth explode with the impact of his blow. Shards of her teeth were floating around in her blood-filled mouth. John had shattered her whole front grill. She turned to look at him as he talked to her. She spit in his face. Pieces of teeth and blood splattered John's face. He didn't flinch. He calmly opened her door and said, "Let's go."

Little Johnny hopped out of the PT Cruiser and said, "What do we do now?"

"Open the back of the Magnum so I can get in with my little friend here," John instructed. "Lock your car up and Tino's, and get in the driver's seat of this fine automobile that I drove up in, and take us away from here."

John had René by her arm guiding her to the back of the Magnum. When it popped open, he pushed her in and climbed in behind her.

"Has your friend there said anything yet?" John asked Tino.

"Nope. She's been as quiet as a church mouse."

"Church house mouse," John was correcting his hip son. Tino missed it.

"You're a smart girl," John continued. "What's your name?"

"Marie," she muttered.

"Keep your mouth shut and you'll live, Marie. Open it and I'll remember you shooting my son's tires out on his car." He smiled at her.

Marie looked from John to Tino and just nodded. She had just witnessed what happen to René. She did not want to be a victim like her girlfriend.

Little Johnny hopped in the driver's seat and they pulled off. He looked in the rearview mirror at his pops. He could see that his pops had regained his confidence. They caught eye contact, and for once in Little Johnny's life he could see his father's approval. He's finally proud of me. Little Johnny smiled broadly.

"Where to, Pops?" he asked.

"Back to Canton's, son," John said as he winked at his son.

Little Johnny smiled like a kid who just got his first bike for Christmas. As he headed toward the freeway his thoughts were on brighter days between him and his father.

Too bad there would be none of that.

***

"So you mean to tell me that since you've been home these events have occurred?" Kristene asked. Her mind was spinning out of control at Bone's account of how he came across the diamonds.

Bone didn't tell them about the drugs. But he did explain how DuVall and John were responsible for a lot of the prostitutes being burned with hot glass pipes and other hot objects. He left out most of the details, but Mr. Chin and Kristene knew that two hoes had stumbled across the diamonds by 'accident' while cleaning up behind DuVall's fatal 'accident.'

"No, Kristene," Bone sighed, "It happened the night before I came home. Stop trying to put me right in the middle, so you can have another excuse to stay away from me."

"*I'm* not putting you in the middle of it," she said matter-of-factly, "Your hoes are."

Bone had never given Kristene full details on his activities with the chicks that worked the streets. She suspected that he hustled with them and fucked them, but she never got a vivid picture like the one she just heard.

"Not *my hoes*, them hoes," Bone countered firmly.

Mr. Chin saw an argument coming on fast. He raised his hand for them to stop. He knew that Kristene's ears were burning with the realization that her husband was really hanging out with prostitutes on such an intimate level. For them to just hand over a bag of diamonds to him upon his release from prison, that meant that they were paying homage to a real hustler in their circle. *Everyone gets their chance*, Mr. Chin thought. *If they were real about their business*.

"William," Mr. Chin started, "I am most grateful to know you right now. If it were not for your perseverance to the street life I would be out of a great deal of money. But I no longer have that worry, so I too must pay homage."

Bone already knew that Mr. Chin was going to bless him. He just had to let him know that he already had a buyer, so that he could keep the better part of the bread. In spite of the fact that the diamonds belonged to Mr. Chin, Bone would control the sale. Without a '*real*' selfish intent Bone had to make sure that his family circle, and his circle of renegade hoes had more than enough to move on in life.

"I already have a buyer, Papasan." Bone stated. "Now, how much was your deal for with DuVall?" He was all business.

"Because I consider you family, William, I will be straight forward. He was offering Ten million which I gladly accepted. Unfortunately, he had an *'accident'* before we could finalize our deal." Mr. Chin smiled slyly.

Bone couldn't contain his excitement. "And what kind of homage were you going to pay me off of ten million, Papasan?" Bone was grinning from ear-to-ear.

"I will give you three of the ten," Mr. Chin replied. "But, your smile tells me that that is nothing compared to what you will actually walk away with."

"It will be just enough to wipe away a few sorrows that I have caused." Bone looked over at Kristene.

Mr. Chin nodded in agreement and said, "Go. Take care of your business, son, and I will see you when?"

"I'm waiting on a call right now," Bone stated. "If all goes according to schedule I will have my bizness completed by midnight." Bone smiled.

"And I will be right here until around two a.m," Mr. Chin replied. "Be careful, son."

They all rose from their seats.

As Kristene and Mr. Chin embraced Bone went to get Imani away from the video games. She had been bouncing from one machine to another for over an hour now.

"You ready to go, stinky?" Bone asked.

"Five more minutes, Daddy," Imani replied "I have to get through one more level to be Queen Bee."

"Okay, Queen Bee. I'm going to get you a plate of food to go, but when I come back, Queen Bee or not, we be leaving."

"Okay daddy. Now could you please back up? You're messing with my concentration."

"Buzz!" Bone said real close to her ear.

"Da-Dee!" Imani cried.

Bone gathered up three plates to-go, Kristene, and his daughter. On his way out of the door Mr. Chin pulled him aside. He gave the food to Imani, the keys to Kristene, and they went to the truck.

Once they left Mr. Chin said, "You be careful, because John and his sons are looking for you and those girls right now. I also had my own scouts in the field, but I will call them in. Watch out for John," he said firmly. "He is highly upset and scared right now."

"The next time you talk to John," Bone announced, "You tell him that you found me. Tell him that I will be here tonight at twelve-thirty."

"Why?"

"Because he has done some unnecessary things in his search for something that *he* lost," Bone replied.

Mr. Chin knew all too well about the itch for vengeance. He would accommodate William.

"I will make sure that he is at your disposal."

***

Bone let Kristene drive. She said that she wanted to get used to driving a big SUV, so Bone let her roll. Imani was asleep before they hit the freeway, and Bone was too caught up in his own thoughts for conversation. Kristene kept looking over at him, but he kept his mouth shut.

Kristene's mind bounced around the idea of her husband with over three million dollars just a day after getting out of prison. The idea of prostitutes supplying the merchandise to get the money; the thought of him enjoying the money with them more than her. She didn't think he would do that, though. Imani didn't come from some street hooker. After about fifteen minutes of those thoughts Kristene finally said something.

"What do you want me to do, Willie?" She asked.

Bone was thrown off balance by her question. He did not expect her to volunteer herself for underworld activity. It felt strange to him. It also let him know that she was ready for him to come home. Did the money have something to do with it? Hell yeah.

"What you've always done, Kristene," Bone replied warmly. "Let me handle my bizness in these streets, and open your doors to me when I'm done."

"Are you really ready to come home?"

"I'm eight million dollars ready," Bone declared.

"Eight!" Kristene cried.

"Ssshh," Bone whispered. "Don't wake up my stinky." He leaned his seat back, cut the TV on in the console, and put his feet on the dashboard. "Go by Martin Cadillac, baby girl."

Kristene knew exactly where that was. They drove passed it every day for a whole year when they were staying with her sister.

"Why?" She asked.

"So we can order an Escalade ESV Executive Edition," Bone declared. "I can't ride with my feet on the dashboard all the time."

***

Hassan was part owner of a nightclub in Hollywood called Forbidden City. After his meeting with Bone and Barry, Hassan immediately started pulling cash together. He was not about to let this deal get away from him. It wasn't every day that you ran across a guy with a bag of diamonds at such an outstanding price.

Hassan was in the back of the nightclub with his partner Kebah Habek. Kebah was selling alcohol at the bar and ecstasy pills under the tables. Business was good and the feds stayed clear. Hassan was a well-established man in downtown Los Angeles. He stuffed the right pockets.

"Are you sure it's a good investment?" Kebah asked.

"As sure as I was when I invested in you," Hassan replied.

Kebah couldn't argue with that. He loaded the three extra big duffel bags into Hassan's Range Rover.

Hassan drove off. He had to call Willie so that they could finalize their deal.

"Where is that damn phone number?"

Chapter Twenty-two

Karin and Alisha were sitting in the food courts in the Northridge Mall. Alisha had insisted that they shop for Bone first. Now, after all of his bags were tucked away in the trunk of the car, they stopped off to grab a bite to eat.

"They got every culture food there is except soul food," Alisha complained.

"Well," Karin started, "I suggest that you get two all-beef patties, special sauce, lettuce, cheese, pickles, onions, on a sesame seed bun." They both started laughing as they went up to stand in line in front of McDonald's.

While Alisha was ordering Karin's phone rang. She looked at the screen: Private. *A date*, she thought. Most tricks never revealed the number that they were calling form for fear of a return call. Some called from home while their wives were in the shower.

"Yeeess," Karin whispered.

"Where's your pimp?" John demanded. He was furious. René and Marie wouldn't give him any information, and they were calling his bluff: "Just kill us," they both said to him. If he got what he wanted out of Karin he would accommodate them. Bitches.

Karin didn't recognize the voice. It sounded like the guy was talking through clenched teeth. *Pimp? Who was this dude looking for?* Karin wondered.

"You're talking to the only pimp that makes money off of this ass," she replied. Alisha looked at her quizzically. Karin shrugged. If Alisha could hear her she was talking too loud. She stepped out of line and sat back down.

"Who is this, anyway?"

"Don't play no games with me, bitch!" John cried. "Give me Bone's number!"

She caught his voice that time: John. He sounded a little mad and a lot scared.

So what.

"Hey, John!" She cried. "Now why would you call me out of my name? That's not nice."

"Don't taunt me, Karin," John said calmer than before. He had to check himself. "I got two of your girlfriends with me right now, and if I don't get Bone's number, they die. If you want to see René again you'd better start rattling some numbers off."

How in the hell did they get caught like that? Karin's mind started calculating from going to pick up Brooklyn to being kidnapped. That didn't add up.

"Are you still there?" John asked. This was not going as well as he expected.

"Oh, I'm here," Karin was in her zone. "Before we go any further in this conversation though, I must speak to my girlfriends."

"Well," John laughed, "René is not up for too much conversation. You see, she is lacking her Colgate smile at the moment." He passed the phone to Marie.

"This mother fucker hit René in the mouth with his pistol!" Marie cried. "Don't give him shit, Karin!" She found her voice once she figured John for a chump.

"See," he started, "Everybody is just fine…so far."

"You just might get your wish, then. Our terms though, John. You see," Karin laughed. "Tricks don't run shit in our streets."

"You listen…"

"No!" She barked, "You listen to this, trick. Take your Caller ID block off, call me back so that your number is in my phone, and we'll be in touch." Karin ended the call.

Alisha sat across from her now, but she only heard a brief part of the verbal exchange.

"What was all of that about?" She asked.

"René and Marie got caught slippin' going to get Brooklyn. Now John is holding them and demanding to talk to Bone."

"Where's Brooklyn."

"I have no idea," Karin said bitterly. "If she would've just stayed put last night this wouldn't be going down right now."

Her phone rang. She looked at the screen and then showed Alisha. Big John, 562-529-8809.

Karin was right, Alisha thought. The big blame was on her, though. Those diamonds were causing a lot of problems for them. *Maybe we should've just given them back, and keep the dope and stay bound to the street hustler's life. Damn that!* She thought.

"We need to finalize this shit before this trick kills someone we care about," Alisha stated.

"Are you thinking what I'm thinking?" Karin asked.

"Make the calls," Alisha replied.

*** *** ***

"Daddy, can we get XBOX put in?" Imani asked. They were riding in the back of the Cadillac Escalade Executive Edition while Kristene did the test-driving.

"Yes, baby," Bone replied.

"And a DVD Player?"

"Yes, baby."

"MP3?"

"Yes, baby."

"Playstation Two?"

"Imani, where did you get this technical bug from?"

"Mommy told me that money ain't a thang now!" Imani snapped her fingers three times when she said, "ain't a thang".

Bone was overjoyed to see his daughter so happy. There were so many times that he had let her down. To see her spirits high was priceless. Nothing would stand in the way of her happiness from there on out.

"In that case," Bone joined her by snapping his fingers. "I think we'll need at least five TV's in here, right?"

"With two Alienware Laptops for bizness!" Imani added.

"Now that's the bizness!" Bone agreed and gave her a hi-five.

"What are you two so excited about?" Kristene asked.

"Hush, Ms. Daisy, and drive," Bone said. They broke out laughing.

His phone rang.

Bone looked at the screen: Karin.

"What's going on, kid?" He had to be careful how he talked around Imani. She was a smart little girl.

"We got a situation, love," Karin stated the facts. "Meet us at the Bat cave."

"The Batcave!" Bone cried. He looked up front at Kristene. She watched him through the rear-view mirror. He made a gesture to cut the ride short; a hand slicing across his throat. Kristene sighed audibly and looked over at Imani who was watching her father intensely. She sighed again. Bone sighed too, but there was unfinished business in the streets. "I'm with my daughter and my wife." He tried that line, but he already knew that they needed him.

Karin hated to pull Bone from his family. If she could handle the situation by herself she would. The streets always tore families apart. Bone's family was no different. She hated it, but they needed him.

"We need you, Willie," she said reluctantly.

"I'm on my way," he hung up.

"Where we going, Daddy?" Imani asked.

"Not we, baby. Just me."

Imani turned away from him and looked out of the window. She wanted her daddy all to herself. She was tired of sharing him with the streets. Imani had every right to have her lip poked out. When she spoke you cold hear the sorrow in her voice.

"When will I see you again, Daddy?"

"We're going to Magic Mountain tomorrow!" Bone said cheerfully. He hoped that it would work.

"Really, Daddy?" Imani asked suspiciously.

"As long as your mama don't stand in our way." He shifted the conversation and the blame nicely.

Imani looked up at her mother. Kristene was waiting to turn up into the dealership, so she wasn't looking at her daughter.

"Mommy, you're not standing in our way, huh?" Imani asked.

Kristene pulled in and parked. She turned her seat around (swivel seats) to face Imani and Bone. Her face was drawn up in a tight frown, too. She was tired of Bone being so quick to answer the streets when they called him.

"So you can blame me? No, baby," Kristene said gloomily. "I'm not standing in you guys' way." She looked at Bone. "I would like to go, too. Can I?"

They were both looking at him with pleading eyes. This part of the game was not cool. Leaving your family. Time and time again Bone had left and came back with no more than what he left with. Sometimes he never came back. Street life was cold. It takes you farther than you're willing to go…keeps you longer than you're willing to stay…makes you pay more than you're willing to pay.

Damn!

"Listen," Bone sighed. "This will be my last night out in the streets, ladies. If I don't take care of…"

"She is too young for this conversation," Kristene interrupted him.

"She deserves this just as much as you do." Bone shot back.

"What? Being abandoned?" Kristene countered.

His phone rang again.

"What!" Bone yelled.

"Did I catch you at a bad time, Willie?" Hassan asked.

Bone smiled. He opened the door and motioned for his daughter to get out. Kristene got out of the front seat to deal with the car salesman.

"No time is bad with me," Bone replied as he and his daughter walked toward the Escalade that they were driving.

"I have your money together," Hassan announced.

"That was quick." They had discussed their deal only five hours earlier.

"I don't play when it comes to business, Willie," Hassan said flatly. "Where can we make our exchange?"

"Downtown."

"Meet me in front of the Staple Center in ten minutes." Bone was excited. If he didn't come back tonight eight million would take his place just fine.

Maybe.

"I'll be in a green Range Rover," Hassan stated.

"Ten minutes," Bone hung up. He reached down and picked up Imani. Giving her a thumbs-up he said, "Money ain't a thang, baby girl!"

***

Kristene knew the streets better than Bone did so she drove. She also drove faster than him. She pulled up on Figueroa Street and Bone pointed at the Range Rover. Kristene whipped in behind it. Bone got out and Hassan met him between the two trucks.

"There is five million in each bag," Hassan said as he unzipped them all.

Bone slid him the pouch with the diamonds in it. He was awestruck at all that money staring at him. He zipped the bags shut. He turned around and motioned for Kristene to open up the back of the Escalade. He turned back toward Hassan and extended his hand. "Two stones from you and our bizness is done."

Hassan dug in the bag and dropped three stones in Bone's hand. "That is because I like your style." They shook hands.

Bone hefted one bag out and started for the back of his truck. Kristene jumped out and followed suit. She was excited and scared at the same time. At the back of the Escalade Bone dumped the last bag in and grabbed her arm.

"Didn't think it was real did you?"

"Let's drive and talk," she said anxiously.

With the money secure in his truck Bone led Kristene back to Hassan's Range Rover.

"This is my square peg of a wife, Hassan. Meet Kristene."

"A pleasure," Hassan replied. "You have a very resourceful respectful husband."

Kristene just nodded in agreement. Her nerves were on edge. Transactions in the underworld were not a part of her make-up.

"Go, Willie," Hassan said. He could sense Kristene's unease. "Live a comfortable life with your family."

"Thanks, Hassan." They shook hands again and left.

In the truck Kristene took deep breaths to slow down her heart.

"You alright?" Bone was concerned.

"We're…rich…ba…by," she said between breaths.

Bone started laughing as they pulled off. He looked in the back seat at Imani and said, "All of sudden your mama wants to say 'we'. Why is that, baby?"

"It's the money, Daddy."

Chapter Twenty-three

John walked into Canton's with a little pep in his step. He had a bargaining tool which meant that the diamonds were in his grasp. It was evident that René was Bone's top girl, or one of his top girls. If not some other dude would have the diamonds. He would come for her. *He'd better*, thought John.

Mr. Chin wasn't sitting at his table so John went to the counter and rang the bell. Danny came out from the back.

"My father is out right now," Danny said flatly.

"It's important that I speak with him Daniel," John replied.

Danny motioned for John to take a seat at the table. Once John sat down Danny took a seat directly across from him. He didn't like John, so he stared at him; two eyes burning John's flesh like hot coals.

"I'm a little thirsty," John said casually.

"State your business, John. Your thirst is not important. Ten million dollars. That is what is important around here."

"And I have two bargaining chips parked in the alley that will help me achieve that." John shifted in his seat. He was uncomfortable sitting under Danny's deadly gaze. "I just need a place to negotiate with this Bone character.

Mr. Chin had informed Danny on what was going on. They both didn't think that John would find anybody, though.

"Let me see them," Danny said.

They got up and went through the kitchen to the alley. They walked to the back of the Dodge Magnum and Little Johnny clicked the latch. John smiled at Danny and raised the door. Danny froze.

"René!"

Covered in blood from her lips all the way down her shirt, to the crotch of her pants, you could see it. She wasn't afraid, though. Danny's eyes met hers; René had murder written all over her face.

Danny had met her six years earlier at a birthday party for Bone. She was introduced to Danny as Bonnie, Bone was Clyde. Danny didn't know the white girl.

"What the hell did you do to her?" Danny couldn't hide his concern. It was hard for him to conceal his emotions when it came to someone he loved. He loved Bone like a brother and René was his girl, so she got that same love.

Bone is not going to like this one bit, Danny thought.

"She had a run-in with a perverted dentist," John stated and laughed.

Danny didn't find that funny at all. At that moment he felt like shooting John in his mouth. Later, though.

Danny looked at René pleading for him to help her. He winked his eye at her.

"Follow me out to Ms. Sue," he finally said. "You can do your negotiation on deck while I attend to this woman down below."

"Why so much concern, Daniel?" John asked. "This is just a street whore with sticky fingers."

"I have a sister and a mother," Danny pointed out. "I would want someone in this cruel game to look out for them if they ever needed it." Danny winked at René once again as he shut the hatch.

John felt a wave of guilt engulf him at the thought of all of the abuse that he saw his mother go through. Years later here he was doing the very thing that he vowed not to do. Disrespect a woman. This case was different, though. *They put themselves in a position to get mistreated like this*, he thought. *Didn't they?*

Danny walked back into the restaurant. He emerged ten minutes later with a leather trench coat on and leather gloves. He jumped in his Acura Legend and pulled out of the alley. John was close behind him. They were headed to the ocean. To Ms. Sue.

To set the stage.

***

Kristene pulled up in from of the Batcave. After she calmed down from the initial shock of seeing all of that money, she settled into some cool conversation with Bone. They talked about the

good old days and even laughed at some dark times in their life. Money sure did change the tone quick. They were breezing through memories because there was no chance of reliving those old days. Out with the old and in with the new.
Hopefully.

They were parked behind Karin's car. Bone pulled his phone out and called her. There was no need to wake the whole house up on what he was carrying. Some thirsty crooks frequented the Batcave.

"Hey, love," Karin answered.

"You and Alisha come outside for a minute and bring your keys." Bone hung up.

"Why are you calling them out here, Willie?" Kristene was irritated. She wasn't ready to meet her husband's whores.

"You don't take a big duffel bag of money in a place like the Batcave." Bone heard the irritation in her voice. "And don't sound like that. When I open up this full-scale salon these two women will be permanent fixtures."

"To do what? Hair in the front and give head in the back?" Kristene asked flatly.

"Wow!" Bone cried. "That's a good idea."

Kristene swung at him for being silly. Bone ducked her hand and looked at her in shock. She wasn't being serious. Bone wasn't crazy. Money changes frowns to smiles. They both started laughing.

"Shhh," Kristene whispered. "You'll wake up Imani up."

Karin and Alisha came down the driveway dressed alike. They were both dressed in all black; boots, tight jeans, sports bras, and leather trench coats.

"Here comes Bone's Angels," he announced.

Kristene swung again.

"Watch them hands, woman," Bone warned Kristene, "Get out and say hello to eight million dollars."

Kristene would not be intimidated by street hookers. She looked in the back to make sure that Imani was still asleep and got out.

"Ladies," Bone started, "This is my wife. Karin, Alisha, meet Kristene."

"You are more pretty in person, Kristene," Karin stated. "I've heard so many loving stories and seen so many pictures. I feel like I know you already." Karin knew how to ease tension.

Alisha was a little different. She looked at Kristene as a threat. She always knew that Bone had a wife but seeing her changed the game. Alisha kept her cool, though.

"It's a pleasure, Kristene. I've heard a lot about you." They shook hands.

Kristene on the other hand was speechless. Over the years she thought that her husband went out to the streets and totally denounced his union with her. Quite the opposite. He went out there bragging about her, letting all of the girls know that he was spoken for up front. Leaving no room for error on their part.

Yeah right.

Who were they trying to fool? Kristene thought. She knew that they were just another part of the street life, so whether they were ugly ducklings, or beautiful swans, they were just a part of a lifestyle that she had to fight in order to keep her husband at home.

That's why they were separated. Kristene felt that she shouldn't have to fight the streets for *her* husband. *He should bring his butt home on his own*, she thought.

"Okay, stop sizing each other up," Bone ordered. "Karin, pop your trunk. Kristene, pop the back of this truck. Alisha, come and get this bag."

They all started shuffling around glad to have something to do. At the back of the truck Bone grabbed Alisha around her waist.

"Why is your lip poked out?" He asked her warmly.

"They got René, baby," Alisha said, not wanting to show her feelings about meeting Kristene, "We gotta get..."

"Listen." He pulled her closer to him. "I know who stood by me these last forty months. She is not a threat to you." Bone gave her a reassuring smile.

Alisha smiled back at him and let out a sigh of relief. Then she tried to act tough.

"She better not be, boy."

"How could she be when you made this happen?" Bone unzipped one of the bags.

Alisha saw all of that cash and jumped into his arms. She kissed him all over his head, face, and neck. Most of it was pure excitement the rest was for show.

He's mine, Kristene.

"You dumped them stone that fast?" She asked as he let her down.

"I ain't no chump, girl," Bone said proudly. "I'm wit' da' bizness!" He zipped the bag back up, pulled it out of the back and handed it to her.

Alisha immediately headed for Karin's trunk. She wasn't naïve about Batcave patrons.

Bone pulled a stack of hundreds out of another bag grabbed his leather coat and closed the hatch. He walked around to the driver's side where Kristene sat. He wanted to get her reaction from the show Alisha had just put on.

"Give me your phone so that I can put my number in it," he eyed her.

She handed it to him and said, "I'll take the rest of this money to your mom's."

"Oh no you don't," Bone totally objected to that idea. "She ain't taking her cut. I'll issue it to her." Ms. J will take a whole bag if it was left up to her. "Take it to your house and put it in the closet. Call me when you get home so I know you made it safely."

Kristene got out of the truck, grabbed Bone's head with both of her hands and kissed him long, and hard.

"Wow!"

It had been over five years since they kissed. A wave of emotions smothered Kristene. She did not want to let him go. She wouldn't let him go. Not anymore. When this issue he was dealing with was over she would take her husband back home. She refused to lose him again to the streets.

"Whoa, baby girl," Bone said once they separated. "Do you know how long it's been since we did that?"

"Five years, nineteen days, and eight hours." Kristene stated matter-of-factly."

Bone stared at her wide-eyed.

"Yeah," Kristene smiled. "I've been counting." She jumped back into the truck. "Now kiss your daughter so we can go."

Bone opened the back door and kissed Imani on her forehead. Kristene turned her seat to face him before he closed the door.

"When this is over you call me and I'll come get you," she said. "I want you home."

"Why?" Bone asked. "Because of all this money?"

"Because Imani needs her daddy."

And I need my husband, she thought to herself.

Bone stared at her for a long moment.

She meant it.

He closed the door and backed up.

Kristene started up the truck and pulled out. She stopped next to Karin's car and rolled the window down, "Bye Karin."

"See you later, love," Karin replied.

Kristene wasn't done with her goodbyes. "Come here for a second, Alisha."

Alisha walked up slowly. "What's up?" She asked flatly.

"Please make sure that *my* husband makes it home to *me* safe and sound," Kristene whispered and drove off laughing.

"Bitch," Alisha muttered.

"Okay," Bone said after he witnessed the exchange, "Lace me up on what's going on before we go up in here." He looked over at Alisha. "Un-poke that lip, Alisha. We got unfinished bizness to handle."

***

"Mr. Bone!"

"Boss Hog!"

They were embracing. Bone and Boss Hog went back about fifteen years. Bone was hustling with a Cuban ho at the time, and Boss Hog claimed that she beat him out of some money. The trick got tricked. Boss Hog thought that he could buy a renegade permanently and got duped. In his frustration at how things turned out he lashed out, and Bone pistol-whipped him. A week later Bone saved him from two jacker's out for his Cutlass on Dayton wires. Boss Hog proved to be a great asset, too. He was married to a Hispanic woman whose brothers were connected. As long as he treated their sister right he never had to worry about high prices in the dope game. Cocaine was dirt cheap and the marijuana was free. Free weed?

Great asset.

They were all in a den that was built onto the back of Boss Hog's house. He did all street business in the den. There was a play-pen couch, an easy chair, a pool table, dart board, and a fish tank back there. The typical lounge room, except for the thugs inside it. Since Boss Hog had started running with Bone he learned how to pay street thugs to do his dirty work. There were plenty of out-of-work ex-convicts floating around Artesia Blvd, and in order to keep them from plotting on your operation, you threw business their way. Tonight they would make some bread.

"You know the crew right?" Boss Hog asked.

"Oh, yeah," Bone replied. "That's Erin Love, Billy Seals, and Stevie Bradford." Bone knew them all well.

"There you go with that bullshit, William." Billy had a smirk on his face. "Always puttin' a brothaz real shit in the streets."

"Okay, okay...Billy!" Bone smiled at him.

None of them ever used their real names in the streets, but each one knew the other. Between the sub-stations and the prisons they all frequented, the real came out. Erin was "Baby Slick; six-four, black as coal, at two hundred and eighty pounds. Bill was Dirty "B"; six-three and a half, three hundred solid pounds, high yellow, with a long ponytail. Dirty B was a pretty boy with a hidden agenda. Stevie was "Low Down"; five-three, a hundred and twenty pounds, with coke-bottle glasses. Low Down was as black as the ace of spades, bald-headed, with a scar running down the left side of his face from a robbery gone bad; just the right crew for the task at hand.

"Gentlemen," Bone started, "We got a small mission tonight, with a big pay-off." He strolled over to the pool table and stood beside it. Bone pulled out four stacks of hundred dollar bill; ten thousand a stack. He laid them on the table.

"Ten grand a piece." Bone looked at their faces for a shocked looked. There was none. "Is that enough?"

The all nodded in agreement. All business. Boss Hog got ten G's just for his accommodations.

Bone began to lay out his plan to the most treacherous dudes he had ever come across in the streets. Actually, in his whole life. It made him wonder just how crazy he would get in certain situations--birds of a feather.

At the end of Bone's presentation, Karin brought in a duffel bag full of hoodies and leather gloves, so they all could suit up. They were about to get hard in the paint.

***

There was a mellow breeze blowing through the Marina. It was just enough to blow the women's dressed up and mess up the men's hair. A summer breeze off of the coast of Southern California was cool for some--salty for others.

Four men and two women boarded Ms. Sue. Ms. Sue was a 98-foot yacht; an express cruiser with four staterooms, a top-deck Jacuzzi, with limed oak paneling on the deck floor. The main salon housed the bar and dining room. Retractable glass panels separated the main salon from the aft deck. Soft-touch vinyl couches and lounge chairs were positioned on the aft-deck for a lounge area.

Center stage.

"I'm going to take this one below to get her cleaned up," Danny said. "If you want a drink the bar is right here." He retracted the class panel. Danny tapped the top of the bar as they descended into the hull.

"See what kind of beer the Chinos drink, Little Johnny," John said. "If they don't have beer pour some cognac for everybody. You like cognac?" He asked Marie.

She just nodded then said, "I need to use the bathroom."

"Tino," John said, "Take the lady to the restroom down below."

They both got up and went downstairs. There was a bathroom right at the bottom of the steps, so they didn't have to go far. When Marie opened the door Tino tried to go in with her.

"It cost money to watch me pee, son," she said and closed the door in his face.

"Bitch," he muttered. Tino wished that his dad would've hit her in the mouth for what she did to him.

Down the hallway in the Master Stateroom Danny whispered to René, "You okay? He asked."

She nodded.

"Bone will be here later on tonight. He and my dad talked this afternoon. He's got a plan for that asshole up top. Okay?"

She just nodded. René did not want to talk. She didn't want to hear how she sounded without her teeth, and she especially didn't want anyone to see.

"I got a sweat suit and a T-shirt in the closet," Danny continued. "You can go in the bathroom and get cleaned up. Okay?"

René nodded.

"I got a cousin that's a dentist," Danny offered. "You want me to call him?"

She shook her head. René knew that she should have somebody look at her mouth. All of that would have to wait. She wanted to see Bone re-pay John for what he had done to her.

Danny got up and got the clothes out of the closet. He set them down on the toilet seat with two towels. "If you need more towels let me know." He walked over to the mini-bar. "You want a drink?"

René nodded. She wished that Marie were in the room with them. René wanted a hit of cocaine.

In the bathroom down the hall Marie was running sink water while she hit her pipe. She had so much dope on it you would've thought that she was in the kitchen frying bacon. As she blew the smoke out Marie started to feel like she was walking in a dark tunnel. She sat down on the toilet. *I have to get René and myself away from these punks,* she thought. Only a punk would hit a woman in her mouth with a pistol. A faggot might do it, too.

Marie lit up a cigarette as her mind floated down that dark tunnel of cocaine induced thoughts. As she drifted along, she started to see light. There was a small obstacle between her and that light; a little risky getting passed it, but she had to try it. She had to get René some help. Marie cut the sink water off and came out.

"It's all yours, little boy," she said to Tino as she blew cigarette smoke in his face.

He pushed her toward the stairs.

Back on deck they both took a seat; Marie on one of the couches and Tino in a lounge chair. Marie sat as close to the rail as possible and as far away from them as she could.

John picked up on her distance from them and picked up her drink and brought it to her. He sat down right next to her. As straight as she shot who knew what other tricks she knew.

"You don't want to be anti-social do you?" John handed her a drink.

"You drink out of it first," Marie ordered.

"Do I look that clever?"

"No, but that China man does."

John took a sip and tried to pass it to her.

Marie picked up his snifter and drank from it.

"This one will do for me," she smiled at him.

"Whatever. Your friends are taking their sweet little time in calling me. I think I'll call them so that they can bring me my merchandise and take you back to your world."

"Fine with me," Marie said. She flicked her cigarette into the water.

John reached in his pocket for his phone.

Marie reached in her pocket for her cigarette pack. She offered him one.

John declined. He punched in Karin's number.

Marie cupped her hands around her mouth and struck her lighter.

John put the phone to his ear.

Marie still inhaled.

John's lips started moving.

Marie was back in the tunnel.

With one swift move, Marie poked him in the eye with her hot pipe. She leaned into him hard trying to burn all the way though to his brain. John screamed. Marie was on top of him. She looked over her shoulder and saw Little Johnny pulling his pistol out to shoot her. Marie stepped in John's lap and dove over the side of the yacht. She heard two small pops in her tunnel. The windows shattered on the yacht in front of her. Little Johnny missed. She hit the water.

Splash.

Marie swam under the yacht to the other side. She came up slowly for air, got it, and went under the next boat. She went under two more boats until she came up on a walkway. The sun had just gone down, so outside of the lights along the walkways, all was dark. Marie did her best work in the dark. After all, she was a Lady of the Night. She was going to get her girlfriends and Bone. After all, it was their mess, anyway. She would help them get René off of that boat and smother those punks, though. Marie smiled to herself. "This is better than chasing cars."

Chapter Twenty-four

"Aaah!" John screamed into the phone. "Shoot this bitch!" he screamed into Karin's ear. "Get her off of me!"

Karin held the phone away from her ear. The screams felt like they were piercing her brain. She made out whom the scream belonged to, though. John. One of her girlfriends was fighting him and winning.

She walked over to Bone and handed him the phone.

"Who is this?" He asked.

"A victim," she smiled. "Either René or Marie attacked their captor right as he made the call, because I heard him screaming, 'shoot the bitch' and, 'get her off of me.'"

"It's about time one of them caught him slippin'," Bone said. He put the phone to his ear, but he couldn't make out what they were saying. All he heard was a lot of different dudes yelling.

Someone picked up the phone.

"Find that bitch and bring her back to me with her lungs full of salt water."

They were at a Marina, Bone thought, *Which one?*

"Hello!" John yelled into the phone.

Bone pulled the phone away from his ear. "You don't have to yell, kid," he said, with a trace of humor in his voice. "I can hear you're having a problem with your guests."

"Oh, yeah!" John yelled. "You're gonna hear these bitch's brains splatter on the wall if you don't bring them diamonds." John's whole head was on fire. He talked into the phone with both eyes tightly shut.

"Calm down, kid," Bone said casually. "I got your stones. I'm a little busy right now, though, so you'll just have to wait."

"I don't give a fuck what you're do..."

"Now listen up!" Bone hissed. "It's not my fault your bitch-made-ass got caught slippin'. Just be glad I'm being nice enough to give you these punk ass stone back." Bone was tired of this trick. "Now, I'm gonna finish what I gotta do, first. What you need to do is let me know where to meet you around midnight."

John hadn't discussed using Mr. Chin's yacht for the transaction, but so what. They were his diamonds so why not meet on his yacht.

"The Marina in Long Beach," he finally responded. "There will be a red Dodge Magnum in the parking lot. My men in that car will escort you to me."

Ms. Sue, Bone thought. *Good.* He could sleep with the fishes.

"Touch another hair on those two women and you'll come up missin' like Jimmy Hoffa." Bone pressed the end button.

Bone dialed Mr. Chin's number.

"Canton's," he answered.

"I got five of your seven headed your way, Papasan."

Mr. Chin was proud of Willie. He was diverse enough in his game to deal in the underworld on any level. That kind of hustler deserved to be paid homage.

"Give the other two to Ms. J," Mr. Chin instructed.

"Oh, she'll love that!" Bone laughed. "Papasan, where is Danny?"

"He's on Ms. Sue," Mr. Chin paused. "John is out there, son. Don't sink her."

"Not in this lifetime, Papasan."

"Then your stage has been set."

"Okay." Bone was all business. "Look for two lovely ladies dressed in all black in about thirty minutes."

"Be careful, son," Mr. Chin advised Bone one more time.

"You be careful with these ladies I'm sending your way," Bone hung up. He turned to Alisha and Karin. They were all ears.

"Go to Papasan's and come right back," he said firmly. "I don't care what he offers you to stay." Bone started laughin.

Don't worry, love," countered Karin. "We got our trick for the evening already," she grabbed his ass. "And you're throwing around more cash than he would." They all started laughing.

Alisha walked up and grabbed Bone in his crotch. She had an unanswered question, and she searched his eyes for the answer.

She caught a glimpse of it and smiled. "I love you, baby," she whispered.

Bone couldn't find the words to describe the way he felt about Alisha. She was the only woman there for him when he was locked up. Now she had just made him a very rich man. She had been in the right place at the right time, and she loved Bone enough to let him control the score. He owed her more than just a lay in a hotel room. Alisha was responsible for putting a whole lot of people over the hump.

"You know," he wrapped his arms around her waist and pulled her to him, "I don't know what to say right now."

"Tell me you'll keep me on your team after you go home to your wife."

"Alisha..."

"Shhh," she put her finger to his lips. "I'm a ho, Willie. I know the game, baby boy. You got a wife and a down ass bottom bitch: me. You're too good of a man for me to be trippin', so if I gotta share you with Kristene then that's the bizness." She kissed his nose. "Just make sure this bitch right here has a bigger house than she does." She giggled. Alisha had just given Bone a bird in his hand and two in the bush.

Wow!

"You are more amazing than they give you credit for."

"Boy, please!" She slapped him on his chest. "*You* knew I was a sharp bitch when you met me. Thank you for putting me in the spot light. Did I shine?"

"In more ways than one," Bone said passionately.

"Come on, girlfriend," Karin interrupted their moment. "Let's take care of our *bizness* and get our girls back, before you get freaky."

Karin's phone rang.

"Hello?" Bone answered.

"Bone!" Marie yelled. "Come and...get...me," she was pant from running.

"Slow down, home girl. Where are you?"

"I just jumped off a boat in the Marina. They still got René..."

"Marie!" Bone barked. "Catch a cab to the Batcave."

"The Batcave?" She wasn't thinking straight. Then it came to her. "Oh! I haven't been there since you went down."

"Get re-acquainted," he pressed the end button. Bone handed Karin her phone back. "Marie should be a blond."

Alisha and Karin fell out laughing.

"What?" Bone didn't get the joke.

"She is!" They both cried.

***

At the sound of screaming Danny ran up on deck to see what was going on. All he saw was John holding his left eye and his sons were shooting silenced bullets over into the water.

The other girl did some damage and went overboard, he thought.

Good.

The shooting was not good.

"Stop all of that damn shooting, dumb asses!" Danny said bitterly. To John he said, "Let me see your eye."

John removed his hand, but he couldn't open his eye. It hurt too much. He shook his head. "It hurts too bad, Danny."

"I'll get something to wrap it up with."

"Bring René back up here, too," John told him. "I can't afford to let her get away."

Danny descended once again into the hull. This time he was smiling. He walked back in the room to see René's worried eyes.

"Your girlfriend did something to John's eye and jumped ship." He saw a wave of relief come over her face. Danny had found a notepad and a pen earlier, and René was using them to communicate with him.

She was scribbling furiously. She handed the notepad to him. (Marie will go and get Bone now. (Smile). Marie's a crazy white bitch.)

"I just hope that Willie let's her know that I'm on you guys' side." Danny smiled.

René grinned but did not show any part of the inside of her mouth.

Danny felt sorry for René. She reminded him of his sister right now: helpless and scared. She was showing bravery on the surface, but deep down inside there was a strong undercurrent of fear. That made Danny furious. He wanted to kill John himself. René recognized the look on Danny's face. She waved at him to give her the pad back. He handed it to her. She scribbled some big bold letters on it and handed it back to him.

Danny looked at it and smiled. "Very soon, René. Very soon."

She winked at him.

***

Bone's phone rang. "It's about time you called." It was Kristene, "Everything straight?"

"I stopped at Mickey D's for your daughter," she replied.

"I thought that you headed to Sancho's."

"Who the heck is Sancho?" She asked.

"Sancho is whatever guy that took care of you for the past forty months," Bone stated.

"Boy, please," Kristene teased. "Sancho is not worth no ten million dollars. He'll be lucky to get a hundred thousand."

"Who is that fool?" Bone barked.

"Ah-ha. Touched a nerve, huh?" She laughed. "Unlike you, Willie, I honor the vows that we made to each other with God as our witness."

Kristene was a devoted Christian woman with morals and principles like Mother Teresa.

"Anyway," Bone changed the subject. "I'm glad you made it home safe. This issue I'm dealing with will be over soon."

"Do you want me to still come and get you?" The answer to that question would let Kristene know if Bone had changed. His old self would be staying in the streets tonight.

Staying with Alisha.

"When I call you, just meet me at the Batcave," he replied. "You do know how to get there don't cha'?"

"Yes, I know how to get to your Batcave." Kristene hid her excitement. "Be careful, Willie."

Bone knew that he gave her the answer that she was looking for, so he tried his hand. "Don't wear nothing but my jersey when you come." His jersey was just long enough to cover her ass. Seeing her behind the wheel of that Cadillac dressed like that would be a good jumpstart for his hormones.

"Don't push it, boy," she hung up on him.

Damn!

"Boss Hog!" He called out. "Let's ride."

"Call your boy and let him know we're comin'," he said as he came out of the kitchen.

Bone went through his Recent Calls list, found the number and pressed Send.

"Are you ready for my friend?" Hassan asked.

"I'm on my way to you right now," Bone replied.

"Twenty minutes."

"Done." Bone hung up. He turned to Boss Hog and winked.

"Listen up," Boss Hog addressed the thug crew. "Go out to the Marina and post up. As soon as you see that Dodge Magnum snatch whoever's in it up and call."

They all nodded and headed out of the door.

"Hey Hog," Bone almost forgot, "Marie got away and I told her to catch a cab over here."

Boss Hog sighed. "Ericka, If Marie shows up Bone told her to catch a cab over her. Pay for it and let her in the back." Boss Hog waited for his wife to protest.

"Okay!" She yelled from the kitchen.

"You know she only said okay because of you, right?"

"I'm not the one getting caught with my swipe in a ho's mouth that's why." Bone started laughing.

"Fuck you."

***

Danny wrapped John's head up with a wad of gauze under a silk scarf. That would have to be enough for now. He could go to an emergency room after he took care of his business.

If he lived.

"That's all I can do for you, John."

"Huh?" John was caught up in his own thoughts. He couldn't wait until this ordeal was over; a dildo in his son's ass, and now a crack pipe in his eye. A hot crack pipe. This issue was leaving more bad memories than he cared to remember.

"Thanks, Danny," he muttered. "I need to call your father and let him know what's going on." The time was drawing near. He would have the diamonds and this will be over. No more prostitutes, no more drugs; no more headaches. He rubbed his temples to ease the headache that he had.

He downed his drink, too.

Danny walked over and stood behind the bar. It was just him René and John aboard. Tino and Little Johnny were out in the parking lot scoping the scene.

Waiting.

The infected pimple had come to an ugly head. It wasn't just going to pop either. It was going to explode; spreading its poison all over, touching a few people.

Infecting them.

John dialed the number to Canton's.

"This is Chin."

"Mr. Chin, this is John. I'm out here with your..."

"I know where you are, John," Mr. Chin said flatly. "That is not my concern!" he barked at him. "Where is my merchandise?" Mr. Chin wanted to keep John off balance. Mentally. Hopefully, it would give the clear mind of William and his son Daniel, the upper hand in the situation.

"It is en-route, sir. Everything will be taken care of by midnight." John's hand was shaking. He needed another drink. The situation was tense. Someone was going to die.

"For your sake, John, I hope you are telling me the truth." Mr. Chin hung up on him.

John got up and walked to the bar. Instead of pouring a drink, he drank from the bottle.

***

Mr. Chin heard the bell above his front door chime. He looked up and saw two beautiful women walking his way: Ladies of the Night. dressed in all black. One of them carried a big duffel bag.

My money, he thought. Mr. Chin stood up and met them halfway.

"Mr. Chin?" Karin asked.

"That is I, lovely lady." He took Karin's hand and kissed it.

Karin gestured toward the bag that Alisha was setting down. "Here is your money, sir."

"And, thank you," Alisha added.

"And why are you thanking me, young lady?" Mr. Chin asked.

"For the break we needed to get off of the streets."

Mr. Chin looked at both women and just nodded.

After a moment of awkward silence Karin spoke. "We gotta get going, Mr. Chin. We gotta save our girlfriend from some chumps."

"One?" he asked. "I thought that they were holding two women."

"They were," Alisha answered. "Marie did somethin' crazy and got away. She probably burned John with a hot crack pipe or somethin'."

"Good for her," Mr. Chin smiled. "Tell William that I will take a rain check on you two."

They looked at each other and laughed.

Men.

Chapter Twenty-five

The cab pulled up in front of the Batcave. Marie sat up front with the driver. She had been dripping water off of her body when he picked her up, so he suggested that she sit up front where the heater blew directly on her. Marie jumped out of the cab and ran to the back gate.

"Hey, lady!" The Cabbie yelled. "Don't make me shoot you about my money."

"Relax, Ronnie," Marie said softly. "I told you that my homeboy would pay you when we got here. Kick back, man." She rang the bell on the gate.

"He better pay," he grumbled. Forty-eight dollars was a lot of money to Ronnie. *Ten minutes in the back seat with her would clear the tab*, he thought.

Ericka saw the cab pull up and Marie jump out. She could hear the bell on the side gate ringing through the house. Bitch. *How dare that bitch come here showing her home-wrecking ass around here? Bone had better hurry up and get back here*, Ericka thought. She went out of the front door, walked down to the cab, and leaned in the window.

"How much?" She asked the Cabbie.

"Forty-eight dollars and twenty-seven cents."

Ericka tossed two twenties and a ten dollar bill onto the front seat. Ronnie saluted her and pulled off. She turned around and started walking toward Marie. *Is she shivering?* Marie bounced from foot-to-foot on the side of the house. She was cold. Her clothes were wet from her little swim in the ocean and the salt water was irritating her skin. She turned at the sound of the cab pulling off and saw Ericka coming her way.

Damn.

"Listen, Ericka..."

"Are you wet?" Ericka asked.

"Yeah," Marie answered.

"What happened?" Ericka's concern over-rode all of her bitterness. Her mother always told her to help people in need. Marie was in need.

"I jumped in the ocean getting away from these dudes." Her teeth were chattering now, and she was hugging herself.

"Come on in the house. I got something for you to change into while I wash and dry your clothes," Ericka said warmly.

"You don't have to..."

"Come on!" Ericka ordered and headed for the front door.

With no hesitation Marie followed her, relieved that they weren't fighting.

***

Boss Hog pulled in behind the Range Rover and Bone jumped out. He strolled up to the passenger side window, and Hassan gestured for him to get in.

"Willie, I want to do something with you after you take care of your issue." Hassan liked his style. He had a few rough edges that Hassan could use in his circle.

Bone thought for a moment then he spoke. "Why?"

Hassan started laughing. "For one, you are going to need a man with money," he pointed to himself, "To teach you how to get all of that damn cash circulating without legal problems. For two, I got a club in Hollywood that needs that subtle rough edge that you have. For three, I like you, Willie, and you need to see a different side of the game...finer things."

The next level of the game, Bone thought, *a formal invitation, from a respected jewelry dealer, into the big business world.* What more could a convicted felon ask for? "Do I get my clothes tailored for free?"

They both started laughing.

Hassan handed Bone what he asked for, and they shook hands.

"I'll call you Monday after I go and see this parole agent," Bone stated.

"When you come out of his office just come to my jewelry store." Hassan handed him a business card.

Bone got out of the Range Rover and got back in with Boss Hog. "Let's roll," Bone said. As they pulled off he looked over at Hog. He looked tired, not sleepy. Weary. "You ready for a change, fat boy?"

"Change? You mean the penitentiary or the grave?" Boss Hog sighed. "Ain't no other way out for me."

"I got another way, homie!" Bone declared excitedly.

"Nah. I'm ghetto fabulous, Bone. I'll do a lil' somethin' wit' cha', but leave me in the trenches." As they turned to get on the freeway Boss Hog looked over at Bone and smiled. He slammed his foot down on the gas pedal and shot them up the on-ramp of the Harbor Freeway.

"Ghetto fabulous, Bone!" Boss Hog cried and passed Bone the joint.

***

They all pulled up at the Batcave at the same time. Karin jumped out of her car and ran up to Boss Hog's truck. She bounced from foot-to-foot.

"Give me your keys, Hog," she pleaded. "I gotta pee."

"Here," he put his hands out of the window, "Piss right here."

"That's gonna cost you, fat boy," Karin shook her titties in his face. All of the girls had gotten money out of Boss Hog at one time or another. "Come on with the keys, man."

Boss Hog handed her the keys and Karin ran off. He looked over at Bone with a big grin on his face.

"That's why Ericka's gonna blow your fat ass away," Bone stated. "Keep on trickin' with them hoes at the pad, Hog, and you won't have to worry about catchin' a case."

"Let me handle this, Bone," Boss Hog said as he slid out of his truck. He made the inside of his for F-150 look like the inside of an El Camino: stuffy. "Let me do the trickin' and you do the pimpin'.

"I ain't no pimp," Bone declared.

"Yeah, and Bill Clinton didn't get his candle blew out in the Oval Office." Boss Hog started laughing as he walked off.

Bone just shook his head. He got out of the truck and walked over to Karin's car. Alisha sat inside with her head hung low. *What's wrong now?* He thought. As he got closer he saw that it was nothing wrong, but all the way right.

"Fire this up," she said and passed Bone a fat chronic joint. Alisha got out of the car and said, "Let's go see if Marie made it."

"Oh, yeah," Bone remembered. "Let's get the bizness from her before she goes into full blond-mode."

***

"This is bullshit, man," Little Johnny complained. "We should just go and torture this bitch until she tells us where her fucking pimp is hiding with the diamonds."

Tino and Little Johnny were sitting in the parking lot of the Marina. Tino was nervous. He had done some tough-guy stuff before, but he was never comfortable with it. He just hoped that this situation didn't call for him to be some Dirty Harry that he wasn't.

"I need some cigarettes," Tino said, and got out of the car to walk over to the gas station.

As he walked out of the parking lot a Kawasaki ZRX 1100 pulled in, followed by a 2001 Monte Carlo. Baby Slick was on the motorcycle; Dirty 'B' and Low Down were in the Monte Carlo. Baby Slick spotted the Red Dodge Magnum and pulled right up on the driver's side. He gestured for Little Johnny to roll down his window. *This must be Bone*, Little Johnny thought. *He came by himself. Idiot.*

Little Johnny rolled down his window. "We've been expecting you," he said sarcastically.

With his left hand Baby slick raised his helmet. "Did you expect this?" He pulled his right hand out of his coat pocket and fired.

Little Johnny was not expecting that.

Baby Slick waved his homies over. Dirty 'B' pulled in next to the Magnum on the passenger side. He and Low Down got out. Dirty 'B' reached behind his seat for the rope while Low Down slid into the Magnum's passenger seat.

"This fool is snorin', Baby Slick," Low Down started laughing.

"Man, just tie the pink-toe up, so we can go get us a drink." Baby slick pulled out his phone to call Bone while Low Down and Dirty 'B' tied Little Johnny up.

Phase one was complete.

***

Behind a row of bushes outlining the parking lot Tino watched in total shock as three dudes were stuffing his brother into the trunk of a car. He dug in his pocket for his phone. He left it in the car. It was up to him to help his brother.

"Shit," he muttered.

***

Bone's phone rang. "Talk to me, I talk back!" He cried.

"Check it out, Bone," Baby Slick started, "We got pink-toe tied up and in the trunk of the Monte 'C'. What next?"

The hunter's scout has been captured, Bone thought. *Time to go and take the hunter down.*

"Good job," Bone replied. "Now, there's a yacht out there name Ms. Sue. Find her and just post up. We're on our way. If anybody leaves before we get there send Dirty 'B' behind them and call. Other than that, don't move." He hung up.

Bone looked over at Marie running her mouth to Karin and Alisha. Boss Hog stood off to the side watching her licking his lips like a hungry lion. Marie would not be staying behind.

"Marie," Bone called out, "Change clothes with Karin. You're going with me."

"She can't fit my clothes, Bone," Karin whined. She was mad because she knew that she was being left behind.

"She could if she had a trick that wanted her in all black, huh?" It wasn't a question. Bone knew that they exchanged clothes all the time. Whether they fit or not, they would make it look good. Their profession called for it. "Besides," he continued, "Marie can shoot better than all of us. I need her on point."

"I wanna blow that punks head off, anyway!" Marie added.

Karin sighed. She got up and took off her coat. She tossed it over Marie's head. "My shit better come back like I give it to you, bitch. If not," Karin smiled, "You'll sell ass for me until *I* decide you've re-paid me."

"What about my jersey dress, Karin?" Marie countered. "I haven't seen that in two months."

"You said it was too long for you!" Karin got loud. "As a matter-of-fact, I gave you ten dollars for that dress. Gas money if I remember the story right. Don't start, Marie!" Karin yelled.

Hooker's hang-ups: clothes. Bone had heard every clothes argument and every make-up discussion in the world. He once saw a girl get stabbed over an eye brow pencil. *This was not the time to be entertained by two hoes on some otha shit,* he thought.

"Come on, Karin," Bone said coolly, "Shake that ass out of them jeans and shit, baby, so we can go."

"Yeah, Karin," Boss Hog added.

They all looked over at him.

Beads of sweat formed on his forehead and he licked his lips furiously.

The whole den roared with laughter.

Ericka stood in the doorway shaking her head.

***

Tino's mind raced. Three dudes had his brother tied up and stuffed in the trunk of their car. He had no phone to contact his dad for help, and he didn't have the heart to take all three dudes on by himself. Fear gripped him to the point of immobility. *How in the hell am I going to get my brother free? Three against one. They had to have guns. I can't even shoot straight,* he thought.

He took out a cigarette. As soon as he struck the match to light it he instantly regretted it. All three guys looked in his direction. He blew the match out just as fast as he lit it and stood still. It didn't matter now—they were coming his way.

***

"Did you see that shit, Dirty 'B'?" Low Down asked. He pointed at the bushes that separated the parking lot from the street.

"It looked like somebody flicked a lighter in them bushes, huh?" Dirty 'B' asked.

"Yep." Low Down got out of the car and walked over to Baby Slick. He was the unofficial leader of their mission. "We got us a fan," Low Down informed Baby Slick, and pointed toward the bushes again.

Baby Slick gestured for Dirty 'B' to join them. As they all started walking toward the row of bushes Baby slick said, "Fan out."

They all took out silenced pistols and cocked them. At about two car lengths apart, they converged on the spot where they saw the light.

Baby Slick slipped in between a tree at the start of a line of bushes. He peaked around the bushes. Nothing. He waved for his boys to move in on the spot.

Low Down ran and jumped over the bush directly in front of him. Nothing. He looked under the truck in front of him. Nothing.

Dirty 'B' squatted down right in front of the bushes and looked in them. Nothing.

Baby Slick walked toward them, but he was looking under every car in between. He didn't see anybody. When he got up on Low Down and Dirty 'B' he looked at them strange.

"I saw a lighter flick damn it!" Low Down barked.

"I saw it, too," Dirty 'B' confirmed the sight.

"Go get a drink, Low Down." Baby Slick sound disgusted. "Maybe that'll help you see better. Dirty, go back to the car while I go and look for this boat," he shook his head. "You niggaz ain't shit unless you loaded."

They all walked off.

In the back of the truck Tino let out a soft sigh of relief.

***

John's vision was blurry. He had not one, but three too many cognacs. It didn't matter. With the way things were going, Bone wouldn't show up with the diamonds. *I'll kill René and*

Danny will kill me, John thought. *That's why Danny was hanging out anyway; to put a bullet in my head*, he mused.

Twelve midnight. Fifteen minutes, and I'll just shoot both René and Danny. Yeah, right. That will make my situation just that much more lovely. Kill Mr. Chin's son. Might as well bite down on a bullet myself, John thought, as things came into focus and blurred once again.

Way too much cognac.

***

Bone, Alisha, and Marie pulled up next to the Monte Carlo. Low Down and Dirty 'B' were both turning up bottles wrapped up in paper bags.

"Where's Baby Slick?" Bone was irritated.

They both pointed toward the public restroom. Bone got out of the car when he saw Baby Slick. He walked over to him.

"Why did you give them cats something to drink, Slick?"

"Come one, Bone," he replied. "You know them niggaz ain't shit unless their head is a little fuzzy."

Baby Slick had a point, Bone thought. There was no doubt in Bone's mind that Low Down and Dirty 'B' couldn't handle the job. A stiff drink to the liver just made it easier to deal with street situations.

"Alcohol to them is like weed to me," Bone finally conceded.

Baby Slick just nodded.

"I located the boat." Baby Slick gave Bone the business. "Two dudes and René. I got some chump tied up in the Monte 'C'."

"You're missin' one," Bone observed. "Marie said that it was four dudes.

Baby Slick's eyes got wide. "There was somebody watchin' us from behind those bushes," he pointed, "But we didn't catch him."

"I told you to keep a lid on this can!" Bone barked. "No flaws and no gaps, Slick."

"Come on, Bone," Baby Slick was unmoved by Bone's outburst. "Let's go get René and melt these marks down."

Bone sighed. Flaws and gaps in the game get filled up in an ugly way. "The China man is my boy, Slick," he stated. "Just remember that much and you won't have no problem out of me."

"And if I don't?" Baby Slick was teasing Bone.

"Then I sock you up like I did before I went down." Bone smiled as he threw a jab in Baby Slick's direction.

They walked back over to the cars. Everybody stood around. Ready. "Pop the trunk and throw that clown over your shoulder, Dirty 'B'," Baby Slick commanded.

Dirty 'B' popped the trunk and was about to pull Little Johnny out of the trunk, but Bone stopped him. Bone recognized the face instantly. Although it was a younger version, there was no question in Bone's mind who the kid belonged to.

"Marie," he started, "What's this kid's name?"

Marie walked over to the trunk and looked inside. "That's the one that they call Little Johnny."

"Johnny Cantwell," Bone smiled. "Johnny Cantwell, and Steven Stone. Two unsuccessful thieves. They used to do small-time robberies. Started doing speed real bad and robbed one of my girls for five ounces and fifteen hundred." Bone lifted Little Johnny out of the trunk and slung him over his own shoulder. "Let's see how Papa John reacts to me bringing junior to him."

***

On the outskirts of the parking lot Tino watched Bone carrying his brother toward Ms. Sue. He never saw his brother again.

Chapter Twenty-six

René heard footsteps on the walkway. A lot of them. She looked to her right and saw them coming. Her eyes showed the smile that her mouth did not. Her head had been throbbing every since John had hit her in the mouth. René wasn't dwelling on the loss of her teeth, though. At the moment she just wanted her head to stop pounding. The sight of her friends coming down the walkway made her headache subside.

John must've heard the footsteps, too. He watched the group of underworld players coming his way. He cocked his pistol, grabbed René and sat down on the port side of the lounge. He looked over at Danny who was behind the bar. Danny's look told John that he was on his own.

Alisha and Marie boarded Ms. Sue first. They each took a position in front of the bar. Alisha winked at René and fanned back her trench coat: twelve gauge.

Baby Slick boarded next and stood right next to the steps. Bone boarded right behind him with Little Johnny on his shoulder. Low Down and Dirty 'B' stayed on the walkway.

John's eyes got as big as silver dollars at the sight of Bone carrying his son. *What in the hell was Willie doing here?* He wondered.

"Willie?" It was evident that John was confused. "What are you doing he…" Then it dawned on him. "Bone." *How could I be so stupid*, John thought. He had never put two and two together. The man who knew all about the hoes on Artesia Blvd.

Willie Braxton.

"Who else would come, but the only man who can get his candle blew out for free on Artesia," Bone smiled. "Johnny Cantwell," Bone said as he laid Johnny junior on the couch at the starboard side of Ms. Sue. "I brought you a gift. I don't like the new look you got going on." He talked about the eye patch.

"If you hurt my boy..."

"Shut up, chump!" Bone cut him off. He looked over a Danny and said, "Take us out to sea, bro."

"Untie us and we're off," Danny replied.

Baby Slick motioned to his boy's on the walkway to take care of that.

Low Down and Dirty 'B' untied Ms. Sue as Danny started her up. With the ropes slung aboard their job was done. It was the easiest ten grand that they had every made in their life.

John was stunned. He was sobering up. Not only had he run into an old enemy, but also the boat that he was on was owned by his enemies advocate. Wow. *How in the hell do I get out of this?* He wondered.

"Look, Willie..."

"It's Bone, John," he corrected him quickly. "Family and friends call me Willie. You're too damn pink to be family, and you fucked off our friendship years ago."

So he remembered that stunt me and Steve pulled on that hooker in the Motel 6. If I'd known that she was working for Willie, we would've given her a pass, John thought.

 Too late now.

"Okay, Bone," John stated, "Just give me the diamonds, untie my son and you can be on your way."

Bone started laughing. As Danny started pulling out of the slip, Bone sat down. He untied Little Johnny and sat him up in the corner of the couch. He looked over at John and laughed some more.

"Haven't you noticed something, John?" Bone waved his hand at his crew. "You ain't in control of this here show, kid. You lost control the day you met her." he pointed at René. "But, if it's stones that you want," Bone dug in his coat pocket and tossed John a pouch, "Then here."

As soon as John stretched his hand out to catch the pouch René tore away from him and ran to Bone's side. John wasn't concerned with her anymore. He had that familiar pouch back in his possession. He opened it up to examine the contents and froze.

While John was examining the content of the pouch Bone waved Baby Slick over to the couch. He came over to where Little

Johnny was positioned and waved some smelling salt under his nose. He was coming around slowly, so Baby Slick slapped him.

At the sound of the slap, John snapped out of his shocked state of mind. John had been dealing with diamonds for fifteen years and what he saw in the pouch were not diamonds. Bone had tossed him a pouch of zircons… *His boy is slapping my son on top of all of that*, he fumed.

"Hey mother…," John raised his pistol.

"Hey what, motha fucka!" Alisha barked. She had that pistol-grip-pump 12 gauge trained on him.

He lowered his gun. "What the fuck are these, Bone?" John questioned the stones in the pouch.

Bone wasn't listening. He was looking at René funny. "You alright?" He asked her.

She just nodded.

"What the fuck do that mean?" No one told Bone what John had did to René. "Talk to me, baby girl. Did he hurt you?"

He doesn't know, René thought. "My mouf," she said, and opened her mouth for Bone to see.

Bone's eyes turned into slits. He did not look like anything normal. It was as if a demon had just possessed his mind. Bone was no longer present. He allowed every demonic spirit that he had ever fought in his whole life, to take control of his every move. Marie watched him. She saw the transformation going on in his mind and followed suit.

"Give me that pistol, punk!" Marie barked as she pulled the pistol-grip gauge she had.

John hesitated.

She jacked it off.

"Shoot that fool, Marie!" Bone said bitterly as he stood up.

John slid her his gun. She didn't shoot him.

"When I tell you to do somethin', bitch," Bone snatched the gauge from her, "I mean that!" Bone stuck the barrel against John's left knee and pulled the trigger.

Everyone heard John scream, but Bone. He saw with tunnel vision. Blind fury was in control. Bone nodded at Baby Slick, who slapped Little Johnny in the mouth with his pistol. Once again, he was asleep.

"That kneecap was for Lisa," Bone said as he jacked off the 12-gauge--(click-clack)-- ejecting the spent shell.

"John, you hit this woman in her mouth!" Bone pointed at René. "A woman? Regardless to her working the streets, she's still a woman." He smiled a sinister grin. "If I remember correctly your pop's abused your mother, and you promised her that you would never harm any woman. Oh yeah, I remember real well. So, for you going against what you promised your mother, it's time for some brutal punishment." Bone looked at Alisha, and then at René.

They both nodded in agreement.

"Then it's settled." Bone showed that sinister grin again. "You two tie this clown up like you did his son when you were in the valley."

Alisha gave Marie the 12-gauge she had, shook off the backpack she had on, and opened it up. Inside, were strips of nylon rope and a few sex toys. Alisha set two dildos out on deck along with the rope.

"You won't need those dildos," Bone informed them. "This is going in instead." He held up the gauge.

This wasn't in the plan he told me, thought Baby Slick. He had to bring Bone back from the abyss in his mind. If you were gonna smoke somebody, then that's what you do. Torture was a whole different trip that Baby Slick wasn't down with.

"Bone," Baby Slick said cautiously, "Let's just blow these fools heads off, toss them overboard, and be done with this bizness."

"Fuck that, Baby Slick!" Bone yelled. "I want him to feel what Lisa feels…what René feels…what Shelley felt." He was emotional.

"Oh, he feels it all right," Marie broke in. "I stuck a hot crack pipe in that asshole's eye socket." She laughed

"And you just blew his kneecap off with a gauge," Baby Slick continued. "That's enough torture, Bone. If you're gonna smoke this fool, bang and get it over with."

"If?" Bone looked at Baby Slick crazy, but he was claming down. He wasn't a malicious cat, but the sight of René's mouth had sent him on one. "If?" He repeated. "First, he robbed and beat up my first ho, then he played a part in burning up Shelley. Now, he done knocked out René's grill..."

Pop—Pop!

From the corner of the couch Little Johnny shot wildly. He was dazed, seeing double, but he managed to get off two good rounds: one grazed the back of Bone's head the other one went through his left calf.

"Ah, fuck!" Bone growled through clenched teeth.

Boom! (Click-clack) Boom!

Marie spun on Little Johnny and let him have it. She peppered every inch of his body between his head and his knees. He leaned forward and slowly laid down on the couch.

"Junior!" John cried. His legs were tied but not his arms. He reached out and grabbed Alisha, pulling her into him; he used her as a shield. It was useless. Danny walked up behind him and dumped a nine-millimeter bullet into his skull.

It was over.

Bone felt a little dizzy, so he sat down. The back of his head was burning, and his leg was going numb.

René walked over to him and examined his head. "Is juss a scratch?" she said with her hand over her mouth.

That was all Bone needed to wash away the rest of the anger that was in him. He busted out laughing.

He couldn't help it.

"Ash-shole," she muttered as she punched him in his arm.

"It's okay, baby girl," Bone managed between laughs. "Doctor Beecham is gonna straighten you out."

***

While Baby Slick and Marie tossed the bodies overboard, and René cleaned up the deck, Danny and Alisha patched Bone up. Alisha was a Registered Nurse, so she dressed his leg up like the professional that she was.

"I don't know where you got that torture bullshit from," Alisha said, "But you need to deal with them demons."

"I did flash kinda hard, huh." It wasn't a question.

"Yeah," Danny added, "It almost got your red ass killed." Danny was rubbing A&D Ointment on the graze that Bone had on the back of his head.

"Where's my phone?" Bone asked as he searched his pockets.

"You set it on top of the bar," Danny informed him.

"Why in the hell did I do that?"

"You were dizzy, and you thought your phone was a drink," Alisha replied. "You tipped it up to your mouth thinking that it was a drink. When you got nothing out of it you set it down like an empty glass." Alisha smiled as she replayed the scene in her mind.

Bone looked embarrassed. He shook that look quickly and asked, "Could you get my phone, woman…on the rocks?"

They all laughed.

Once Alisha was gone Danny let out a low whistle. "Where did you get *'that'* one, Willie?"

"Out of a tent."

                                        ***

Bone limped down the walkway to Kristene waiting for him. He called her from the yacht. He didn't feel like going back to the Batcave.

With a lot of effort Bone finally pulled himself up into the Escalade. "Damn, woman," he complained, "You coulda helped a brotha out." When he looked over at her, she was pointing at the very-revealing jersey.

"*You* wanted to see me like this," she stated. "Not everybody else."

"To be honest with you, I didn't think you would come like that."

"Good," she replied. "Now you'll stop testing me like that." Kristene pulled out and asked, "What happened to you?"

"I got shot," he tried to sound casual about it.

"Shot!" She cried. "I told you these streets are no good." She growled and backhanded him in his chest.

"Gee, thanks for so much concern." Bone looked over at her and said, "Don't have a panic attack on me, woman."

Kristene was breathing really fast. She pulled over into the gas station to calm down.

Bone was worried. "You okay?" She wasn't responding to him. He opened his door and jumped out. "Aaahh!" He cried, and limped around to the driver's side. He opened the door and said, "Climb over."

Kristene climbed over the armrest and relaxed in the passenger seat.

Bone stood there admiring how she looked in that jersey. He shook the thought out of his head, climbed in behind the wheel and pulled off. It was time for him to leave the streets. He never knew how much if affected Kristene until now. He looked over at her consciously working at controlling her breathing. He couldn't admire that.

They rode home in silence. The only sound was soft jazz flowing through the speakers at a low volume.

Anything to calm Kristene's nerves.

Bone eased onto the Long Beach freeway. He was headed home. Home with his wife.

Behind him a red Dodge Magnum followed at a safe distance.

Chapter Twenty-seven

Imani walked into her mother's room about six-thirty in the morning. She saw more than the normal lumps of her mother under the cover.

"Daddy!" Imani cried, as she jumped in the bed.

"Hey, stinky!" Bone hid the pain he felt in his leg. "You ready for Magic Mountain today?"

"You know it," she beamed. "Just me you and mommy, right?"

"Once she wakes her lazy butt up." Bone positioned himself over her, ready to start tickling her.

"Don't even think about it," Kristene mumbled.

"Too late!" He cried. "Tickle, tickle, tickle!" Bone had his hands under her clenched armpits. "Get her feet, baby."

"Got'em, Daddy!" Imani was enjoying both of her parents on a bright Sunday morning. Finally.

"Okay, okay!" Kristene cried. She laughed so hard that it hurt. "Ooo—kaaayy!"

After their tickling session was over, they all got out of the bed. Imani ran off to her bathroom to take a shower. Kristene went to the bathroom to use it, and Bone limped right in behind her.

She sighed audibly. "I gotta get use to this again. You and I haven't shared a bathroom in a long, long time."

"Remind me to have a urinal added in our next bathroom."

"I heard that," Kristene countered. "You won't turn my new home into a prison dormitory."

Kristene's phone rang. That was her way to get him out of 'her' bathroom. "Go answer the phone while I finish up in here."

Bone stood in the bathroom looking stupid, anyway, so he gladly left. When he got to the phone he looked at the Caller ID and smiled.

"Braxton residence," he said when he picked up the receiver.

"Hey, son," Joyce said with relief all in her voice. "I see you made it home."

"I'm needed down here, right?"

"That you are," she agreed. Joyce paused before she spoke again. "So, how did it go yesterday?"

"It went just fine. Why do you ask?" Bone wasn't giving her the answer she was looking for.

"You know what I'm talkin' 'bout, boy."

"Why does everybody keep callin' me, boy? I am...a...man!"

"Stop playin' with me," Joyce said firmly. "Did you sell them?"

"Yeah, mama," he finally gave in. "You're no fun."

"That's my boy!" Joyce announced. She didn't hear his last comment. "Okay," she turned all business. "This is what we need to do. We..."

"We need to let me take my family to Magic Mountain today, and we'll discuss bizness next week."

Joyce wasn't listening. "You see, it's just that..."

"Mama," Bone said calmly, "The bill collector won't ring your phone on a Sunday. Go to church, and let me take my family out for some fun. Okay?"

She paused for a moment. Reluctantly she said, "Have fun, baby."

Bone hung up. He slowly rose up from the bed. His leg was stiff. As he made his way back to the bathroom, his cell phone rang. He walked over to his coat draped over a chair, pulled his phone out and answered it.

"Speak," he said flatly.

"Bone!" Road Rash yelled. "Raina got popped last night. I gotta go bail her out, bro."

"Calm down, Rash." Bone winced as he sat back down on the bed.

"What in the *fuck* do you mean calm down?" Rash countered. "This is my wife that we're talking about. I'm going to go and bail her out, and I'm using your money."

Bone just smiled to himself. He couldn't blame his buddy for being so excited. If that shoe was on his foot, he would've used Rash's money first and called later.

"You got enough cash, Rash Ass?"

"Hell yeah!" Rash answered excitedly. His attitude went from worry to excitement in a flash. "I sowed up a hundred blocks in two days." He was exaggerating but not by much.

"Go get your ol' lady, fool!" Bone was laughing. "And be careful not to get caught up yourself."

"No shit, huh?" It wasn't a question. "This shit is straight nitro-dust. Have you tried it?" Rash wanted to talk.

"Bye, Rash Ass," Bone hung up.

His leg was throbbing and he didn't have any painkillers. *A joint and a drink*, he thought.

Bone got up and made his way to the bathroom. He poked his head in to see Kristene in the shower. Her silhouette was inviting, but the pain in his leg was not letting him fulfill those desires.

"I'm going to put some gas in the Caddie, baby girl."

"Don't smoke that joint inside that truck," Kristene replied. "Your daughter is still blind to your vices."

"I see you're not," he mumbled.

"What?"

"Yeah, okay," he shut the door.

On his way out of the front door, his daughter caught sight of him from the kitchen.

"Where you going, Daddy?" Imani sounded worried.

"I'm just going to fill the truck up with gas, baby."

She sighed audibly. "I'm going." she declared.

Wow, Bone thought.

She was almost petrified of him leaving her. His presence was definitely needed in his daughter's life.

"Come here, baby," he whispered. He had to be clever. If not, she was not going to let him leave by himself. He squatted down and winced. She walked over to him slowly. "You stay here and make sure your mama don't try to run off with our money."

"Mommy's not like that." Imani was not convinced.

"You don't know her like I do," he tried again. "I remember one time I sent her to the store to get you some diapers, and I didn't see her for two whole days." Bone crossed his fingers.

"Really?"

He nodded.

"I'll make sure that she doesn't get away, Daddy," she said. "You just hurry up, because I don't think I can stop her from leaving. She's '_way_' bigger than I am."

Bone fell over laughing.

"Okay...baby," he said between laughs. He got up slowly and walked out.

While he let the truck warm up he rolled up a joint. Once he was done, he backed out of the driveway and headed up the hill.

Barry was out on the front porch reading the newspaper and drinking tea. Bone pulled up in the driveway and rolled the window down.

"Your boy cashed me out last night," he informed Barry.

"That's the bizness, as you say," Barry smiled from ear-to-ear. He got up and walked down to the truck.

Bone got out and lit the joint. He pulled on it real hard and offered it to Barry.

"Too early," Barry turned it down. He looked at the bandage on Bone's leg, "What happened?"

"Graze," Bone answered off handedly.

Barry let it go at that.

"Take my," Bone pulled on the joint again, "Mama...out today." He was hitting the joint way too hard. He started coughing and coughing. Finally, Bone sounded like he was all out choking. His lungs were on fire. He passed the rest of it to Barry.

Bone was high.

"Two-hitter quitter, kid," Barry said and flicked the cherry off of it.

Bone climbed back into the truck. That weed came down on him fast and hard.

"You sure don't act like you got millions, Willie," Barry observed.

"I'm taking calculated steps," Bone replied. "If I don't, I'll be broke and thirsty in a year."

Smart boy, Barry thought.

"We'll go to the round table, Big 'B'!" Bone smiled.

Barry nodded as Bone backed out of the driveway. He shot up the street to the stop sign. He had no idea which way was the closest gas station. He went left. The gas station was up two blocks ahead. He pulled into the first lane of pumps. A black Lexus was on his bumper urging him to pull down to the last pump in the lane. Bone pulled down to accommodate the Lexus. He got out to pay for his gas. So did the driver of the Lexus.

Clad in skin-tight biker shorts and a sports bra, the driver of the Lexus was a seasoned white woman. Firm legs, flat stomach, apple bottom, and her breasts stood up at attention. With a long braided ponytail down to the middle of her back, she was the epitome of a seasoned vet.

"Beauty always goes before a thug," Bone stated. With his leg wrapped up, and a band-aid across the back of his head, Bone fit a thug's description.

"I like a roughneck on occasion," she said seductively as she walked out of the station.

Bone watched her sway out of the door. He turned and looked at the station attendant with raised eyebrows. Bone paid for his gas and said, "Give me a pen and paper." He slid a five dollar bill into the pay slot.

The attendant took the five and slid Bone the pen and paper.

Bone strolled up to the lady while she was struggling with the gas nozzle.

"Here," Bone handed her the pen and paper while he grabbed the nozzle from her. "Let me help you with this." Once her gas was pumping, he went over to get his own pump going. She slid in behind him.

"I hope I put the right information on this paper for you," she said as she slid it into his back pocket. She caressed his ass before she pulled her hand away.

"A number and address will do for me," He turned to look at her, "And you, just fine." Bone replied smoothly.

"I like a confident man," she shot back at him.

"Confidence and Viagra," Bone joked.

She laughed softly.

"When should I expect to hear from you, uh…?"

"William," Bone took her hand in his and kissed it. Bone couldn't help himself at times. A single white broad, older than he was by at least ten years, driving a brand new Lexus, had to have a few dollars for a handsome black man.

"I'm Jan," she said softly, "Mr. Distinguished. A polished thug. We're gonna have fun. So, when will I hear from you, William?"

"I'll surprise you," Bone replied.

"And I will *definitely* do the same," Jan stated.

Bone's pump stopped as well as Jan's. They both didn't need too much gas before their tanks were full. Bone stuck his nozzle back on the pump and started toward the Lexus to do the same.

"I got that, William," Jan said softly. "I'll be waiting to hear from you."

"You won't have to wait long," Bone walked back into the station to get his change.

Jan pulled off.

She didn't need her change.

She looked over at her passenger and smiled.

"You did real good, Jan." Tino patted her leg. "Real good."

ALSO AVAILABLE BLACK FRIDAY

ESCAPING THE ALLURE OF THE GAME 2

"THE GAME AIN'T OVER"

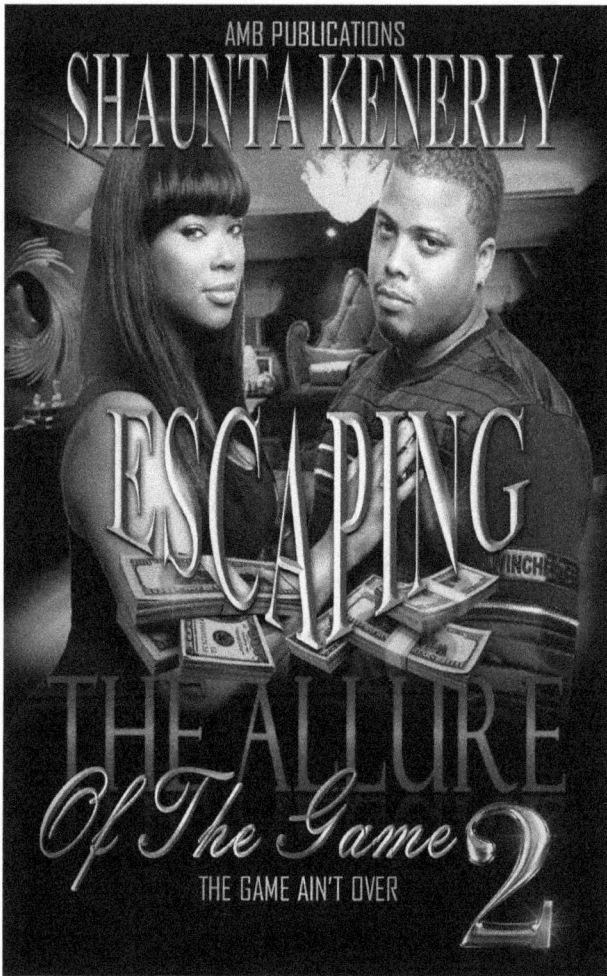

AMB PUBLICATIONS
SHAUNTA KENERLY
ESCAPING
THE ALLURE
Of The Game 2
THE GAME AIN'T OVER

COMING SOON!

ESCAPING THE ALLURE OF THE GAME
THE MOVIE

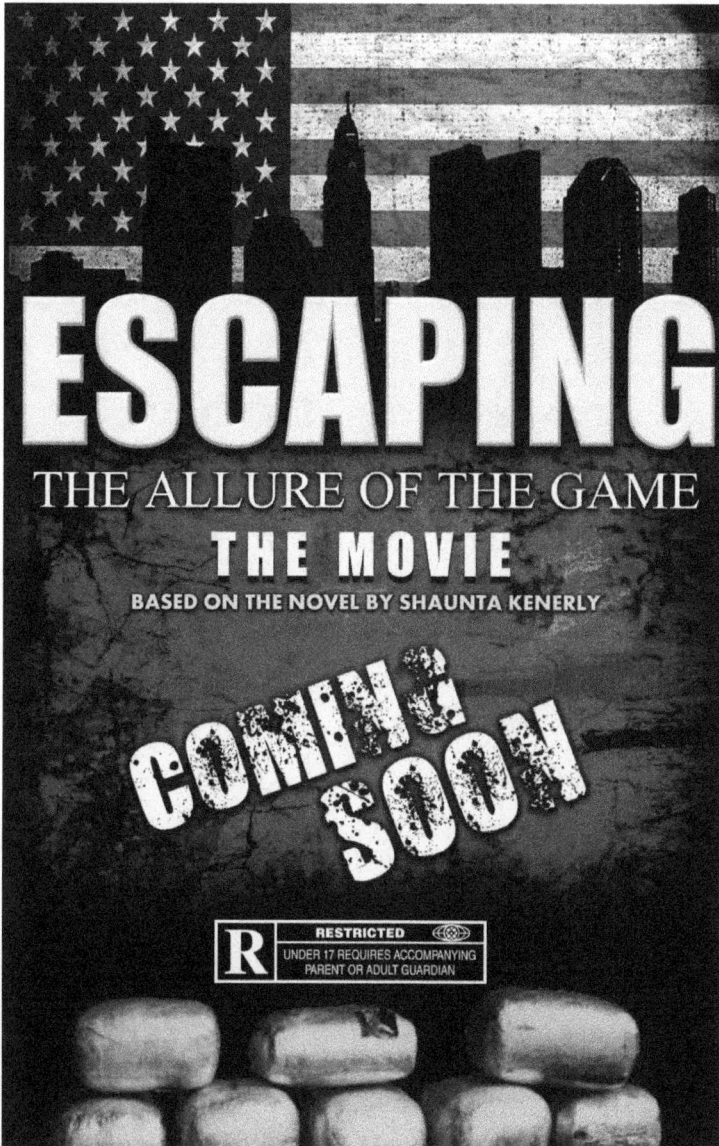

Also Available From AMB/KP

Chosen by Nicole Michelle

Treasure by Shaunta Kenerly

Sweatin by Miss Kim

Hood Bound by Aija M. Butler

The Boutique by Dannaye Carter

Check us out today where books are

sold!!!

www.ingramcontent.com/pod-product-compliance
Lightning Source LLC
Chambersburg PA
CBHW051821040426

42447CB00006B/309